Mastering Time Series Analysis and Forecasting with Python

Bridging Theory and Practice Through Insights, Techniques, and Tools for Effective Time Series Analysis in Python

Sulekha Aloorravi

www.orangeava.com

Copyright © 2024, Orange Education Pvt Ltd, AVA™

All rights reserved. No part of this book may be reproduced, stored in a retrieval system, or transmitted in any form or by any means, without the prior written permission of the publisher, except in the case of brief quotations embedded in critical articles or reviews.

Every effort has been made in the preparation of this book to ensure the accuracy of the information presented. However, the information contained in this book is sold without warranty, either express or implied. Neither the author nor **Orange Education Pvt Ltd** or its dealers and distributors, will be held liable for any damages caused or alleged to have been caused directly or indirectly by this book.

Orange Education Pvt Ltd has endeavored to provide trademark information about all of the companies and products mentioned in this book by the appropriate use of capital. However, **Orange Education Pvt Ltd** cannot guarantee the accuracy of this information. The use of general descriptive names, registered names, trademarks, service marks, etc. in this publication does not imply, even in the absence of a specific statement, that such names are exempt from the relevant protective laws and regulations and therefore free for general use.

First published: March 2024
Published by: Orange Education Pvt Ltd, AVA™
Address: 9, Daryaganj, Delhi, 110002, India

275 New North Road Islington Suite 1314 London,
N1 7AA, United Kingdom

ISBN: 978-81-96815-10-3

www.orangeava.com

Dedicated To

My Loving Husband:

Dileep

My Strength and Support System

About the Author

Sulekha Aloorravi is a professional with over 18+ years of experience along with a diverse background and several key roles. She is currently the Vice President in the Banking industry, where she also specializes as a Data Scientist. In addition to her corporate role, Sulekha is also a mentor with Great Learning. Her contributions in the academic field have been recognized and cited.

Her expertise extends into the realm of engineering and data science, with a noted deep understanding of various technologies and systems. This technical proficiency is further exemplified through her work as an author. Sulekha has written "*Metaprogramming with Python*," a guide for programmers on writing reusable code to build smarter applications.

This combination of roles in both the corporate and academic sectors, along with her contributions to the field of programming through her publication, highlights Sulekha Aloorravi's multifaceted expertise and her significant presence in the fields of data science, business management, and technology.

Sulekha is a passionate advocate for the use of data science to solve real-world problems. She has a strong track record of success in identifying and extracting valuable insights from large datasets, which she has then used to improve business processes, optimize data-driven solutions, and make better-informed decisions. In addition to her technical expertise, Sulekha is also a highly effective communicator and collaborator. She has a proven ability to work with cross-functional teams to translate complex data into actionable insights that can be readily understood and adopted by business.

About the Technical Reviewer

Dileep Vuppaladhadiam is an accomplished leader in the field of Artificial Intelligence and Machine Learning (AI/ML) with a remarkable 18-year track record of shaping the industry. His expertise spans a wide spectrum of domains, including solution design, data architecture, data engineering, data science, and the practical application of artificial intelligence and machine learning technologies.

Throughout his career, Dileep has played a pivotal role in deploying cutting-edge AI/ML-based applications, employing rigorous data science methodologies to empower data-driven decision-making. His achievements include the successful implementation of numerous AI/ML solutions, both on-premises and in cloud environments, delivering substantial business value.

Dileep's academic journey is equally impressive, featuring multiple majors encompassing accounting, economics, finance, business administration, data science, artificial intelligence, business analytics, and business intelligence. His commitment to education extends beyond his own studies, as he has also served as a dedicated coach, mentor, and faculty member, inspiring and guiding countless aspiring data scientists.

His professional footprint spans diverse sectors, including Manufacturing and Industrial, Information Technology, Banking, Finance, Retail, Travel and Tourism, and Consulting. Dileep has had the privilege of leading Research and Development, Technical Consultancy, and Support teams, bringing innovative solutions to renowned organizations such as IBM, Capgemini, Barclays, HSBC, HomeCredit, Mindtree, and Infosys.

Currently, Dileep holds the prestigious position of Vice President at Wells Fargo, where he plays a pivotal role in guiding the global enterprise towards achieving significant and sustainable business value. His focus centers on harnessing the power of robust and scalable data engineering and data science approaches tailored to the modern business landscape. Through his leadership, he champions data-driven business and technical transformations, enabling the creation of substantial value on a global scale.

Acknowledgements

I am deeply grateful to my family for their unwavering support and encouragement throughout the journey of writing this book. Their love, understanding, and patience have been my anchor, enabling me to devote countless hours to research, writing, and revision. To my spouse Dileep, whose belief in me never wavered, and to my nephew Sai Sathvik, whose boundless energy and laughter filled my days with joy and inspiration, I owe a debt of gratitude beyond words.

Thank you for your sacrifices, your understanding during late nights and weekends spent at the keyboard, and for being my constant source of motivation. Your love and encouragement have been instrumental in bringing this project to fruition. I am forever grateful for your unwavering support and belief in me.

I extend my sincere gratitude to the publishers for their guidance, expertise, and support throughout the publication process. Their dedication to excellence and commitment to providing valuable resources to readers have been instrumental in bringing this book to successful completion. I am deeply grateful for their collaboration and unwavering belief in the importance of this work.

To the readers, I offer my heartfelt thanks for choosing this book as a resource on your journey to mastering time series analysis with Python. Your interest and engagement inspire me to continue striving for clarity, depth, and relevance in my writing. It is my hope that the knowledge shared within these pages will empower you to tackle complex data challenges with confidence and creativity.

Thank you for your trust, curiosity, and commitment to lifelong learning. Your feedback and insights are invaluable, and I am honored to have the opportunity to contribute to your growth and success in the field of data science.

Preface

Welcome to "*Mastering Time Series Analysis and Forecasting with Python.*" In this book, we embark on an exploration of time series analysis, a foundational pillar of data science with far-reaching applications across industries. Whether you are a seasoned data scientist seeking to deepen your understanding of time series methods or a beginner eager to unlock the potential of Python for analyzing sequential data, this book is designed to be your comprehensive guide.

The field of time series analysis encompasses numerous methods, algorithms, and techniques tailored to uncover patterns, trends, and insights within sequential data. Through a hands-on, practical approach, we delve into the fundamental concepts of time series analysis, explore state-of-the-art methodologies, and provide step-by-step tutorials to implement these techniques using Python libraries such as pandas, NumPy, Matplotlib, Statsmodels, and more.

As you journey through the pages of this book, you will learn how to visualize time series data, extract meaningful features, build predictive models, and evaluate their performance. From classical methods like ARIMA and exponential smoothing to modern approaches like machine learning and deep learning, we cover a diverse array of techniques to suit various data scenarios and business requirements.

Each chapter is crafted to provide both theoretical foundations and practical applications, ensuring that you not only understand the underlying principles but also gain the skills to apply them effectively in real-world projects. Along the way, you will encounter Python code examples, illustrative plots, and hands-on exercises to reinforce your learning and deepen your understanding.

This book comprises 9 chapters, each a complete module in itself, serving as your comprehensive guide to mastering time series in Python. Whether you are analyzing financial data, forecasting sales, predicting demand, or studying sensor readings, the techniques presented in this book will equip you with the tools and knowledge to tackle a wide range of time series challenges. I invite you to embark on this journey with me and discover the fascinating world of time series analysis with Python.

Chapter 1 Introduction to Time Series: In this chapter, we embark on a journey to explore the fundamental concepts of time series analysis and its applications across various domains. We begin by introducing the concept of time series data and its significance in analyzing sequential data. Through real-world examples, we demonstrate how time series analysis plays a crucial role in diverse industries such as finance, healthcare, manufacturing, and more. Whether you're a beginner or an experienced practitioner, this chapter serves as an essential primer for understanding the role of time series analysis in modern data science applications.

Chapter 2 Overview of Times Series Libraries in Python: In this chapter, readers will embark on an exploration of popular time series libraries in Python, gaining insights into their features and applications through practical examples and illustrations. Beginning with Pandas, the versatile library provides robust capabilities for handling time series data, followed by an examination of NumPy's role in numerical computing for time series analysis. The chapter further delves into Statsmodels, showcasing its capabilities for statistical modeling and forecasting. Additionally, readers will be introduced to other significant libraries such as Prophet and AutoTS, which offer advanced features for time series forecasting and modeling. Through this comprehensive exploration, readers will acquire the knowledge and tools necessary to harness Python's capabilities for effective time series analysis.

Chapter 3 Visualization of Time Series Data: In this chapter, readers will be introduced to a myriad of time series visualization techniques facilitated by Python libraries. Beginning with an overview of time series visualization libraries in Python, the chapter delves into basic plotting functionalities using matplotlib, providing a foundational understanding of visualizing time series data. Subsequently, readers will explore advanced visualization capabilities using seaborn, enabling them to analyze complex temporal patterns and relationships with ease. The chapter culminates with an exploration of interactive time series visualizations using plotly, empowering readers to create dynamic and interactive plots that facilitate deeper insights into time series data. Through practical examples and step-by-step guidance, readers will gain proficiency in leveraging Python's visualization tools for effective time series analysis and interpretation.

Chapter 4 Exploratory Analysis of Time Series Data: In this comprehensive chapter, readers will embark on a journey through the foundational aspects of time series data analysis. Beginning with the essential tasks of loading and inspecting time series data, readers will gain proficiency in navigating diverse datasets.

Through an exploration of descriptive statistics, readers will uncover key insights into the characteristics and distributions of time series data, laying the groundwork for deeper analysis. The chapter further delves into advanced techniques such as time series decomposition, stationarity analysis, and autocorrelation analysis, equipping readers with the tools to discern underlying patterns and structures within time series data. Additionally, readers will explore the significance of rolling statistics in capturing temporal trends and variability, enabling them to extract meaningful insights from dynamic datasets. With practical examples and illustrative explanations, this chapter serves as an indispensable guide for mastering the fundamental principles of time series data analysis.

Chapter 5 Feature Engineering on Time Series: In this illuminating chapter, readers will delve into the intricate realm of feature engineering for time series data. Beginning with the exploration of univariate feature engineering techniques, readers will learn how to create lag-based features, compute rolling statistics, derive expanding window statistics, and calculate exponential moving averages. Through practical examples and step-by-step explanations, readers will gain a profound understanding of each technique's application and significance in uncovering temporal patterns and relationships within univariate time series data. The chapter further advances into the realm of multivariate feature engineering, where readers will discover how to craft lag-based multivariate features, generate interaction terms-based features, and derive aggregated features. By mastering these techniques, readers will acquire the expertise to extract valuable insights and enhance the predictive power of their time series models, propelling their data science endeavors to new heights.

Chapter 6 Time Series Forecasting – ML Approach Part 1: In this enlightening chapter, readers will embark on a captivating journey through a myriad of time series forecasting techniques and models. Commencing with a deep dive into the intricacies of Autoregressive Integrated Moving Average (ARIMA), readers will unravel the essence of this foundational model and its application in capturing temporal patterns and trends. Subsequently, the chapter illuminates the process of Seasonal Decomposition of Time Series (STL), providing insights into dissecting time series data into its constituent components of trend, seasonality, and noise. Moving forward, readers will delve into the realm of Exponential Smoothing Models, exploring their efficacy in capturing underlying patterns and making accurate predictions. Furthermore, the chapter unveils the prowess of Facebook Prophet, shedding light on its intuitive interface and robust forecasting capabilities. Lastly, readers will be introduced to Support Vector Machines (SVM), a powerful machine learning algorithm adept at handling non-linear relationships and making accurate predictions in time series data. Through practical examples and insightful explanations, readers will emerge equipped with the knowledge and skills to navigate the intricate landscape of time series forecasting, empowering them to unlock valuable insights and drive informed decision-making in their data-driven endeavors.

Chapter 7 Time Series Forecasting – ML Approach Part 2: In this interesting chapter, readers will embark on a captivating exploration of diverse machine learning algorithms tailored for time series forecasting. Beginning with a comprehensive overview of Hidden Markov Models (HMM), readers will uncover the intricacies of this probabilistic framework and its application in capturing latent states and transitions within time series data. Subsequently, the chapter delves into the realm of Gaussian Processes, revealing their inherent flexibility and ability to model complex relationships in time series data. Moreover, readers will discover the art of developing machine learning-based approaches for time series forecasting, harnessing the predictive power of algorithms such as Support Vector Machine (SVM), K-Nearest Neighbour (KNN), Random Forest, and Gradient Boosting. Through practical examples and insightful discussions, readers will gain invaluable insights into the diverse array of machine learning techniques available for time series analysis, empowering them to make informed decisions and extract actionable insights from their data.

Chapter 8 Time Series Forecasting – DL Approach: In this captivating chapter, readers will embark on an enlightening journey into the realm of deep learning for time series forecasting. The exploration begins with a deep dive into Long Short-Term Memory (LSTM) networks, unraveling the inner workings of these powerful recurrent neural networks designed to capture long-term dependencies in sequential data. Through practical examples and insightful discussions, readers will gain a comprehensive understanding of how LSTM networks can be effectively applied to time series forecasting tasks. Additionally, the chapter explores the application of Gated Recurrent Units (GRUs), another variant of recurrent neural networks known for their efficiency in modeling sequential data. Furthermore, readers will delve into the realm of Convolutional Neural Networks (CNNs), uncovering how these versatile architectures can be adapted to extract meaningful features from time series data for forecasting purposes. Armed with this knowledge, readers will be equipped to leverage the full potential of deep learning techniques for tackling a myriad of time series forecasting challenges with confidence and proficiency.

Chapter 9 Multivariate Time Series, Metrics, and Validation: In this comprehensive chapter, readers will embark on a comprehensive journey through the fundamental concepts and techniques essential for understanding and analyzing time series data. Beginning with the crucial step of loading and inspecting time series data, readers will learn how to effectively explore the structure and characteristics of their datasets. Subsequently, the chapter delves into the realm of descriptive statistics, providing readers with valuable insights into summarizing and understanding the statistical properties of time series data. The exploration continues with an in-depth examination of time series decomposition techniques, enabling readers to disentangle the underlying components such as trend, seasonality, and noise within their data. Furthermore, readers will learn how to perform stationarity analysis to assess the stability of time series data over time, followed by a thorough review of autocorrelation and partial autocorrelation functions to identify temporal dependencies. Finally, the chapter concludes with an exploration of rolling statistics, empowering readers with the ability to analyze trends and patterns in their time series data using moving averages and other rolling window techniques. Through practical examples and step-by-step explanations, readers will gain a solid foundation in time series analysis, equipping them with the knowledge and skills needed to navigate the complexities of real-world time series datasets with confidence and precision.

This book presents a comprehensive and accessible guide to mastering the intricacies of time series data analysis. Through a comprehensive coverage of theoretical concepts, practical examples, and hands-on Python code, this book equips readers with the knowledge and skills needed to navigate the complexities of time series data across diverse domains such as finance, healthcare, manufacturing, and beyond. From the foundational principles of time series analysis to advanced forecasting models and techniques, each chapter offers invaluable insights and actionable strategies for harnessing the power of time series data to derive meaningful insights and drive informed decision-making.

Downloading the code bundles and colored images

Please follow the links or scan the QR codes to download the *Code Bundles and Images* of the book:

https://github.com/OrangeAVA/Mastering-Time-Series-Analysis-and-Forecasting-with-Python

The code bundles and images of the book are also hosted on
https://rebrand.ly/e6e2d8

In case there's an update to the code, it will be updated on the existing GitHub repository.

Errata

We take immense pride in our work at **Orange Education Pvt Ltd,** and follow best practices to ensure the accuracy of our content to provide an indulging reading experience to our subscribers. Our readers are our mirrors, and we use their inputs to reflect and improve upon human errors, if any, that may have occurred during the publishing processes involved. To let us maintain the quality and help us reach out to any readers who might be having difficulties due to any unforeseen errors, please write to us at :

errata@orangeava.com

Your support, suggestions, and feedback are highly appreciated.

DID YOU KNOW

Did you know that Orange Education Pvt Ltd offers eBook versions of every book published, with PDF and ePub files available? You can upgrade to the eBook version at **www.orangeava.com** and as a print book customer, you are entitled to a discount on the eBook copy. Get in touch with us at: **info@orangeava.com** for more details.

At **www.orangeava.com**, you can also read a collection of free technical articles, sign up for a range of free newsletters, and receive exclusive discounts and offers on AVA™ Books and eBooks.

PIRACY

If you come across any illegal copies of our works in any form on the internet, we would be grateful if you would provide us with the location address or website name. Please contact us at **info@orangeava.com** with a link to the material.

ARE YOU INTERESTED IN AUTHORING WITH US?

If there is a topic that you have expertise in, and you are interested in either writing or contributing to a book, please write to us at **business@orangeava.com**. We are on a journey to help developers and tech professionals to gain insights on the present technological advancements and innovations happening across the globe and build a community that believes Knowledge is best acquired by sharing and learning with others. Please reach out to us to learn what our audience demands and how you can be part of this educational reform. We also welcome ideas from tech experts and help them build learning and development content for their domains.

REVIEWS

Please leave a review. Once you have read and used this book, why not leave a review on the site that you purchased it from? Potential readers can then see and use your unbiased opinion to make purchase decisions. We at Orange Education would love to know what you think about our products, and our authors can learn from your feedback. Thank you!

For more information about Orange Education, please visit **www.orangeava.com**.

Table of Contents

1. **Introduction to Time Series** 1
   - Structure 2
   - Overview of Time Series 2
   - Applications of Time Series Across Industries 2
     - *Usage in Finance and Economics* 3
       - Stock Market Analysis 3
       - Market Risk Analysis 4
       - Credit Risk Analysis 6
       - Analysis of Economic Conditions 7
     - *Usage in Sales and Marketing* 9
       - Forecasting of Retail Sales 9
       - Seasonality Analysis and Planning 10
       - Inventory Management 11
       - Marketing Campaign Analysis 13
       - Customer Segmentation 15
     - *Usage in Healthcare* 16
       - Analysis of Patient Features in Treating Comorbidities ... 16
       - Disease Detection and Prediction 18
     - *Usage in Weather and Environmental Science* 19
     - *Usage in Transportation and Traffic Management* 21
   - Preparation of Time Series Data 22
   - Conclusion 24
   - References 24

2. **Overview of Time Series Libraries in Python** 27
   - Structure 27
   - Pandas for Time Series 28
   - NumPy for Time Series 39
   - Prophet for Time Series 42
   - AutoTS for Time Series 55
   - Conclusion 59

  References 60

3. Visualization of Time Series Data **61**
  Structure 61
  Introduction to Time Series Visualization Libraries of Python 62
    Exploring Matplotlib and Its Uses 62
    Exploring Seaborn and Its Uses 64
    Exploring Plotly and Its Uses 71
  Basic Time Series Plots with Matplotlib 74
    Line Plot 74
    Scatter Plot 75
    Box Plot 78
    Histogram 81
  Advanced Time Series Visualization with Seaborn 83
    Heat Map 84
    Pair Plots 88
  Interactive Time Series Visualization with Plotly 90
    Area Plot 90
    Candlestick Plot 91
  Conclusion 92
  References 93

4. Exploratory Analysis of Time Series Data **95**
  Structure 95
  Loading and Inspection of Time Series Data 96
  Understanding Descriptive Statistics 99
    Mean 100
    Median 100
    Mode 101
  Exploring Time Series Decomposition 103
    Trend 103
    Seasonality 103
    Level 104
    Noise 104
  Performing Stationarity Analysis 108
    Augmented Dickey-Fuller Test 109

   Kwiatkowski–Phillips–Schmidt–Shin (KPSS) Test.......................... 112
 Reviewing Autocorrelation and Partial Autocorrelation..................... 114
   Autocorrelation... 114
   Partial Autocorrelation 116
 Exploring Rolling Statistics 118
 Conclusion 122
 References 122

5. Feature Engineering on Time Series 125
 Structure 125
 Univariate Feature Engineering 126
   Creating Lag-Based Univariate Features.. 126
   Calculating Rolling Statistics 130
   Computing Expanding Window Statistics...................................... 133
   Calculating Exponential Moving Averages.................................... 139
 Multivariate Feature Engineering 143
   Creating Lag-Based Multivariate Features 148
   Creating Interaction Terms-Based Features 149
   Creating Aggregated Features... 152
 Conclusion 155
 References 155

6. Time Series Forecasting – ML Approach Part 1 157
 Introduction 157
 Structure 157
 Data Introduction 158
 Understanding Autoregressive Integrated Moving
 Average (ARIMA)... 158
   Model Documentation 159
 Application of ARIMA on Time Series Data 161
 Illustrating Exponential Smoothing Models... 167
   Model Documentation 167
   Application of Simple Exponential Smoothing on
   Time Series Data... 168
   Double Exponential Smoothing 172
   Application of Double Exponential Smoothing on

  Time Series Data..174
  Triple Exponential Smoothing...178
   Application of Triple Exponential Smoothing on
   Time Series Data...179
 Exploring the Prophet Algorithm...183
   Application of Prophet on Time Series Data.....................184
 Conclusion..189
 References..190

7. Time Series Forecasting – ML Approach Part 2 191
 Introduction 191
 Structure 191
 Data Introduction 192
 Applying Hidden Markov Models (HMM)..192
   Application of HMM on Time Series Data 194
 Understanding Gaussian Process 198
   Application of Gaussian Process on Time Series Data.................. 199
 Developing a ML-Based Approach for Time Series Forecasting.....203
 Applying Support Vector Machine... 207
   Application of SVM on Time Series Data 209
 Applying K-Nearest Neighbor (KNN)..212
   Application of KNN on Time Series Data......................... 213
 Implementing with Random Forest 216
   Application of Random Forest on Time Series Data 219
 Implementing with Gradient Boosting 221
   Application of Gradient Boosting on Time Series Data.................225
 Conclusion... 228
 References.. 228

8. Time Series Forecasting - DL Approach 231
 Structure 231
 Data Introduction 232
 Understanding Long Short-Term Memory Networks 232
 Developing a Deep Learning-Based Approach for
 Time Series Forecasting 242
 Applying Gated Recurrent Units 248

　　　　Application of GRU on the time series data 251
　　　Applying Convolutional Neural Networks 256
　　　　Application of CNN on the time series data 258
　　　Conclusion 263
　　　References 264

9. Multivariate Time Series, Metrics, and Validation 265
　　　Structure 265
　　　Data Introduction 266
　　　Understanding Vector AutoRegression 267
　　　　Application of VAR on Time Series Data 268
　　　Applying Vector Error Correction Model 276
　　　Application of VECM on Time Series Data 278
　　　Understanding VARMAX 289
　　　Application of VARMAX on Time Series Data 290
　　　Metrics for Time series 296
　　　Conclusion 297
　　　References 297

Index 299

CHAPTER 1
Introduction to Time Series

Time is the most important dimension of our lives and all the changes happen around the world constantly because of the impact of time. As human beings with access to enormous technology, we collect a lot of data over time with or without realizing it. Understanding the data that we collected over time and utilizing the information we derived from it to make things better helps in human evolution and the evolution of technology for the betterment of this world. The concept of time series comes in handy to perform this analysis.

Whether you are a data scientist, data analyst, data engineer, or Python programmer who works on data that deals with time, you will benefit from the content of this book. Let us together explore the value of time series data and learn how to derive more insights throughout this learning journey.

We will begin this chapter by introducing time series, then examine its applications in various domains across the industry such as finance, healthcare, manufacturing, and more. Finally, we will conclude this chapter by discussing methods for preparing time series data.

Structure

In this chapter, the following topics will be covered:
- Overview of Time Series
- Time Series Usage in Different Domains
- Preparation of Time Series Data

Overview of Time Series

Data collected over regular intervals of time is termed time series data. This can be data collected every second on your mobile phone, data collected throughout the day on your smartwatch, or even data collected manually by someone every hour of the day for a continuous period of one month, among other examples. All of this data, collected for specific purposes, can be used to understand patterns and derive insights for one or more use cases. As time goes on, more data gets collected, and the repository of such large data becomes a rich source of information that can be explored and analyzed to make informed decisions.

Time series data also helps in identifying hidden patterns in the data collected over time. It can provide information on trends, such as the upward and downward movements of the price of oil in the market, as well as seasonality, such as the right time to sell gift items in your shop.

The analysis of time series data can be performed by applying various powerful techniques using programming languages such as Python, R, and many more. You can understand the data simply by exploring it and examining its statistical information, such as measures of central tendency. Alternatively, you can apply machine learning and deep learning to the data to identify hidden insights or to predict and forecast the future. This book covers a wide range of these concepts and provides examples of where they can be applied.

Applications of Time Series Across Industries

Time series data is of extensive use in various industry domains. To understand the examples of time series data in various domains, we will be using the UCI machine learning repository's datasets widely throughout this book. You can find these datasets at https://archive.ics.uci.edu/ml/datasets. Let us explore some of the industry domains here.

Usage in Finance and Economics

Finance and Economics are an integral part of the world's economy. Large amounts of data are accumulated in these domains across the industry. The study of the patterns in this data is very crucial for effective financial decision-making in a constantly changing economic landscape. Some of the applications of time series data in finance and economics will be explored in this section.

Stock Market Analysis

Stock markets are an excellent source of time series data. Trades in stock markets happen during business hours every weekday on several investment products across multiple industry sectors. Using the stock market data, we can analyze market conditions, predict future stock prices, make trading decisions, and manage individual investor interests.

An example of daily stock market time series data for Lenevo Group Limited, sourced from https://finance.yahoo.com/, is represented in the following table (see *Figure 1.1*):

Daily high price of LNVGY Ticker for March 2023

Date	High
01-03-2023	18.719999
02-03-2023	18.59
03-03-2023	18.639999
06-03-2023	19.23
07-03-2023	19.200001
08-03-2023	18.98
09-03-2023	18.6
10-03-2023	19.299999
13-03-2023	19
14-03-2023	18.91
15-03-2023	18.379999
16-03-2023	18.450001
17-03-2023	19.290001
20-03-2023	18.65
21-03-2023	18.620001
22-03-2023	18.74
23-03-2023	20.809999

Figure 1.1: *Time series data of stock prices*

The trend line for the preceding stock market prices can be reviewed in the following chart (see *Figure 1.2*):

Figure 1.2: Time series trend of stock prices

Figure 1.2 demonstrates the behavior of the daily high prices of LNVGY stock over 23 days. A simple analysis of the trend of the stock can explain when the prices were high and when the prices were low during these 23 days.

Market Risk Analysis

Market risk analysis is another type of analysis that can be performed in financial markets to understand the factors that can adversely impact market performance. Time series data is an important factor or input that is used to analyze market risk. Value-at-risk is one of the statistical measures that is majorly used to analyze market risk. Historical market data, such as market prices, spreads, volatilities, interest rates, and more, are used in the analysis. The volatility index, denoted by VIX, is an example of market risk analysis input data. VIX is a volatility index measure calculated based on exchange-specific index option prices, denoting the expectation of volatility for a stock market.

An example of India VIX time series data for NIFTY index option prices is sourced from https://www1.nseindia.com/products/content/equities/indices/historical_vix.htm and is represented in the following table (see *Figure 1.3*):

Introduction to Time Series

Daily VIX for India

Date	Open	High	Low	Close	Prev. Close	Change	% Change
01-Mar-23	14.02	14.02	12.275	12.995	14.02	-1.03	-7.31
02-Mar-23	12.995	13.55	11.1	12.97	12.995	-0.03	-0.19
03-Mar-23	12.97	12.97	11.98	12.18	12.97	-0.79	-6.09
06-Mar-23	12.18	12.4725	11.8375	12.2675	12.18	0.09	0.72
08-Mar-23	12.2675	12.8475	11.8975	12.45	12.2675	0.18	1.49
09-Mar-23	12.45	12.8425	11.78	12.725	12.45	0.28	2.21
10-Mar-23	12.725	13.8175	12.725	13.4125	12.725	0.69	5.4
13-Mar-23	13.4125	16.4275	13.4125	16.215	13.4125	2.8	20.89
14-Mar-23	16.215	16.6425	15.0025	16.2175	16.215	0	0.02
15-Mar-23	16.2175	16.505	14.5175	16.295	16.2175	0.08	0.48
16-Mar-23	16.295	17.355	13.95	16.2175	16.295	-0.08	-0.48
17-Mar-23	16.2175	16.2175	14.6	14.7675	16.2175	-1.45	-8.94
20-Mar-23	14.7675	17.22	14.52	16.0075	14.7675	1.24	8.4
21-Mar-23	16.0075	16.035	14.0825	15.0825	16.0075	-0.93	-5.78
22-Mar-23	15.0825	15.0925	14.2425	14.8075	15.0825	-0.28	-1.82
23-Mar-23	14.8075	15.0575	13.9025	14.49	14.8075	-0.32	-2.14

Figure 1.3: *Time series data of India VIX*

India VIX is based on the NIFTY index option prices. The trend lines for the preceding India VIX can be reviewed in the following chart (see *Figure* 1.4):

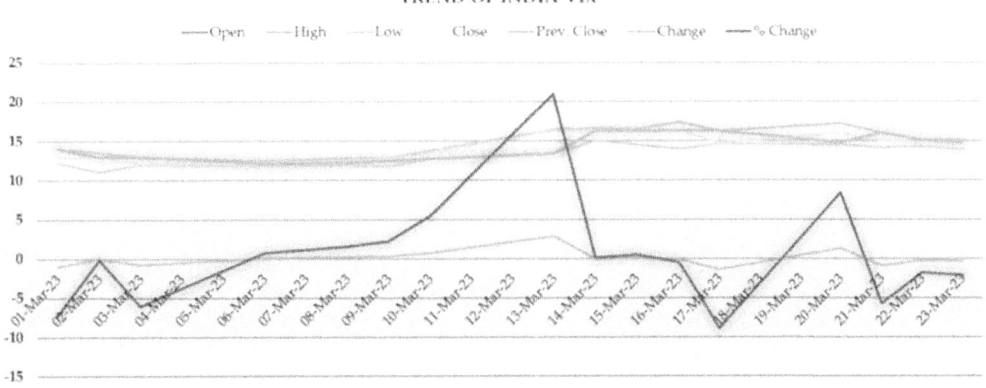

Figure 1.4: *Trend lines of India VIX*

The preceding figure represents the trends of multiple variables of India VIX over 23 days. A trend analysis of each of these variables can help us understand how each variable has performed by itself, as well as with respect to other variables.

Credit Risk Analysis

In finance, lending or loans is a major financial product for many banks and financial institutions. Lending is a process that always poses a threat of credit risks. Credit risk analysis is performed by financial institutions before entering into any lending contract either with customers who are individuals/retailers or with counterparty firms. Credit risk analysis involves various calculations and scorings using historical time series data with multiple variables related to the credit behavior of counterparties. The statistical measures such as the probability of default, loss given default, and exposure at default are derived from the time series data to understand the creditworthiness of a customer or counterparty.

An example of a credit risk dataset generated specifically for this chapter can be seen in *Figure 1.5*:

Loan repayment ledger by date

Date	Loan Repayment Amount (USD)
10-01-2022	500
10-02-2022	500
10-03-2022	500
10-04-2022	500
10-05-2022	500
10-06-2022	500
10-07-2022	500
10-08-2022	500
10-09-2022	500
10-10-2022	500
10-11-2022	500
10-12-2022	500
10-02-2023	1020
10-03-2023	500

Figure 1.5: *Loan repayment time series data*

Introduction to Time Series

The trend line for the preceding loan repayment ledger can be reviewed in the following chart:

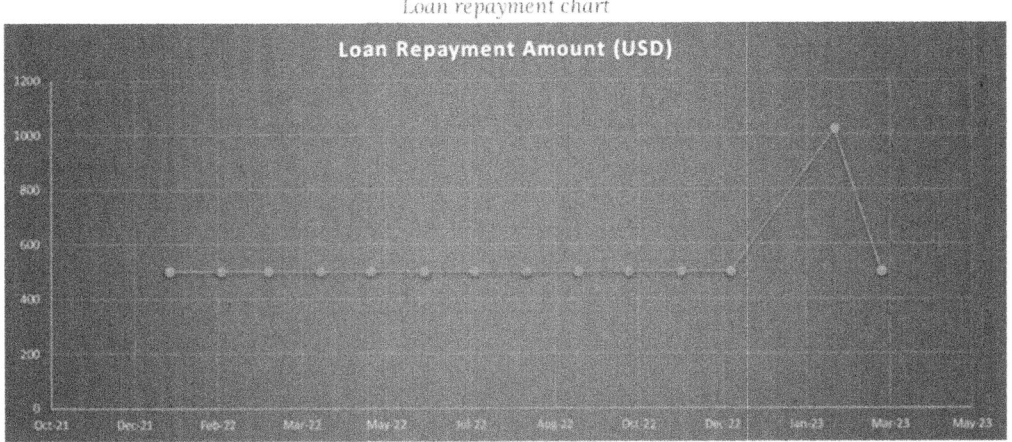

Figure 1.6: *Trend line for loan repayment*

The trend line in *Figure* 1.6 shows the credit behavior of a customer. During the month of January 2023, no repayment was made, and the repayment happened during February 2023 along with a penalty of $20. The credit behavior of a customer becomes an input for the bank while calculating the credit score, thus influencing the lending decision of banks for future loans.

Analysis of Economic Conditions

Time series data can be used to analyze economic indicators such as inflation rates, interest rates, and GDP of a nation, and forecast future values for informed decision-making.

Inflation rate, in general, indicates the percentage increase in the price of goods over time. Similarly, interest rate, in general, denotes the percentage increase of interest on loans borrowed by customers of a financial institution. GDP, or Gross Domestic Product, is a measure with a time dimension that indicates the market value of finished products within a country.

An example of GDP time series data for the United States is sourced from https://data.worldbank.org/indicator/NY.GDP.MKTP.CD and is represented in the following table (see *Figure* 1.7):

Annual GDP of United States

Year	GDP
2011	$ 1,55,99,72,81,23,000.00
2012	$ 1,62,53,97,22,30,000.00
2013	$ 1,68,43,19,09,93,000.00
2014	$ 1,75,50,68,01,74,000.00
2015	$ 1,82,06,02,07,41,000.00
2016	$ 1,86,95,11,08,42,000.00
2017	$ 1,94,77,33,65,49,000.00
2018	$ 2,05,33,05,73,12,000.00
2019	$ 2,13,80,97,61,19,000.00
2020	$ 2,10,60,47,36,13,000.00
2021	$ 2,33,15,08,05,60,000.00

Figure 1.7: *GDP data of the United States*

The preceding data in *Figure 1.7* shows the GDP values of the United States, starting from the year 2011 to 2021. Forecasting the GDP for subsequent years through time series forecasting techniques is one of the use cases of time series data in economics.

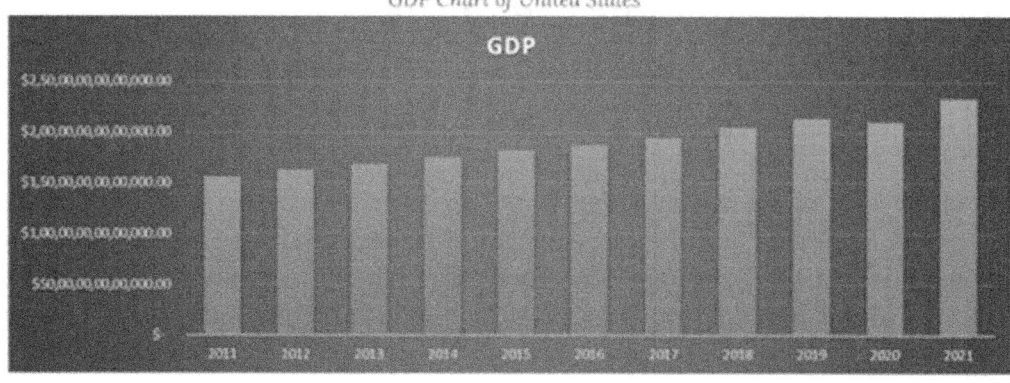

Figure 1.8: *Trend of the GDP of a country*

The year-on-year view of GDP along with a trend of movement can be observed from the preceding chart in *Figure 1.8*. From the chart, it is evident that there is a constant upward trend in GDP, except for the year 2020.

These are some of the applications of time series data in finance. However, there are many more applications, such as investment portfolio management, algorithmic trading, pricing strategies, macroeconomic analysis, and more. With this understanding, let us further explore the usage of time series data in sales and marketing.

Usage in Sales and Marketing

Sales and marketing are domains that are related to each other, as the growth in one drives the growth in the other. There are numerous uses of time series data in these two domains. Some of the applications will be explored in this section.

Forecasting of Retail Sales

Time series data can be used to study the pattern of sales of various products in a supermarket daily and forecast sales for the near future. This helps the management to plan their production and inventory. Sales forecasting can be performed using multiple time series analysis techniques, which will be further studied in subsequent chapters of this book, along with case studies.

Let us now look at an example of time series data that can become an input to sales forecasting. The sample data for this example is downloaded from https://archive.ics.uci.edu/ml/datasets/Sales_Transactions_Dataset_Weekly. This data, as shown in *Figure* 1.9, lists products in rows, the time in weeks in the columns, and the values being weekly sales numbers.

Weekly Sales by Product

Product_Code	W0	W1	W2	W3	W4	W5	W6	W7
P1	11	12	10	8	13	12	14	21
P2	7	6	3	2	7	1	6	3
P3	7	11	8	9	10	8	7	13
P4	12	8	13	5	9	6	9	13
P5	8	5	13	11	6	7	9	14
P6	3	3	2	7	6	3	8	6
P7	4	8	3	7	8	7	2	3

Figure 1.9: Weekly purchase quantity of products

Forecasting the purchase quantity for each product is one of the use cases of time series data in sales. Let us look at the weekly purchase trend of each product in *Figure* 1.10.

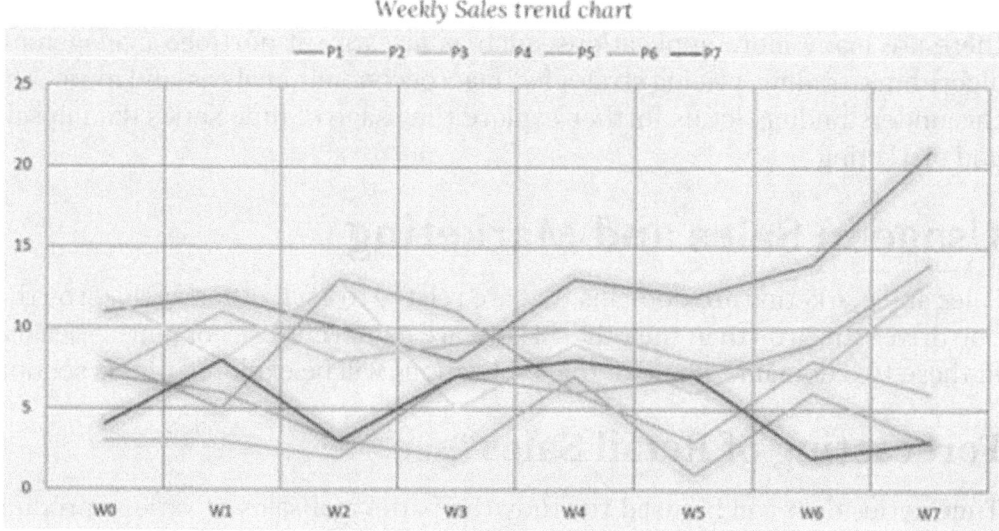

Figure 1.10: *Purchase trend of products*

The purchase quantity of each product in *Figure 1.10* follows a specific pattern. For instance, product P1 has an upward purchase trend over time. This observation can help management to produce or stock more of Product 1 to handle the upcoming demand.

Seasonality Analysis and Planning

Seasonality can be considered as the repetition of a particular behavior at a specific point in time, which is observed as a continuous trend in sales patterns. For example, the sales of air conditioners go up every summer, and the sales of gift articles go up during every festival season such as Christmas to the new year. These are known patterns, but there may also be a lot of unknown seasonal patterns in the sales of products that are not visible evidently by looking at the data. Such patterns can be analyzed by performing a seasonal analysis of the time series data.

An example of time series data depicting the trends of sales quantity of consumer products, which can be used to analyze seasonality is downloaded from https://archive.ics.uci.edu/ml/datasets/online%20retail. A sample of the dataset is presented in *Figure 1.11*:

Introduction to Time Series

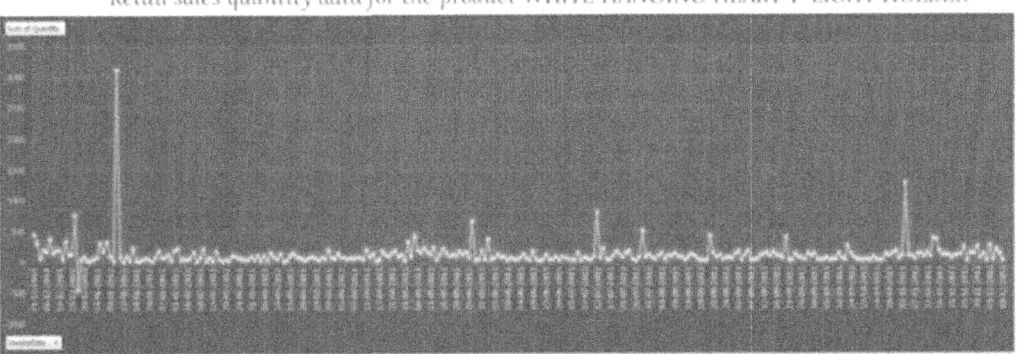

Figure 1.11: Retail dataset

The sales quantity in the dataset can be further analyzed to identify seasonal patterns, as represented in *Figure 1.12*:

Figure 1.12: Sales quantity from 2010 to 2011

The spikes in the data in *Figure 1.12* can be further analyzed in detail for seasonal sales and the reason behind them. Such analysis can help in managing the inventory of the product to handle the spikes in demand.

Inventory Management

Sales forecasting through time series analysis will, in turn, help in managing the stocks in the inventory for specific products that are in demand. Managing inventory efficiently also helps in avoiding excess inventory stocking and the storage costs that will be incurred. Stocking excess inventory in cases of perishable goods such as FMCG (fast-moving consumer goods) like milk, vegetables, baked food, and more, can increase the losses for a retail business.

To explain the benefit of inventory management, let us look at an FMCG inventory and sales dataset generated specifically for this chapter, as shown in *Figure 1.13*. This dataset was generated between 1st January 2023 and 31st January 2023 for four FMCG products: milk, bread, tomatoes, and mangoes. The data is divided into inventory quantity and sales quantity for each day. The inventory quantity denotes the inventory stocked at the beginning of the day, while the sales quantity denotes the sales that happened by the end of the same day.

Sales and Inventory dataset

Date	Inventory				Sales			
	Milk	Bread	Tomatoes	Mangoes	Milk	Bread	Tomatoes	Mangoes
01-Jan-23	100	200	75	80	67	22	18	72
02-Jan-23	100	200	75	80	1	36	66	34
03-Jan-23	100	200	75	80	89	107	30	20
04-Jan-23	100	200	75	80	93	22	74	9
05-Jan-23	100	200	75	80	75	90	16	32
06-Jan-23	100	200	75	80	60	2	14	24
07-Jan-23	100	200	75	80	51	28	14	70
08-Jan-23	100	200	75	80	61	116	53	33
09-Jan-23	100	200	75	80	66	174	37	20
10-Jan-23	100	200	75	80	55	142	5	21
11-Jan-23	100	200	75	80	54	80	9	15
12-Jan-23	100	200	75	80	4	25	52	0
13-Jan-23	100	200	75	80	65	38	24	69
14-Jan-23	100	200	75	80	42	141	35	61
15-Jan-23	100	200	75	80	65	62	61	70
16-Jan-23	100	200	75	80	42	20	22	70
17-Jan-23	100	200	75	80	53	14	30	16
18-Jan-23	100	200	75	80	97	94	31	37
19-Jan-23	100	200	75	80	50	196	19	30
20-Jan-23	100	200	75	80	61	157	8	9
21-Jan-23	100	200	75	80	33	119	69	18
22-Jan-23	100	200	75	80	55	175	0	10
23-Jan-23	100	200	75	80	84	104	15	47
24-Jan-23	100	200	75	80	74	188	48	31
25-Jan-23	100	200	75	80	75	50	3	39
26-Jan-23	100	200	75	80	36	121	37	49
27-Jan-23	100	200	75	80	39	20	35	61
28-Jan-23	100	200	75	80	59	92	52	47
29-Jan-23	100	200	75	80	49	23	57	45
30-Jan-23	100	200	75	80	45	38	24	29
31-Jan-23	100	200	75	80	48	167	25	50

Figure 1.13: *Sales and Inventory of FMCG*

A study of each individual product inventory stock vs. sales is depicted in *Figure 1.14*:

Figure 1.14: *Inventory vs. Sales trend of FMCG products*

Let us look at the trend of one example product from *Figure* 1.14. The inventory quantity of milk for all 31 days of January 2023 has been continuously 100, whereas the actual sales have changed each day, with very low sales on 2nd and 12th January compared to high sales on 4th and 18th January. This analysis gives an idea to decide on what should be the appropriate daily inventory stocking of milk based on the expected demand.

Marketing Campaign Analysis

While marketing new or existing products or services, campaigns are conducted to increase their reach through various channels. For instance, a new broadband service of a telecom provider might conduct a campaign by printing advertisements and delivering them to prospective customers inside a mall or by doing a door-to-door delivery of the advertisement brochures in a particular prospective locality. The other way they might conduct a campaign is by reaching out to prospects through social media platforms or by posting advertisements on websites. The reach of these campaigns can be analyzed through various analytical methods and tools. The types of data that get collected through these campaigns are time series in nature and help in analyzing various customer behavioral aspects that can help in generating leads through prospects.

To examine an example of campaign time series data, let us look at the bank campaign dataset available at https://data.world/data-society/bank-marketing-data. A sample data from this dataset is presented in *Figure 1.15*. The dataset in *Figure 1.15* has the following input variables: age, job, marital status, education, credit default, loan details, mode of contact, last contacted month and day of the week, last contact duration, number of contacts during the campaign, last contact time gap, campaign outcome, employment variation rate, consumer price index, consumer confidence index, daily indicator, and quarterly indicator.

Banking campaign data

month	may	may	may	may	may	may	may	may
day_of_week	mon	mon	mon	mon	mon	mon	mon	mon
age	56	57	37	40	56	45	59	41
job	housemaid	services	services	admin.	services	services	admin.	blue-collar
marital	married	married	married	married	married	married	married	married
education	basic.4y	high.school	high.school	basic.6y	high.school	basic.9y	professional.course	unknown
default	no	unknown	no	no	no	unknown	no	unknown
housing	no	no	yes	no	no	no	no	no
loan	no	no	no	no	yes	no	no	no
contact	telephone	telephone	telephone	telephone	telephone	telephone	telephone	telephone
duration	261	149	226	151	307	198	139	217
campaign	1	1	1	1	1	1	1	1
pdays	999	999	999	999	999	999	999	999
previous	0	0	0	0	0	0	0	0
poutcome	nonexistent	nonexistent	nonexistent	nonexistent	nonexistent	nonexistent	nonexistent	nonexistent
emp.var.rate	1.1	1.1	1.1	1.1	1.1	1.1	1.1	1.1
cons.price.idx	93.994	93.994	93.994	93.994	93.994	93.994	93.994	93.994
cons.conf.idx	-36.4	-36.4	-36.4	-36.4	-36.4	-36.4	-36.4	-36.4
euribor3m	4.857	4.857	4.857	4.857	4.857	4.857	4.857	4.857
nr.employed	5191	5191	5191	5191	5191	5191	5191	5191
y	no	no	no	no	no	no	no	no

Figure 1.15: Sample data of a bank campaign

The input variables in this dataset can be used to perform time series campaign analysis and understand the campaign outcome. This kind of analysis will help in further product development as well as enhancing the reach of existing products to more prospective customers and helps in an effective lead generation too.

Customer Segmentation

Customer segmentation is the process of clustering customers into various segments based on their historical behavioral analysis. Customer segmentation can be performed focused on the product for which a specific segment of customers' needs to be targeted. Let us look at an example of input time series data that can be used to understand customer behavior and perform customer segmentation.

To understand this, let us examine individual household electric consumption data from https://archive.ics.uci.edu/ml/datasets/Individual+household+electric+power+consumption. The electric consumption patterns and timings of a household can help the electricity department to segment the customer under a specific bucket and ensure efficient power supply management in a well-planned and optimized manner. A sample data of individual household power consumption is provided in *Figure 1.16*.

Date	Time	Global_active_power	Global_reactive_power	Voltage	Global_intensity	Sub_metering_1	Sub_metering_2	Sub_metering_3
31-12-2006	00:00:00	0.21	0	243.1	0.8	0	0	0
31-12-2006	00:01:00	0.302	0.114	242.52	1.4	0	0	0
31-12-2006	00:02:00	0.32	0.152	242.71	1.4	0	0	0
31-12-2006	00:03:00	0.318	0.156	243.35	1.4	0	0	0
31-12-2006	00:04:00	0.318	0.162	244.4	1.4	0	0	0
31-12-2006	00:05:00	0.314	0.16	243.9	1.4	0	0	0
31-12-2006	00:06:00	0.314	0.158	243.83	1.4	0	0	0
31-12-2006	00:07:00	0.378	0.232	244.16	2	0	0	0
31-12-2006	00:08:00	2.494	0.25	241.62	10.2	0	1	0
31-12-2006	00:09:00	2.46	0.244	240.68	10.2	0	1	0
31-12-2006	00:10:00	0.74	0.276	243.01	4.6	0	2	0
31-12-2006	00:11:00	0.39	0.282	243.29	2	0	1	0
31-12-2006	00:12:00	0.39	0.28	243.07	2	0	1	0
31-12-2006	00:13:00	0.392	0.288	244.16	2	0	2	0
31-12-2006	00:14:00	0.392	0.29	244.39	2	0	1	0

Figure 1.16: *Sample dataset to understand consumer behavior*

The input variables of this dataset consist of data and time of power consumption, household global minute-averaged active power, household global minute-averaged reactive power, minute-averaged voltage, household global minute-averaged current intensity, sub-metering 1 for kitchen, sub-metering 2 for laundry room, and sub-metering 3 for the water heater.

A simple time series analysis can be performed by reviewing the power consumption over time for this household to understand the customer and segment them accordingly. *Figure 1.17* is a sample view of the power consumption on 31st of December 2006.

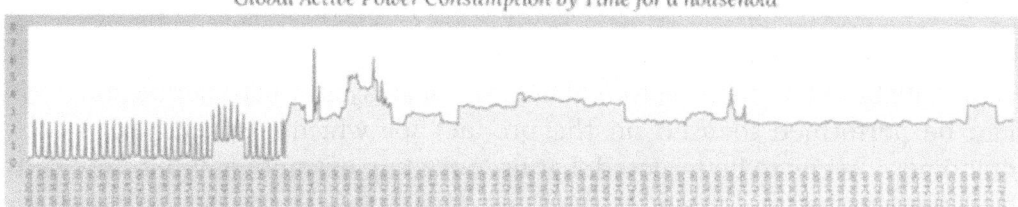

Figure 1.17: Minute-wise power consumption of a household

Observing daily patterns, the quantity of power consumed, and the timing of power consumption can help in segmenting this household into an appropriate bucket such as heavy users, moderate users, or limited users.

Other areas where time series data can be utilized in Sales and Marketing include marketing research, trend analysis, product development, pricing analysis, and many more. With this understanding, let us move on to the next section on the applications of time series data in the healthcare industry.

Usage in Healthcare

Time series analysis is an important and effective technique in understanding healthcare data, identifying disease patterns and frequencies, predicting the chances of comorbidities in patients, identifying the intensity and spread of communicable diseases, and many more use cases. Let us discuss some of these applications along with example datasets in this section.

Analysis of Patient Features in Treating Comorbidities

Understanding various health attributes of patients going through the same or similar diseases helps in identifying the right treatment procedures and developing more suitable drugs for specific diseases. This can be performed by studying the health parameters of patients over a specific time and will help medical practitioners and pharmaceutical manufacturers to make the right decisions in disease treatment and drug manufacturing, respectively.

Let us look at this possibility by exploring an example dataset on diabetes from https://archive.ics.uci.edu/ml/datasets/Diabetes. This dataset consists of the readings of 70 patients for various codes, as explained in *Figure 1.18*.

Introduction to Time Series

Health parameter codes for diabetes patients

code	description
33	Regular insulin dose
34	NPH insulin dose
35	UltraLente insulin dose
48	Unspecified blood glucose measurement
57	Unspecified blood glucose measurement
58	Pre-breakfast blood glucose measurement
59	Post-breakfast blood glucose measurement
60	Pre-lunch blood glucose measurement
61	Post-lunch blood glucose measurement
62	Pre-supper blood glucose measurement
63	Post-supper blood glucose measurement
64	Pre-snack blood glucose measurement
65	Hypoglycæmic symptoms
66	Typical meal ingestion
67	More-than-usual meal ingestion
68	Less-than-usual meal ingestion
69	Typical exercise activity
70	More-than-usual exercise activity
71	Less-than-usual exercise activity
72	Unspecified special event

Figure 1.18: *List of Health parameter codes from the Diabetes dataset*

A sample dataset of records for patient ID: 68 is displayed in *Figure 1.19*:

Figure 1.19: *Sample of Health coefficients of patients from the Diabetes dataset*

From this time series dataset, the health check parameters and values related to 70 patients with diabetes can be analyzed to understand the health conditions of patients on time and provide the right kind of treatment.

Disease Detection and Prediction

Another use case in healthcare is in the field of detecting or predicting disease in a patient by analyzing the data of similar patients. Predicting a disease or detecting it in advance can help in the precautionary treatment and in avoiding the disease before it manifests or aggravates in a patient. Very high accuracy is required in such use cases since an error can lead to incorrect treatment, which can be harmful or fatal to patients. An example of a healthcare dataset that can be used for the detection of probable coronavirus deaths can be downloaded from https://data.world/covid-19-data-resource-hub/covid-19-case-counts . This dataset has multiple variables in a time series, and the number of probable deaths due to coronavirus in a particular locality can be predicted or forecasted using machine learning or deep learning algorithms. A sample of the dataset is presented in *Figure 1.20*.

Covid-19 cases dataset of Albany

REPORT DATE	PEOPLE POSITIVE CASES COUNT	COUNTY NAME	PROVINCE STATE NAME	CONTINENT NAME	DATA SOURCE NAME	PEOPLE DEATH NEW COUNT	COUNTY FIPS NUMBER	COUNTRY ALPHA 3 CODE	COUNTRY SHORT NAM	COUNTRY ALPHA 2 CODE	PEOPLE POSITIVE NEW CASES COUNT	PEOPLE DEATH COUNT
01-04-2020	240	Albany	New York	America	New York Times	1	36001	USA	United States	US	14	2
02-04-2020	255	Albany	New York	America	New York Times	0	36001	USA	United States	US	15	2
03-04-2020	267	Albany	New York	America	New York Times	2	36001	USA	United States	US	14	4
04-04-2020	280	Albany	New York	America	New York Times	2	36001	USA	United States	US	26	6
05-04-2020	306	Albany	New York	America	New York Times	2	36001	USA	United States	US	12	8
06-04-2020	319	Albany	New York	America	New York Times	1	36001	USA	United States	US	14	9
07-04-2020	333	Albany	New York	America	New York Times	0	36001	USA	United States	US	14	9
08-04-2020	342	Albany	New York	America	New York Times	1	36001	USA	United States	US	9	10
09-04-2020	379	Albany	New York	America	New York Times	2	36001	USA	United States	US	37	12
10-04-2020	426	Albany	New York	America	New York Times	2	36001	USA	United States	US	47	14
11-04-2020	446	Albany	New York	America	New York Times	2	36001	USA	United States	US	20	16
12-04-2020	478	Albany	New York	America	New York Times	0	36001	USA	United States	US	32	16
13-04-2020	499	Albany	New York	America	New York Times	1	36001	USA	United States	US	21	17
14-04-2020	535	Albany	New York	America	New York Times	4	36001	USA	United States	US	36	21
15-04-2020	548	Albany	New York	America	New York Times	5	36001	USA	United States	US	13	26
16-04-2020	581	Albany	New York	America	New York Times	0	36001	USA	United States	US	33	26
17-04-2020	619	Albany	New York	America	New York Times	0	36001	USA	United States	US	38	26
18-04-2020	648	Albany	New York	America	New York Times	0	36001	USA	United States	US	29	26
19-04-2020	682	Albany	New York	America	New York Times	7	36001	USA	United States	US	34	33
20-04-2020	687	Albany	New York	America	New York Times	2	36001	USA	United States	US	5	35
21-04-2020	704	Albany	New York	America	New York Times	1	36001	USA	United States	US	17	36
22-04-2020	737	Albany	New York	America	New York Times	0	36001	USA	United States	US	33	36
23-04-2020	758	Albany	New York	America	New York Times	5	36001	USA	United States	US	21	41
24-04-2020	805	Albany	New York	America	New York Times	1	36001	USA	United States	US	47	42
25-04-2020	899	Albany	New York	America	New York Times	1	36001	USA	United States	US	94	43
26-04-2020	948	Albany	New York	America	New York Times	2	36001	USA	United States	US	49	45
27-04-2020	979	Albany	New York	America	New York Times	0	36001	USA	United States	US	31	45
28-04-2020	1009	Albany	New York	America	New York Times	0	36001	USA	United States	US	30	45
29-04-2020	1067	Albany	New York	America	New York Times	2	36001	USA	United States	US	58	47
30-04-2020	1165	Albany	New York	America	New York Times	6	36001	USA	United States	US	98	53

Figure 1.20: *Sample COVID-19 cases data*

This data shows the reporting date of COVID-19 cases in Albany, along with demographic details and the number of detected positive cases, as well as the number of deaths. A study of the correlation between location, the number of positive cases, and the number of deaths over a period might be a possible use case to forecast the number of deaths at a future point in time. *Figure 1.21* depicts the direction of movement of COVID death count vs. positive cases count.

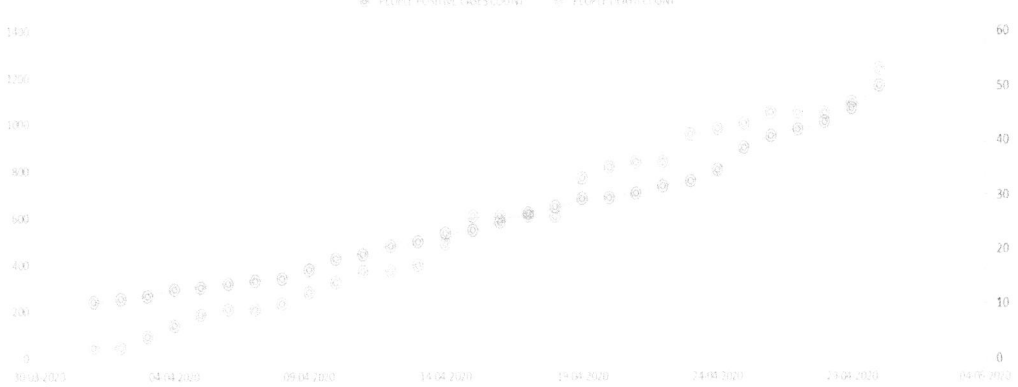

Figure 1.21: COVID positive cases vs. deaths

These are some examples of time series applications in the healthcare industry. With this understanding, let us look at a few more domains and examples where time series data can be effectively utilized for educated decision-making.

Usage in Weather and Environmental Science

Weather and climate analysis is another important domain where time series data is widely used. Analyzing historical climatic conditions and studying weather patterns helps in forecasting future weather conditions in specific seasons and periods. Applications of models on climate data can increase the accuracy of such forecasts. Another use case would be in predicting disaster situations such as earthquakes or volcano eruptions in a locality based on historical data modeling. Time series analysis of weather data can also help in identifying the impact of pollution or deforestation on the environment and taking the right measures to control the depletion of natural resources.

Let us look at an example of a climate and environment dataset from:

https://archive.ics.uci.edu/ml/datasets/Greenhouse+Gas+Observing+Network.

This dataset contains a time series of greenhouse gas (GHG) concentrations at 2921 grid cells in California created using simulations. A sample of the GHG data is represented as follows:

Sample GHG dataset

Region	Time period 1	Time period 2	Time period 3	Time period 4	Time period 5	Time period 6
Region 1	0.000119211	0.00012144	0.000119234	0.003364916	0.01007477	0.01868644
Region 2	0.000129082	0.000121438	0.000119239	0.02664775	0.08732145	0.1146594
Region 3	0.000123167	0.000121439	0.000119233	0.1085916	0.4469747	0.5421139
Region 4	0.000120406	0.00012144	0.000119233	0.003971372	0.06156554	0.1189335
Region 5	0.000119544	0.000121439	0.000119233	0.003057116	0.01026343	0.01421324
Region 6	0.000119741	0.000121439	0.000119233	0.000149049	0.005107149	0.03263646
Region 7	0.07996896	0.000342311	0.000152469	0.3214087	2.747699	3.389921
Region 8	0.02318376	0.000152633	0.000490664	0.06955806	1.571334	2.717854
Region 9	0.1544369	0.00050707	0.00174998	0.05243933	0.4825722	0.4569814
Region 10	0.000263868	0.000121496	0.000132802	0.03189226	1.241558	1.627293
Region 11	0.1060105	0.002890401	0.1886558	0.9680126	2.987851	1.228453
Region 12	0.0115642	0.000635318	0.01463407	3.610982	71.04779	28.74756
Region 13	0.0001	0.000144546	0.000100001	0.000100272	0.0409545	0.01554544
Region 14	42.66028	28.79044	34.31854	42.8645	0.05703437	0.1920971
Region 15	0.000543986	0.1783792	0.0362916	0.04007686	0.213956	1.381346
Synthetic observation	23.84779	38.19709	19.8772	25.36687	47.67966	38.01834

Figure 1.22: *Greenhouse gas data*

In *Figure* 1.22, rows 1–6 represent the regions where the greenhouse gas concentration was observed, and row 17 represents the concentration of synthetic observations. Columns of this dataset represent 6-hour intervals of GHG concentration levels.

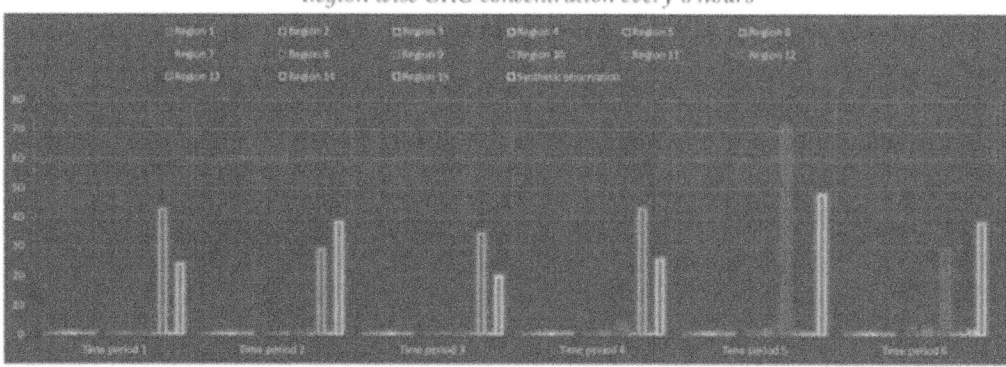

Figure 1.23: *Comparison of GHG concentration between regions*

The preceding *Figure* 1.23 shows an example of how greenhouse gas concentrations vary in various regions of a particular location. With this understanding, let us further explore the applications of time series data in transportation and traffic management.

Usage in Transportation and Traffic Management

The transportation and traffic management domain can also make use of time series data to effectively plan public transportation, public safety, manage traffic flow in heavy traffic regions, timing of road-related construction work, and many more. The transportation department can plan the timings and frequencies of public transportation, such as buses and trains, using the historical number of passengers traveling in different regions during the days of a week. Optimal planning can also help in cost-saving and pollution management. Another use case of time series data will be in traffic control, where traffic management can be effectively handled by focusing on the days and timings of heavy traffic flow and redirecting traffic to avoid traffic jams and delays for the public. Analyzing historical traffic flows can also help public departments plan the timing of road construction or repair work so that the public is not impacted during their peak hours of travel. Efficient traffic flow management can also minimize the number of road accidents and enhance public safety.

Let us look at an example of time series data that can help study the behavior of urban traffic. The behavior of the urban traffic of the city of Sao Paulo in Brazil dataset is downloaded from https://archive.ics.uci.edu/ml/datasets/Behavior+of+the+urban+traffic+of+the+city+of+Sao+Paulo+in+Brazil. A sample of this dataset is represented in *Figure 1.24*.

Figure 1.24: Sample data of behavior of the urban traffic of the city of Sao Paulo in Brazil

A simple graphical analysis of all the variables of time series data from the dataset in *Figure 1.24* can be reviewed in *Figure 1.25*:

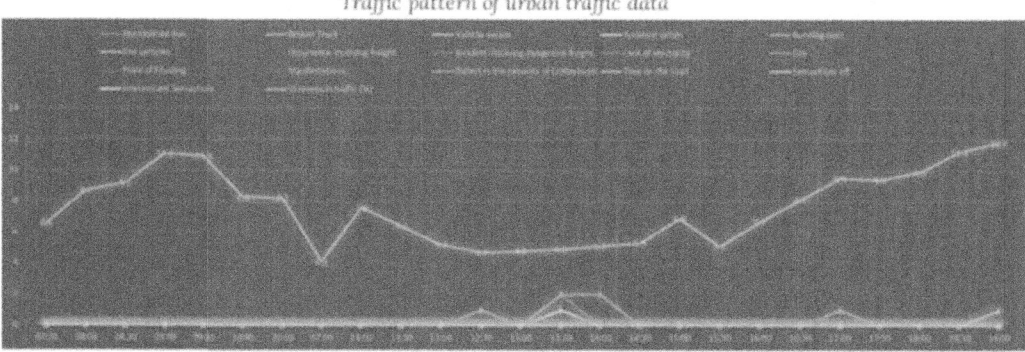

Figure 1.25: *Traffic pattern analysis with respect to time*

From the preceding graph in *Figure 1.25*, we can observe that slowness is more impacted by timing rather than scenarios like a broken truck or an accident. Even when there were two broken trucks, two immobilized buses, and one accident victim at 1:30 pm, the traffic movement was still faster compared to 9:00 am or 7:00 pm when there were no blocking scenarios.

These are some of the applications of time series data in various industry domains. In the next section, let us explore the steps required to prepare time series data for analysis.

Preparation of Time Series Data

In this section, let us learn about how to collect and prepare time series data, and the steps involved in the preparation activities.

1. **Data Collection**

    Gathering the time series data required to solve a business problem or use case is the first step in preparing time series data. Data can be gathered in the following ways depending on the problem to be solved:

    - Record data in smart devices at regular intervals of time
    - Record data through everyday activities happening in the business such as daily sales
    - Record data into databases such as bank transactions
    - Record data manually through surveys or forms at regular time intervals

2. **Exploratory Data Analysis**

   Exploratory data analysis is the process of understanding the data and reviewing various properties of the data before getting the data ready to solve a problem.

   Explore the data gathered by:
   - Performing univariate analysis
   - Performing multivariate analysis
   - Reviewing the overall structure of data
   - Reviewing the data types of variables gathered
   - Analyzing the missing values and null values
   - Analyzing the outliers in each variable
   - Performing visualization of the data

3. **Data Cleansing**

   Cleansing the data is the next step where the data is treated and enriched to convert it into a usable form. Following are the steps involved in data cleansing:
   - Missing value treatment
   - Null value treatment
   - Outlier treatment
   - Data type conversion
   - Handling special characters
   - Creation of dummy variables or one hot encoding

4. **Normalization**

   Conversion of numeric variables in the data into a common unit scale is required as part of data preparation so that time series techniques or machine learning algorithms can perform better in predicting using the data.

5. **Resampling**

   The data sometimes might need to be resampled to make it more usable in prediction problems. Two types of resampling can be performed on the data:

- **Upsampling**: Increasing the number of records or increasing the frequency of data when there is not enough data to solve a business problem.
- **Downsampling**: Decreasing the number of records or decreasing the frequency of data when there is more data to solve a business problem.

6. **Trend Analysis**

    Analysis of the direction of movement of the time series data, such as if the data is moving upward or downward over a period.

7. **Seasonal Analysis**

    Analysis of repetitive patterns in the data with respect to specific repetitive times such as daily, weekly, or monthly seasonal patterns.

8. **Featurization**

    Performing feature engineering on the data, such as applying dimensionality reduction techniques when there are a greater number of variables, identifying the relevant input variables through domain expertise, and more.

These are the steps required to prepare time series data for solving problems such as forecasting or prediction from the data, enabling better-informed decision-making using the time series data.

Conclusion

In this chapter, we have learned about an overview of time series data and explored its applications in various domains, including finance and economics, sales and marketing, and healthcare.

Additionally, we discussed its applications in weather and environmental science, as well as transportation and traffic management.

In the next chapter, we will provide an overview of time series libraries in Python with examples and code.

References

- UCI Machine Learning Repository: Data Sets. Available at: https://archive.ics.uci.edu/ml/datasets.php (Accessed: March 26, 2023).

- Yahoo Finance - Stock Market Live, quotes, Business & Finance News (no date) Yahoo! Finance. Yahoo! Available at: https://finance.yahoo.com/ (Accessed: March 26, 2023).

- National Stock Exchange of India LTD. (no date) NSE. Available at: https://www1.nseindia.com/products/content/equities/indices/historical_vix.htm (Accessed: March 26, 2023).

- GDP (current US$) (no date) Data. Available at: https://data.worldbank.org/indicator/NY.GDP.MKTP.CD (Accessed: March 26, 2023).

- Tan, S. C. and San Lau, J. P. (2014) 'Time series clustering: A superior alternative for market basket analysis', in Proceedings of the First International Conference on Advanced Data and Information Engineering (DaEng-2013). Springer, Singapore, pp. 241–248.

- Chen, D., Sain, S.L. and Guo, K. (2012) Data mining for the online retail industry: A case study of RFM model-based customer segmentation using data mining - Journal of Database Marketing & Customer Strategy Management, SpringerLink. Palgrave Macmillan UK. Available at: https://link.springer.com/article/10.1057/dbm.2012.17 (Accessed: March 26, 2023).

- Bank marketing data - dataset by data-society (2016) data.world. Available at: https://data.world/data-society/bank-marketing-data (Accessed: March 26, 2023).

- (no date) UCI Machine Learning Repository: Individual household electric power consumption data set. Available at: https://archive.ics.uci.edu/ml/datasets/Individual+household+electric+power+consumption (Accessed: March 26, 2023).

- Kahn, M. (no date) UCI Machine Learning Repository: Diabetes data set. Washington University, St. Louis, MO. Available at: https://archive.ics.uci.edu/ml/datasets/Diabetes (Accessed: March 26, 2023).

- Covid-19 activity - dataset by COVID-19-data-resource-hub (no date) data.world. Available at: https://data.world/covid-19-data-resource-hub/covid-19-case-counts (Accessed: March 26, 2023).

- Lucas, D.D. et al. (2015) "Designing optimal greenhouse gas observing networks that consider performance and cost," Geoscientific Instrumentation, Methods and Data Systems, 4(1), pp. 121–137. Available at: https://doi.org/10.5194/gi-4-121-2015.

- Ferreira, R.P. (2016) "Combination of artificial intelligence techniques for prediction the behavior of urban vehicular traffic in the city of São Paulo," Anais do 10. Congresso Brasileiro de Inteligência Computacional [Preprint]. Available at: https://doi.org/10.21528/cbic2011-12.1.

CHAPTER 2
Overview of Time Series Libraries in Python

Time series is a very important data point needed for understanding changes in information over time, and the right tools needed to perform an analysis of time series data are available in Python. Many popular libraries have functionalities to handle time series data.

In this chapter, we will explore some of the popular time series libraries in Python, along with examples that help to understand the usage of these libraries. We will begin by introducing the features available in Pandas for handling time series data. Next, we will cover examples using NumPy, followed by Statsmodel. Additionally, we will further provide an introduction to some of the other important libraries such as Prophet and AutoTS.

Structure

In this chapter, the following topics will be covered:
- Pandas for Time Series
- Numpy for Time Series
- Prophet for Time Series
- AutoTS for Time Series

Pandas for Time Series

In this section, let us begin by examining one of the most prominent libraries in Python, which is used for data processing. Pandas is a library heavily used for all kinds of data processing in Python. This library is mainly used for structured data, and its functionalities are intuitive and can be easily handled by developers for various data processing use cases.

Documentation

The documentation for this library is available at: **https://pandas.pydata.org/docs/getting_started/overview.html**

Installation

Pandas can be installed for Python using the following command:

```
pip install pandas
```

Functionalities of Pandas

Pandas is used to handle datasets that are structured in nature. The main feature of this library is the data frames, which are a tabular representation of data. We can load datasets of different formats into Pandas data frames and thereby perform various operations on the data, including cleansing, aggregating, or transforming data. We can also view the structure of the data, perform data type conversions, and conduct exploratory analysis on the data. Pandas also supports time series operations on the data, which we will explore in this section. Official documentation on Pandas time series functionalities can be found at https://pandas.pydata.org/docs/user_guide/timeseries.html.

Let us look at an application of Pandas over time series data in the following case study.

Let us assume a scenario where we would like to analyze the air quality of a city over time. To perform this analysis, let us download the data in CSV format from the UCI Machine Learning repository. In this example, the Air Quality data from https://archive.ics.uci.edu/ml/datasets/Air+Quality will be analyzed for its various attributes, and the time series data will be studied using Pandas.

To begin with, let us first import Pandas into the Python interface and then proceed to read the CSV file into a new Pandas data frame named `airquality_df`. The CSV file has a semicolon (`;`) delimiter:

```
import pandas as pd
```

Overview of Time Series Libraries in Python

```
airquality_df = pd.read_csv("AirQualityUCI.csv", sep = ";")
```

Once the data frame is created, we can start by exploring the data.

Code:

```
airquality_df.shape
```

Output:

```
(9471, 17)
```

The air quality data has 9471 rows and 17 columns. A sample of the data frame can be viewed as follows:

Code:

```
airquality_df.head(5)
```

Output:

Figure 2.1: Air quality dataset

We can further look at the column names and decide if all the columns are needed for the analysis.

Code:

```
airquality_df.columns
```

Output:

```
Index(['Date', 'Time', 'CO(GT)', 'PT08.S1(CO)', 'NMHC(GT)', 'C6H6(GT)',
       'PT08.S2(NMHC)', 'NOx(GT)', 'PT08.S3(NOx)', 'NO2(GT)', 'PT08.
       S4(NO2)',
       'PT08.S5(O3)', 'T', 'RH', 'AH', 'Unnamed: 15', 'Unnamed: 16'],
       dtype='object')
```

In the preceding output, two columns are not needed for this analysis and they will be dropped from the data frame.

Code:

```
airquality_df.drop(labels = ['Unnamed: 15', 'Unnamed: 16'], axis = 1, inplace = True)

airquality_df.columns
```

Output:

```
Index(['Date', 'Time', 'CO(GT)', 'PT08.S1(CO)', 'NMHC(GT)', 'C6H6(GT)',
       'PT08.S2(NMHC)', 'NOx(GT)', 'PT08.S3(NOx)', 'NO2(GT)', 'PT08.
       S4(NO2)',
       'PT08.S5(O3)', 'T', 'RH', 'AH', 'Unnamed: 15', 'Unnamed: 16'],
      dtype='object')
```

The attributes of the dataset consist of date and time followed by the concentration of various gases, temperature, relative humidity, and absolute humidity values. While reviewing the **tail** of the dataset, it is observed that there are null values in the data.

Code:

```
airquality_df.tail(5)
```

Output:

	Date	Time	CO(GT)	PT08.S1(CO)	NMHC(GT)	C6H6(GT)	PT08.S2(NMHC)	NOx(GT)	PT08.S3(NOx)	NO2(GT)	PT08.S4(NO2)	PT08.S5(O3)	T	RH	AH
9466	NaN	NaN	NaN	NaN	NaN	NaN	NaN	NaN	NaN	NaN	NaN	NaN	NaN	NaN	NaN
9467	NaN	NaN	NaN	NaN	NaN	NaN	NaN	NaN	NaN	NaN	NaN	NaN	NaN	NaN	NaN
9468	NaN	NaN	NaN	NaN	NaN	NaN	NaN	NaN	NaN	NaN	NaN	NaN	NaN	NaN	NaN
9469	NaN	NaN	NaN	NaN	NaN	NaN	NaN	NaN	NaN	NaN	NaN	NaN	NaN	NaN	NaN
9470	NaN	NaN	NaN	NaN	NaN	NaN	NaN	NaN	NaN	NaN	NaN	NaN	NaN	NaN	NaN

Figure 2.2: Air quality – null values

The next step to handle this data would be to understand the existence of null values. Let us explore it with **isna**.

Code:

```
airquality_df.isna()
```

Output:

	Date	Time	CO(GT)	PT08.S1(CO)	NMHC(GT)	C6H6(GT)	PT08.S2(NMHC)	NOx(GT)	PT08.S3(NOx)	NO2(GT)	PT08.S4(NO2)	PT08.S5(O3)	T	RH
0	False	False	False	False	False	False	False	False	False	False	False	False	False	False
1	False	False	False	False	False	False	False	False	False	False	False	False	False	False
2	False	False	False	False	False	False	False	False	False	False	False	False	False	False
3	False	False	False	False	False	False	False	False	False	False	False	False	False	False
4	False	False	False	False	False	False	False	False	False	False	False	False	False	False
...														
9466	True	True	True	True	True	True	True	True	True	True	True	True	True	True
9467	True	True	True	True	True	True	True	True	True	True	True	True	True	True
9468	True	True	True	True	True	True	True	True	True	True	True	True	True	True
9469	True	True	True	True	True	True	True	True	True	True	True	True	True	True
9470	True	True	True	True	True	True	True	True	True	True	True	True	True	True

9471 rows × 15 columns

Figure 2.3: *Identifying null records in Air Quality data*

The next step is to understand the total number of null records.

Code:

```
airquality_df.isna().sum()
```

Output:

```
Date            114
Time            114
CO(GT)          114
PT08.S1(CO)     114
NMHC(GT)        114
C6H6(GT)        114
PT08.S2(NMHC)   114
NOx(GT)         114
PT08.S3(NOx)    114
NO2(GT)         114
PT08.S4(NO2)    114
PT08.S5(O3)     114
T               114
RH              114
```

```
AH               114
dtype: int64
```

There are a total of 114 records with null values in the data. From *Figure 2.3*, it is evident that the records with null values also do not have date and time values populated. In such a case, it would be appropriate to clean the dataset by dropping all the null value records.

Code:

```
airquality_df.dropna(inplace = True)
airquality_df
```

Output:

	Date	Time	CO(GT)	PT08.S1(CO)	NMHC(GT)	C6H6(GT)	PT08.S2(NMHC)	NOx(GT)	PT08.S3(NOx)	NO2(GT)	PT08.S4(NO2)	PT08.S5(O3)	T
0	10/03/2004	18.00.00	2,6	1360.0	150.0	11.9	1046.0	166.0	1056.0	113.0	1692.0	1268.0	13.6
1	10/03/2004	19.00.00	2	1292.0	112.0	9.4	955.0	103.0	1174.0	92.0	1559.0	972.0	13.3
2	10/03/2004	20.00.00	2,2	1402.0	88.0	9.0	939.0	131.0	1140.0	114.0	1555.0	1074.0	11.9
3	10/03/2004	21.00.00	2,2	1376.0	80.0	9.2	948.0	172.0	1092.0	122.0	1584.0	1203.0	11.0
4	10/03/2004	22.00.00	1,6	1272.0	51.0	6.5	836.0	131.0	1205.0	116.0	1490.0	1110.0	11.2
...	...	...	...	...	...	...	...	...	...	...	...	...	...
9352	04/04/2005	10.00.00	3,1	1314.0	-200.0	13.5	1101.0	472.0	539.0	190.0	1374.0	1729.0	21.9
9353	04/04/2005	11.00.00	2,4	1163.0	-200.0	11.4	1027.0	353.0	604.0	179.0	1264.0	1269.0	24.3
9354	04/04/2005	12.00.00	2,4	1142.0	-200.0	12.4	1063.0	293.0	603.0	175.0	1241.0	1092.0	26.9
9355	04/04/2005	13.00.00	2,1	1003.0	-200.0	9.5	961.0	235.0	702.0	156.0	1041.0	770.0	28.3
9356	04/04/2005	14.00.00	2,2	1071.0	-200.0	11.9	1047.0	265.0	654.0	168.0	1129.0	816.0	28.5

9357 rows × 15 columns

Figure 2.4: *Clean dataset*

Now that the data has no null or missing values, we can further look at the data types of the data. Since the dataset is a time series, we need to check the suitability of the data to perform a time series analysis.

Code:

```
airquality_df.dtypes
```

Output:

```
Date             object
Time             object
CO(GT)           object
PT08.S1(CO)     float64
```

```
NMHC(GT)            float64
C6H6(GT)             object
PT08.S2(NMHC)       float64
NOx(GT)             float64
PT08.S3(NOx)        float64
NO2(GT)             float64
PT08.S4(NO2)        float64
PT08.S5(O3)         float64
T                    object
RH                   object
AH                   object
dtype: object
```

Let us now specifically examine all columns with the data type as object, excluding the Date and Time columns.

Code:

```
airquality_df[['CO(GT)', 'C6H6(GT)', 'T', 'RH', 'AH']]
```

Output:

	CO(GT)	C6H6(GT)	T	RH	AH
0	2.6	11.9	13.6	48.9	0.7578
1	2	9.4	13.3	47.7	0.7255
2	2.2	9.0	11.9	54.0	0.7502
3	2.2	9.2	11.0	60.0	0.7867
4	1.6	6.5	11.2	59.6	0.7888
...	...	...	...	...	...
9352	3.1	13.5	21.9	29.3	0.7568
9353	2.4	11.4	24.3	23.7	0.7119
9354	2.4	12.4	26.9	18.3	0.6406
9355	2.1	9.5	28.3	13.5	0.5139
9356	2.2	11.9	28.5	13.1	0.5028

9357 rows × 5 columns

Figure 2.5: *Object columns that need data type conversion*

The columns shown in *Figure 2.5* need to be converted to float from object after replacing the comma (,) with decimal point (.).

Code:

```
cleanup = ['CO(GT)', 'C6H6(GT)', 'T', 'RH', 'AH']

for i in cleanup:
    airquality_df[i] = airquality_df[i].apply(lambda x: x.replace(',', '.')).astype('float64')

airquality_df[['CO(GT)', 'C6H6(GT)', 'T', 'RH', 'AH']]
```

Output:

	CO(GT)	C6H6(GT)	T	RH	AH
0	2.6	11.9	13.6	48.9	0.7578
1	2.0	9.4	13.3	47.7	0.7255
2	2.2	9.0	11.9	54.0	0.7502
3	2.2	9.2	11.0	60.0	0.7867
4	1.6	6.5	11.2	59.6	0.7888
...	...	...	...	...	...
9352	3.1	13.5	21.9	29.3	0.7568
9353	2.4	11.4	24.3	23.7	0.7119
9354	2.4	12.4	26.9	18.3	0.6406
9355	2.1	9.5	28.3	13.5	0.5139
9356	2.2	11.9	28.5	13.1	0.5028

9357 rows × 5 columns

Figure 2.6: Columns converted to float

We still have not converted the Date and Time columns into the required data type. Currently, the date column is displayed as object, as shown in *Figure 2.7*:

```
0       10/03/2004
1       10/03/2004
2       10/03/2004
3       10/03/2004
4       10/03/2004
         ...
9352    04/04/2005
9353    04/04/2005
9354    04/04/2005
9355    04/04/2005
9356    04/04/2005
Name: Date, Length: 9357, dtype: object
```

Figure 2.7: Date column as object

We will make use of `pd.to_datetime` from pandas to convert this column into a date.

Code:

airquality_df['Date'] = pd.to_datetime(airquality_df['Date'])

airquality_df['Date']

Output:

0   2004-10-03

1   2004-10-03

2   2004-10-03

3   2004-10-03

4   2004-10-03

          ...

9352   2005-04-04

9353   2005-04-04

9354   2005-04-04

9355   2005-04-04

9356   2005-04-04

Name: Date, Length: 9357, dtype: datetime64[ns]

We still need to convert the `Time` column. Currently, the `Time` column is an object, and the time separator is (.) instead of (:), which needs to be corrected. The `Time` column will then be converted to a time delta using **pd.to_timedelta**.

Code:

airquality_df['Time']

Output:

0	18.00.00
1	19.00.00
2	20.00.00
3	21.00.00
4	22.00.00
	...
9352	10.00.00
9353	11.00.00
9354	12.00.00
9355	13.00.00
9356	14.00.00

Name: Time, Length: 9357, dtype: object

Let us replace a dot with a colon in the `Time` column values.

Code:

airquality_df['Time'] = airquality_df['Time'].apply(lambda x: x.replace('.', ':'))

airquality_df['Time']

Output:

0	18:00:00
1	19:00:00

Overview of Time Series Libraries in Python

2	20:00:00
3	21:00:00
4	22:00:00
	...
9352	10:00:00
9353	11:00:00
9354	12:00:00
9355	13:00:00
9356	14:00:00

Name: Time, Length: 9357, dtype: object

Now that the data is in the right string format, we will convert it into a time delta.

Code:

airquality_df['Time'] = pd.to_timedelta(airquality_df['Time'])

airquality_df['Time']

Output:

0	0 days 18:00:00
1	0 days 19:00:00
2	0 days 20:00:00
3	0 days 21:00:00
4	0 days 22:00:00
	...
9352	0 days 10:00:00
9353	0 days 11:00:00
9354	0 days 12:00:00

9355   0 days 13:00:00

9356   0 days 14:00:00

Name: Time, Length: 9357, dtype: timedelta64[ns]

Finally, let us create a new column named **Timestamp** to combine **Data** and **Time** columns from the data frame.

Code:

airquality_df['Timestamp'] = airquality_df['Date'] + airquality_df['Time']

airquality_df['Timestamp']

Output:

0   2004-10-03 18:00:00

1   2004-10-03 19:00:00

2   2004-10-03 20:00:00

3   2004-10-03 21:00:00

4   2004-10-03 22:00:00

            ...

9352   2005-04-04 10:00:00

9353   2005-04-04 11:00:00

9354   2005-04-04 12:00:00

9355   2005-04-04 13:00:00

9356   2005-04-04 14:00:00

Name: Timestamp, Length: 9357, dtype: datetime64[ns]

With these steps, we have a clean time series dataset that can be used for forecasting or prediction. The final data frame is represented as follows:

	0	1	2	3	4
Date	2004-10-03 00:00:00	2004-10-03 00:00:00	2004-10-03 00:00:00	2004-10-03 00:00:00	2004-10-03 00:00:00
Time	0 days 18:00:00	0 days 19:00:00	0 days 20:00:00	0 days 21:00:00	0 days 22:00:00
CO(GT)	2.6	2.0	2.2	2.2	1.6
PT08.S1(CO)	1360.0	1292.0	1402.0	1376.0	1272.0
NMHC(GT)	150.0	112.0	88.0	80.0	51.0
C6H6(GT)	11.9	9.4	9.0	9.2	6.5
PT08.S2(NMHC)	1046.0	955.0	939.0	948.0	836.0
NOx(GT)	166.0	103.0	131.0	172.0	131.0
PT08.S3(NOx)	1056.0	1174.0	1140.0	1092.0	1205.0
NO2(GT)	113.0	92.0	114.0	122.0	116.0
PT08.S4(NO2)	1692.0	1559.0	1555.0	1584.0	1490.0
PT08.S5(O3)	1268.0	972.0	1074.0	1203.0	1110.0
T	13.6	13.3	11.9	11.0	11.2
RH	48.9	47.7	54.0	60.0	59.6
AH	0.7578	0.7255	0.7502	0.7867	0.7888
Timestamp	2004-10-03 18:00:00	2004-10-03 19:00:00	2004-10-03 20:00:00	2004-10-03 21:00:00	2004-10-03 22:00:00

Figure 2.8: Air Quality dataset processed with Pandas

With this understanding, let us further explore a few examples with NumPy.

NumPy for Time Series

In this section, we will cover another important Python library named NumPy, which can be widely used to perform various numerical computing operations on time series data. NumPy is effective in performing array-wise calculations on the data, while Pandas is widely used to perform data frame processing. Let us look at some of the examples of using NumPy on the Air Quality dataset from our Pandas example.

Documentation

The documentation for this library is available at: **https://numpy.org/doc/stable/**

Installation

NumPy can be installed for Python using the following command:

```
pip install numpy
```

Functionalities of NumPy

NumPy is another important library used for data processing in Python, covering functionalities that perform scientific computing on the data. It can be used for one-dimensional and multi-dimensional array operations on the data. NumPy offers a better performance in scientific computing since it is built on optimized and precompiled C code that makes it faster. The official documentation of NumPy can be found at the following path: https://numpy.org/doc/stable/user/index.html.

In this section, let us look at some of the examples of applying NumPy functionalities on air quality data.

Let us now reuse the `airquality_df` from the Pandas example and perform a few array operations. As a first step, let us import the `NumPy` library using the following command:

```
import numpy as np
```

We can perform various mathematical operations on the time series data using NumPy. Let us now focus on one particular column, `CO(GT)`, from the air quality dataset. This column represents the concentration of carbon monoxide in the air, and it is measured in mg/m^3. We will now perform an array calculation to convert it into parts per million (ppm).

Let us now create a new variable and store the values from `CO(GT)` into an array.

Code:

```
airquality_co_mgm3 = np.array(airquality_df['CO(GT)'])
airquality_co_mgm3
```

Output:

```
array([2.6, 2. , 2.2, ..., 2.4, 2.1, 2.2])
```

It becomes simple to apply the ppm calculation on a NumPy array.

Code:

```
airquality_co_ppm = airquality_co_mgm3 * 0.001
airquality_co_ppm
```

Output:

```
array([0.0026, 0.002 , 0.0022, ..., 0.0024, 0.0021, 0.0022])
```

Overview of Time Series Libraries in Python

Similarly, it is also simple to perform arithmetic operations on elements of multiple arrays using NumPy without writing for loops to perform iterative calculations.

Let us look at an example where we will perform element-wise addition on two arrays to calculate the total presence of non-metallic hydrocarbons and benzene together in the air for each period.

Code:

```
airquality_nmhc_microm3 = np.array(airquality_df['NMHC(GT)'])
airquality_nmhc_microm3
```

Output:

```
array([ 150.,  112.,   88., ..., -200., -200., -200.])
```

Code:

```
airquality_ben_microm3 = np.array(airquality_df['C6H6(GT)'])
airquality_ben_microm3
```

Output:

```
array([11.9,  9.4,  9. , ..., 12.4,  9.5, 11.9])
```

Code:

```
airquality_nmhc_microm3 + airquality_ben_microm3
```

Output:

```
array([ 161.9,  121.4,   97. , ..., -187.6, -190.5, -188.1])
```

Numpy can also be used to perform statistical computations on time series data. Some of the examples are provided in the following code:

Code:

```
np.mean(airquality_co_ppm)
```

Output:

```
-0.03420752377898899
```

Code:

```
np.median(airquality_co_ppm)
```

Output:

0.0015

Code:

np.max(airquality_co_ppm)

Output:

0.0119

Code:

np.min(airquality_co_ppm)

Output:

-0.2

Code:

np.std(airquality_co_ppm)

Output:

0.07765302055281113

These are some of the simple operations using NumPy on time series data. This library has more features that can perform multi-dimensional array operations and more.

With this understanding, let us move further to explore the time series library named Prophet.

Prophet for Time Series

Prophet is developed by Facebook and is widely used for time series forecasting. This library has methods to handle time series functions such as trend and seasonality effectively. Prophet can be used to identify seasonal patterns in data pretty well. This library can be used to build customized models with varied input parameters as required for different use cases. It can also handle large datasets very effectively. It has an API similar to scikit-learn and is simple to fit the model on the data if you are familiar with scikit-learn.

Documentation

The documentation for this library is available at: **https://facebook.github.io/prophet/docs/quick_start.html#python-api**.

Installation

Prophet can be installed for Python using the following command:

```
pip install prophet
```

Functionalities of Prophet

Prophet can be used to:

- Forecast future values in time series data. For example, predicting future sales or stock forecasting.
- Identify outliers or anomalies in the time series data. For example, identification of earthquakes from seismographic readings.
- Visualize time series data and perform exploratory data analysis using the plot functions available in the library.

In this section, let us apply `Prophet` to the `airquality` data. The first step will be to import the `Prophet` library and then reuse the air quality data to perform forecasting.

Code:

```
from prophet import Prophet
```

Let us take a look at the data and discuss the input parameters that will be used for this example.

Code:

```
airquality_df.head(5)
```

Output:

	Date	Time	CO(GT)	PT08.S1(CO)	NMHC(GT)	C6H6(GT)	PT08.S2(NMHC)	NOx(GT)	PT08.S3(NOx)	NO2(GT)	PT08.S4(NO2)	PT08.S5(O3)	T	RH
0	2004-10-03	0 days 18:00:00	2.6	1360.0	150.0	11.9	1046.0	166.0	1056.0	113.0	1692.0	1268.0	13.6	48.9
1	2004-10-03	0 days 19:00:00	2.0	1292.0	112.0	9.4	955.0	103.0	1174.0	92.0	1559.0	972.0	13.3	47.7
2	2004-10-03	0 days 20:00:00	2.2	1402.0	88.0	9.0	939.0	131.0	1140.0	114.0	1555.0	1074.0	11.9	54.0
3	2004-10-03	0 days 21:00:00	2.2	1376.0	80.0	9.2	948.0	172.0	1092.0	122.0	1584.0	1203.0	11.0	60.0
4	2004-10-03	0 days 22:00:00	1.6	1272.0	51.0	6.5	836.0	131.0	1205.0	116.0	1490.0	1110.0	11.2	59.6

Figure 2.9: A glance at air quality data

Air quality data has **datetime** data type for **Date**, **Time**, and **Timestamp** columns. One of these columns will be the time series input feature used for this example.

Code:

airquality_df.columns

Output:

Index(['Date', 'Time', 'CO(GT)', 'PT08.S1(CO)', 'NMHC(GT)', 'C6H6(GT)',

'PT08.S2(NMHC)', 'NOx(GT)', 'PT08.S3(NOx)', 'NO2(GT)', 'PT08.S4(NO2)',

'PT08.S5(O3)', 'T', 'RH', 'AH', 'Timestamp'],

dtype='object')

Let us consider the **Date** column as the time series feature and **RH** (Relative Humidity) column as the dependent variable to start building the forecasting model.

The most granular **datetime** column in this dataset is the **Time** column, but we are using the **Date** column to build the model. Hence, we need to bring the data into an aggregated format to ensure that **Date** becomes the most granular field in the data.

To perform this aggregation, let us create a pivot table on the data with **Date** as the **index** and all other non-**datetime** input variables as **values**, and **mean** as the aggregation function. Once the pivot is created as a data frame, reset the index so that **Date** becomes a column again.

Code:

airquality_df_pivot = airquality_df.pivot_table(index = ['Date'], values = ['CO(GT)', 'PT08.S1(CO)', 'NMHC(GT)', 'C6H6(GT)',

'PT08.S2(NMHC)', 'NOx(GT)', 'PT08.S3(NOx)', 'NO2(GT)', 'PT08.S4(NO2)',

'PT08.S5(O3)', 'T', 'RH', 'AH'], aggfunc = 'mean')

airquality_df_pivot.reset_index(inplace = True)

airquality_df_pivot.head(5)

Output:

	Date	AH	C6H6(GT)	CO(GT)	NMHC(GT)	NO2(GT)	NOx(GT)	PT08.S1(CO)	PT08.S2(NMHC)	PT08.S3(N
0	2004-01-04	-24.251979	-14.525000	2.550000	310.125000	84.375000	146.250000	1063.833333	859.125000	745.583
1	2004-01-05	1.167312	8.662500	-6.362500	-180.208333	73.083333	92.041667	1097.500000	913.708333	918.063
2	2004-01-06	1.533350	12.375000	-31.583333	-200.000000	64.375000	137.375000	1135.583333	1021.875000	898.791
3	2004-01-07	1.624108	12.225000	2.162500	-200.000000	100.375000	125.541667	1130.583333	1038.541667	740.916
4	2004-01-08	1.673521	5.808333	0.983333	-200.000000	47.750000	41.250000	974.166667	792.583333	860.083

Figure 2.10: Pivot data frame for Prophet

To build the forecast model, let us make use of only two columns from the pivot data frame: **Date** and **RH**.

Code:

```
airquality_prophet = airquality_df[['Date', 'RH']].copy(deep = True)
```

Let us now initialize a **Prophet** model object with default parameters. This object is then used to fit the model to the historical data and make predictions for future periods.

Code:

```
model = Prophet()
```

Any data frame provided as input to the **Prophet** model must have columns ds (date type) and y (the time series). Let us rename the columns **Date** and **RH** into **ds** and **y**.

Code:

```
airquality_prophet.columns = ['ds', 'y']
```

The data frame will now look as follows:

Code:

```
airquality_prophet
```

Output:

	ds	y
0	2004-10-03	48.9
1	2004-10-03	47.7
2	2004-10-03	54.0
3	2004-10-03	60.0
4	2004-10-03	59.6
...	...	...
9352	2005-04-04	29.3
9353	2005-04-04	23.7
9354	2005-04-04	18.3
9355	2005-04-04	13.5
9356	2005-04-04	13.1

9357 rows × 2 columns

Figure 2.11: Prophet input

In the next step, we will **fit** the model object on the **airquality** data.

Code:

```
model.fit(airquality_prophet)
```

Output:

22:53:45 - cmdstanpy - INFO - Chain [1] start processing

22:53:46 - cmdstanpy - INFO - Chain [1] done processing

After initializing the model, we use the **make_future_dataframe()** function to create a new data frame with future dates to make predictions for 10 future time periods. The **periods** parameter specifies the number of periods into the future to forecast.

Overview of Time Series Libraries in Python

Code:

```
predictions = model.make_future_dataframe(periods = 10)

predictions
```

Output:

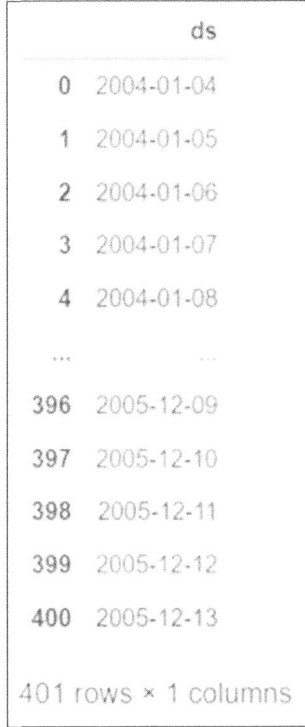

Figure 2.12: *Future data frame*

In this code, let us perform time series forecasting using the **Prophet** library in Python. In this step, let us generate the forecast using an initial **Prophet** model and store it in the forecast variable. We can then display the forecast data frame, containing the columns **ds**, **yhat**, **yhat_lower**, and **yhat_upper** using the tail function.

Code:

```
forecast = model.predict(predictions)
forecast[['ds', 'yhat', 'yhat_lower', 'yhat_upper']]
```

Output:

	ds	yhat	yhat_lower	yhat_upper
0	2004-01-04	58.604980	-4.595090	122.569854
1	2004-01-05	62.174756	0.772726	126.142330
2	2004-01-06	57.088486	-6.946474	117.877430
3	2004-01-07	55.910126	-5.952720	119.467297
4	2004-01-08	59.893307	-2.784357	123.888253
...	...	...	...	...
396	2005-12-09	-4.205317	-67.973420	55.890317
397	2005-12-10	8.086799	-57.272456	73.892317
398	2005-12-11	5.485496	-56.006896	76.144836
399	2005-12-12	9.074445	-51.806818	75.284492
400	2005-12-13	4.007348	-59.913515	70.045901

401 rows × 4 columns

Figure 2.13: Forecasted values

Next, let us call the **plot** function of the model object with the **forecast** as the input, and store the resulting plot in the **chart1** variable.

Code:

```
chart1 = model.plot(forecast)
```

Output:

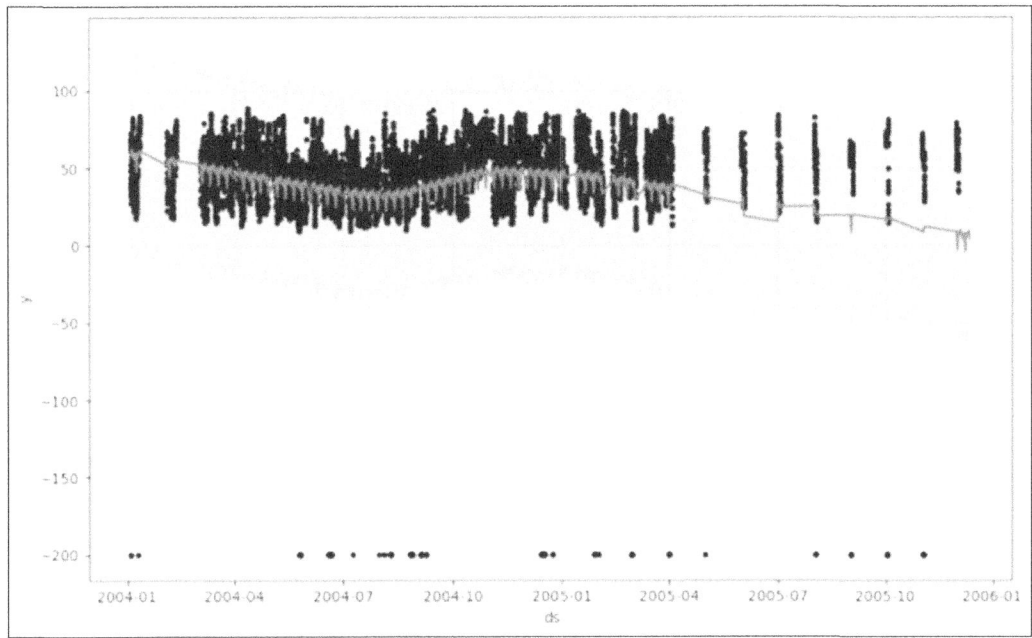

Figure 2.14: Chart 1 displaying forecasts from the initial model

The forecasts in *Figures* 2.13 and 2.14 are not on similar lines to the actual values and will need a rework so that the predictions can be made better.

Let us examine this further by calling the **describe** function on the **airquality_prophet** data frame, which displays descriptive statistics of the **y** column by default.

Code:

```
airquality_prophet.describe()
```

Output:

	y
count	9357.000000
mean	39.485380
std	51.216145
min	-200.000000
25%	34.100000
50%	48.600000
75%	61.900000
max	88.700000

Figure 2.15: Default output of Describe function

In *Figure 2.15*, there is a large difference between the min and 25th percentile of the relative humidity, which denotes the presence of outliers between these percentiles of the data. Let us use the `zn` optional percentiles parameter to display specific percentiles.

Code:

```
airquality_prophet.describe(percentiles = [0.1, 0.2, 0.3, 0.4, 0.5, 0.6,
0.7, 0.8, 0.9]).transpose()
```

Output:

	count	mean	std	min	10%	20%	30%	40%	50%	60%	70%	80%	90%	max
y	9357.0	39.48538	51.216145	-200.0	21.8	30.5	37.2	43.3	48.6	53.6	59.02	64.8	72.1	88.7

Figure 2.16: Percentile spread from min to max

From *Figure 2.16*, we can understand that the values have spiked all of a sudden between **min** and **10%**. This leads to further examination of the values between these percentiles.

Code:

```
airquality_prophet.describe(percentiles = [0.01, 0.02, 0.03, 0.04, 0.05,
0.1]).transpose()
```

Output:

	count	mean	std	min	1%	2%	3%	4%	5%	10%	50%	max
y	9357.0	39.48538	51.216145	-200.0	-200.0	-200.0	-200.0	10.048	15.0	21.8	48.6	88.7

Figure 2.17: Percentile spread from min to 4th percentile

From *Figure* 2.17, we can understand that the value of RH has changed from −200 to 10.048 between the 3rd and 4th percentile of the data. Let us now select a subset of `airquality_prophet` with values between −200 and 10, so that we can decide on the closest number to set a cap on the minimum values.

Code:

```
airquality_prophet[(airquality_prophet['y']>  -200)   &   (airquality_prophet['y']< 10)]
```

Output:

	ds	y
1817	2004-05-25	9.9
1818	2004-05-25	9.8
1819	2004-05-25	9.2
1820	2004-05-25	9.3
1821	2004-05-25	9.2
2851	2004-07-07	9.6
9335	2005-03-04	9.9

Figure 2.18: Values between min and 4th percentile

Let us handle the outlier with a value of **-200** by replacing it with **10** by defining a custom function `replace_outlier`.

```
def replace_outlier(x):
    if (x==-200):
        return 10
    else:
        return x
```

We will then apply the Lambda function and the `replace_outlier` function on the RH column, so that the minimum value of **-200** is replaced by **10**. We have now treated the outlier in the data.

Let us now create a new **Prophet** object and fit it with the modified **airquality_prophet** data frame using the **fit** function.

Code:

model2 = Prophet()

model2.fit(airquality_prophet)

Output:

07:09:34 - cmdstanpy - INFO - Chain [1] start processing

07:09:36 - cmdstanpy - INFO - Chain [1] done processing

<prophet.forecaster.Prophet at 0x1834cb58f40>

Let us create a new set of predictions, **predictions2**, using the **make_future_dataframe** function with a period of **10**.

Code:

predictions2 = model2.make_future_dataframe(periods = 10)

predictions2.tail(10)

Output:

Figure 2.19: Make future predictions data frame

Let us now call the predict function of **model2** with **predictions2** as the input. The resulting forecast will be stored in the **forecast2** variable.

Code:

```
forecast2 = model2.predict(predictions2)
```

Let us look at the last 10 rows of the **forecast2** data frame, containing the columns **ds**, **yhat**, **yhat_lower**, and **yhat_upper** using the **tail** function.

Code:

```
forecast2[['ds', 'yhat', 'yhat_lower', 'yhat_upper']].tail(10)
```

Output:

	ds	yhat	yhat_lower	yhat_upper
391	2005-12-04	45.904337	22.874923	69.397192
392	2005-12-05	44.841863	23.712503	68.366798
393	2005-12-06	43.776227	22.744829	65.255417
394	2005-12-07	44.871648	21.172822	67.325802
395	2005-12-08	45.662218	22.299686	68.496629
396	2005-12-09	43.654390	19.455352	66.120492
397	2005-12-10	45.871133	23.044215	67.522337
398	2005-12-11	45.758592	23.277677	68.326812
399	2005-12-12	44.696118	22.757012	66.693490
400	2005-12-13	43.630482	19.950925	66.105028

Figure 2.20: *Predictions from Model 2*

Finally, let us call the plot function of the **model2** object with **forecast2** as the input, and store the resulting plot in the **chart2** variable.

Code:

```
chart2 = model2.plot(forecast2)
```

Output:

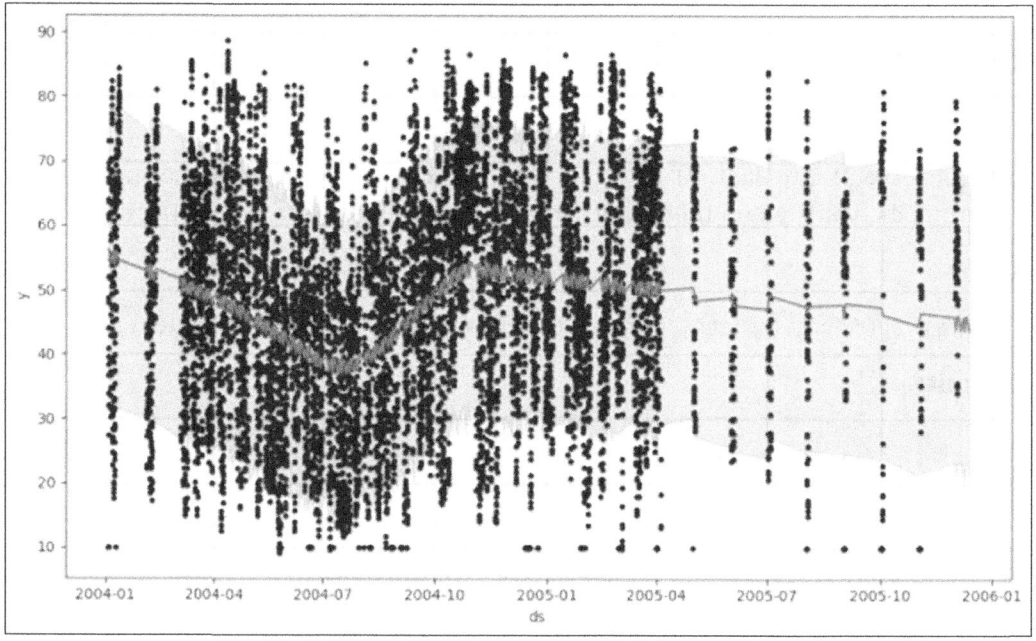

Figure 2.21: Chart from Model 2 predictions

Let us now compare Model 1 and Model 2 to review the predictions before and after the outlier treatment.

	ds	yhat	yhat_lower	yhat_upper		ds	yhat	yhat_lower	yhat_upper
0	2004-01-04	58.604980	-6.913927	130.337454	0	2004-01-04	56.278711	33.358774	78.510063
1	2004-01-05	62.174756	-4.399828	125.480474	1	2004-01-05	55.161466	31.049244	77.824439
2	2004-01-06	57.088486	-9.608240	125.323858	2	2004-01-06	54.041059	30.175516	77.991712
3	2004-01-07	55.910126	-8.177619	120.274434	3	2004-01-07	55.081710	31.986781	77.692731
4	2004-01-08	59.893307	-1.634993	125.559719	4	2004-01-08	55.817509	32.865339	79.054686
...	...	...	...	...	...	...	...	...	...
396	2005-12-09	-4.205317	-67.246897	57.412829	396	2005-12-09	43.654390	19.455352	66.120492
397	2005-12-10	8.086799	-59.539650	73.901251	397	2005-12-10	45.871133	23.044215	67.522337
398	2005-12-11	5.485496	-60.848730	69.109242	398	2005-12-11	45.758592	23.277677	68.326812
399	2005-12-12	9.074445	-58.213262	73.020893	399	2005-12-12	44.696118	22.757012	66.693490
400	2005-12-13	4.007348	-63.097872	69.768663	400	2005-12-13	43.630482	19.950925	66.105028

Figure 2.22: Model 1 forecast vs. Model 2 forecast

The plots of the forecasts are also compared as follows:

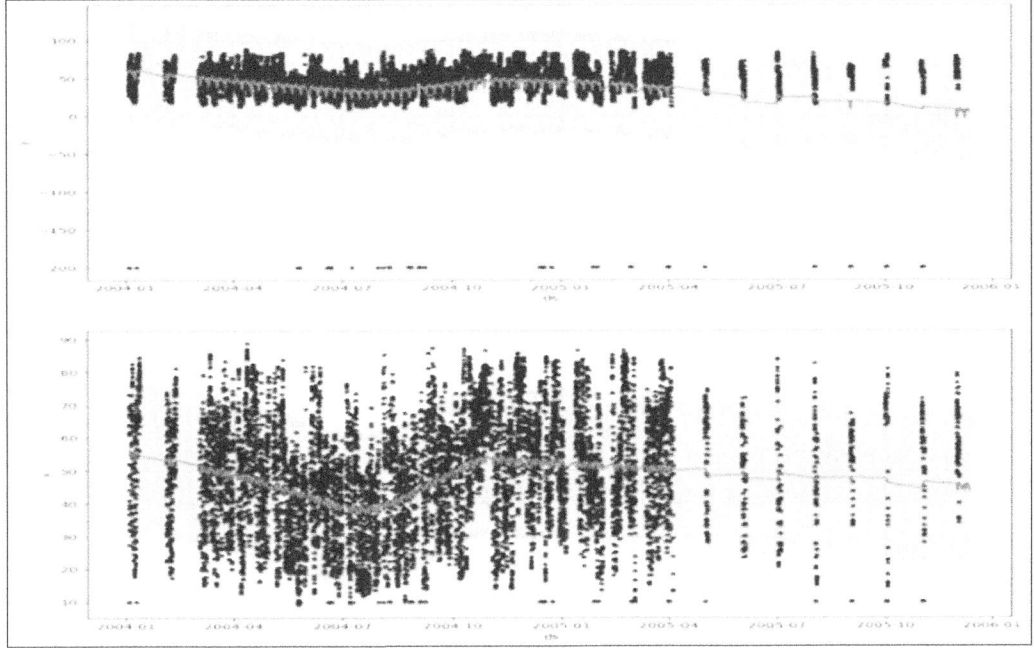

Figure 2.23: Plot of Model 1 forecast vs. Model 2 forecast

From both *Figures* 2.22 and 2.23, the first five rows and last five rows of each data frame represent the comparison between the original data frame's **yhat** and the forecasted rows **yhat** values. Looking at this data, it is evident that the forecasts look more relevant for model 2 compared to model 1.

This is an example of applying Facebook's Prophet library to air quality time series data. With this understanding, let us now look at an example of the AutoTS library.

AutoTS for Time Series

AutoTS is another open-source time series library that performs automatic time series forecasting. It has fit and predict functions similar to sklearn. This library supports univariate and multivariate time series forecasting, as well as multiple machine learning and deep learning models. Similar to Prophet, AutoTS is designed in such a way that developers can easily apply multiple models to the data without prior knowledge of the underlying algorithms. The library can be customized by providing input parameters to the models as required by the use case being solved.

Documentation

The documentation for this library is available at https://winedarksea.github.io/AutoTS/build/html/source/tutorial.html

Installation

Prophet can be installed for Python using the following command:

```
pip install autots
```

Functionalities of AutoTS

As the name implies, AutoTS performs the best model selection by analyzing the data and the conditions provided for a specific use case. This makes the task simple for a data analyst, as the model selection is not a manual process. Time series optimization is also simple in AutoTS, as the hyperparameter tuning also happens automatically. It also handles large datasets in an efficient manner.

Let us look at an example of the use of the **AutoTS** library to perform time series forecasting on the **airquality_prophet** dataset.

In the first step, we will import the AutoTS library and create a new **AutoTS** object called **model3** with a forecast length of 10.

Code:

```
from autots import AutoTS

model3 = AutoTS(forecast_length=10)
```

Next, let us convert the **ds** column of **airquality_prophet** to a **datetime** format and fit the model to the data using the **fit** function. We will specify that the date column is **ds** and the value column is **y**.

Code:

```
airquality_prophet['ds'] = pd.to_datetime(airquality_prophet['ds'], format='%Y-%m-%d')

model3 = model3.fit(airquality_prophet, date_col = 'ds', value_col = 'y')
```

We will then generate predictions using the **predict** function, and assign the result to **prediction3**.

Code:

```
prediction3 = model3.predict()
```

Overview of Time Series Libraries in Python

We can then use the **plot** function to generate a plot of the forecasted values against the actual values:

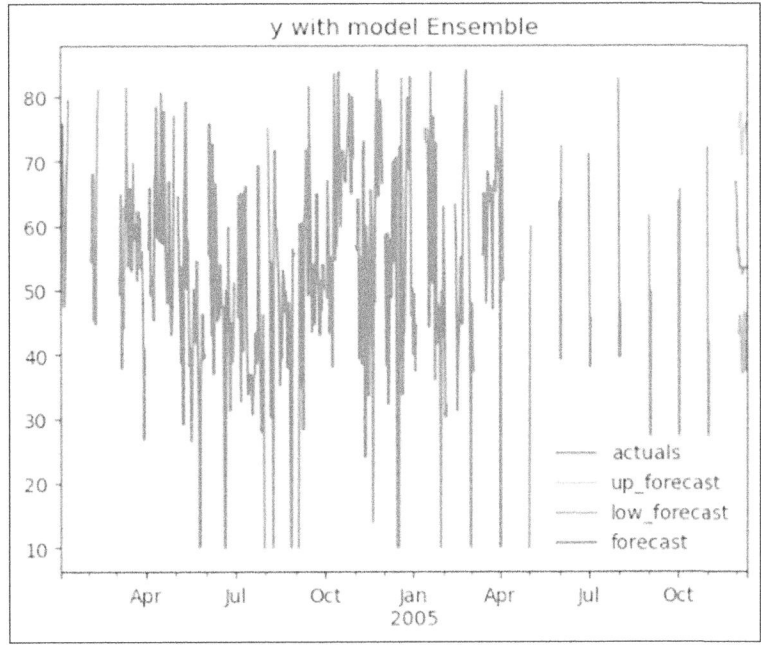

Figure 2.24: Plot of Model 3 forecast

Let us now look at the forecasted values. The model has forecasted upper, lower, and forecast values as follows:

Code:

forecast3 = prediction3.forecast

	y		y		y
2005-12-04	75.125900	2005-12-04	43.203950	2005-12-04	56.247832
2005-12-05	75.592564	2005-12-05	45.926650	2005-12-05	53.312788
2005-12-06	77.506693	2005-12-06	44.877500	2005-12-06	53.312788
2005-12-07	70.713182	2005-12-07	37.591445	2005-12-07	53.312788
2005-12-08	70.947307	2005-12-08	36.943276	2005-12-08	52.274000
2005-12-09	73.268793	2005-12-09	43.169475	2005-12-09	53.312788
2005-12-10	75.592564	2005-12-10	46.421189	2005-12-10	53.312788
2005-12-11	75.592564	2005-12-11	37.413547	2005-12-11	53.312788
2005-12-12	75.592564	2005-12-12	41.755350	2005-12-12	53.312788
2005-12-13	74.448400	2005-12-13	38.144350	2005-12-13	53.312788

Figure 2.25: Forecasted values: upper forecast, lower forecast, and forecast

We can also look at the forecasted values from **AutoTS** by comparing them against the forecasted values of **Prophet** to check if they are similar.

Code:

prediction3.forecast

forecast2[['ds', 'yhat']].tail(10)

Output:

	y		ds	yhat
2005-12-04	56.247832	391	2005-12-04	45.904337
2005-12-05	53.312788	392	2005-12-05	44.841863
2005-12-06	53.312788	393	2005-12-06	43.776227
2005-12-07	53.312788	394	2005-12-07	44.871648
2005-12-08	52.274000	395	2005-12-08	45.662218
2005-12-09	53.312788	396	2005-12-09	43.654390
2005-12-10	53.312788	397	2005-12-10	45.871133
2005-12-11	53.312788	398	2005-12-11	45.758592
2005-12-12	53.312788	399	2005-12-12	44.696118
2005-12-13	53.312788	400	2005-12-13	43.630482

Figure 2.26: Forecasted values – AutoTS vs. Prophet

The AutoTS model provides model results in a user-friendly manner and helps in performing further analysis on the automatic model.

Code:

model3_results = model3.results()

model3_results.columns

Output:

Index(['ID', 'Model', 'ModelParameters', 'TransformationParameters',

'TransformationRuntime', 'FitRuntime', 'PredictRuntime',
'TotalRuntime',

'Ensemble', 'Exceptions', 'Runs', 'Generation',

```
        'ValidationRound',
        'ValidationStartDate', 'smape', 'mae', 'rmse', 'made', 'mage',
        'underestimate', 'mle', 'overestimate', 'imle', 'spl',
        'containment',
        'contour', 'maxe', 'oda', 'dwae', 'mqae', 'ewmae', 'uwmse',
        'smoothness', 'smape_weighted', 'mae_weighted', 'rmse_weighted',
        'made_weighted', 'mage_weighted', 'underestimate_weighted',
        'mle_weighted', 'overestimate_weighted', 'imle_weighted',
        'spl_weighted', 'containment_weighted', 'contour_weighted',
        'maxe_weighted', 'oda_weighted', 'dwae_weighted', 'mqae_weighted',
        'ewmae_weighted', 'uwmse_weighted', 'smoothness_weighted',
        'TotalRuntimeSeconds', 'Score'],
        dtype='object')
```

The results of AutoTS are different compared to the Prophet model, as evident in *Figures* 2.25 and 2.26. Further analysis needs to be performed while building these models to understand which of the two models is providing reasonable predictions. It is worth exploring error parameters such as RMSE, MAE, and others to determine the most suitable model for the air quality data. Additionally, it is better to perform backtesting on the data to calculate accuracy metrics.

With this understanding, let us explore further the various types of visualizations that can be performed on the time series data in the upcoming chapter.

Conclusion

In this chapter, we have learned about an overview of time series libraries in Python data and explored the applications of time series data on the fundamental libraries of Python such as Pandas and NumPy.

We also discussed the applications of time series data in building models using other time series-specific libraries such as AutoTS and Prophet.

In the next chapter, we will delve into an overview of time series data visualization in Python, with examples and code.

References

- Package overview (no date) Package overview - Pandas 2.0.1 documentation. Available at: https://pandas.pydata.org/docs/getting_started/overview.html (Accessed: May 2, 2023).

- S. De Vito, E. Massera, M. Piga, L. Martinotto, G. Di Francia. On field calibration of an electronic nose for benzene estimation in an urban pollution monitoring scenario, Sensors and Actuators B: Chemical, Volume 129, Issue 2, 22 February 2008, Pages 750-757, ISSN 0925-4005, https://archive.ics.uci.edu/ml/datasets/Air+Quality

- NumPy documentation (no date) NumPy documentation - NumPy v1.24 Manual. Available at: https://numpy.org/doc/stable/ (Accessed: May 2, 2023).

- Quick Start (2023) Prophet. Available at: https://facebook.github.io/prophet/docs/quick_start.html#python-api (Accessed: May 2, 2023).

- Tutorial (no date) Tutorial - AutoTS 0.5.6 documentation. Available at: https://winedarksea.github.io/AutoTS/build/html/source/tutorial.html (Accessed: May 2, 2023).

CHAPTER 3
Visualization of Time Series Data

Visualization is the process of understanding data through graphical representations. It plays a very important role in time series analysis as it helps in gaining valuable insights and identifying hidden patterns within the data. There are many libraries in Python that help in performing data visualization of time series data and in exploring patterns, trends, and anomalies within the data.

In this chapter, let us delve into the visualization of time series data with Python. Let us explore various libraries and techniques that would help us derive valuable insights by creating informative plots. This chapter will cover Python libraries such as `Matplotlib`, `Seaborn`, and `Plotly`, which are the most important visualization libraries capable of producing multiple types of charts.

Structure

In this chapter, the following topics will be covered:
- Introduction to Time Series Visualization Libraries of Python
- Basic Time Series Plots Using Matplotlib
- Advanced Time Series Visualizations Using Seaborn
- Interactive Time Series Visualizations Using Plotly

Introduction to Time Series Visualization Libraries of Python

In this section, we will explore some of the libraries of Python with capabilities to visualize time series data. We will cover the following libraries with examples: Matplotlib, Seaborn, and Plotly.

Exploring `Matplotlib` and Its Uses

`Matplotlib` is a widely used library for visualization, providing various plots along with customization of parameters. It can be used to visualize different types and complexities of time series data.

Documentation

The documentation for this library is available at:

https://matplotlib.org/ – Matplotlib – Visualization with Python

Installation

Matplotlib can be installed for Python using the following command:

pip install matplotlib

Functionalities of `Matplotlib`

Matplotlib has various options to visualize data using multiple plot types such as line charts, bar charts, pie charts, box plots, violin plots, histograms, scatter plots, and many more. We will look at some of the relevant examples in this section.

There are various advantages of using Matplotlib on the time series data while working in Python, as follows:

- The data in Python is majorly represented in the form of Pandas data frames or Numpy arrays. `Matplotlib` integrates well with both of these libraries.
- The plots and layouts of this library are highly customizable.
- Matplotlib's clear visualizations help in storytelling and explaining use cases in a more user-friendly manner.

Visualization of Time Series Data

An example of using this library to plot time series data is explained in the following code.

To begin with, let us first import **pyplot** from Matplotlib.

```
import matplotlib.pyplot as plt
```

We can then define two variables named **date** and **sales**. The date variable will hold the dates from January to May 2023, and the sales variable will hold a simulated sales value for these five months.

Code:

```
date = ['Jan-2023', 'Feb-2023', 'Mar-2023', 'Apr-2023', 'May-2023']
date
```

Output:

```
['Jan-2023', 'Feb-2023', 'Mar-2023', 'Apr-2023', 'May-2023']
```

```
sales = [20, 43, 56, 18, 14]
sales
```

Output:

```
[20, 43, 56, 18, 14]
```

We can then plot the sales against dates using the plot function of Matplotlib by adding labels to the chart, x-axis, and y-axis.

Code:

```
plt.plot(date, sales)
plt.xlabel('Date')
plt.ylabel('Sales')
plt.title('An example of matplotlib')
plt.show()
```

The output of the preceding code is represented in *Figure 3.1*.

Output:

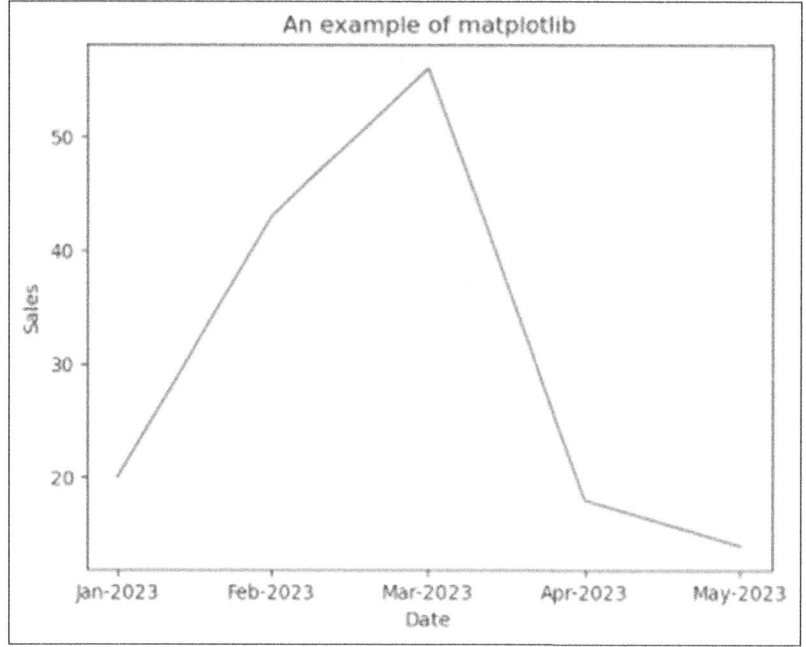

Figure 3.1: An example of Matplotlib

This is one simple example of how to use the Matplotlib library. In this chapter, we will discuss more individual use cases and examples of using this library.

With this understanding, let us now look at a library named `Seaborn` for time series visualization.

Exploring Seaborn and Its Uses

`Seaborn` is another important library for visualizing time series or any type of datasets in Python. This library is built as a wrapper on top of `Matplotlib` with simplified accessibility and usage.

Documentation

The documentation for this library is available at:

https://seaborn.pydata.org/ – **seaborn: statistical data visualization – seaborn 0.12.2 documentation (pydata.org)**

Installation

Seaborn can be installed for Python using the following command:

```
pip install seaborn
```

Functionalities of Seaborn

Seaborn has a simplified API to create various plots and customize views according to user requirements and use cases. Various options are available for numerical and categorical data visualizations in this library.

Seaborn is suitable for creating both simple and advanced visualizations, similar to Matplotlib, but it offers a simpler API that makes it easier to perform exploratory data analysis on time series data.

An example of using this library to plot time series data is explained in the following code.

To begin with, let us first import **seaborn** along with **pandas** and **datetime** libraries, which will be used to perform data processing on the data used for this example:

```
import seaborn as sns

import pandas as pd

from datetime import datetime
```

The online retail sales data used for this example can be downloaded from https://archive.ics.uci.edu/dataset/352/online+retail. This data has the following attributes:

- `InvoiceNo`
- `StockCode`
- `Description`
- `Quantity`
- `InvoiceDate`
- `UnitPrice`
- `CustomerID`
- `Country`

Let us further read the data and review the columns.

Code:

```
df = pd.read_excel('Online Retail.xlsx')
```

```
df.columns
```

Output:

```
Index(['InvoiceNo', 'StockCode', 'Description', 'Quantity', 'InvoiceDate',
       'UnitPrice', 'CustomerID', 'Country'],
      dtype='object')
```

To prepare the data for visualization using seaborn, let us convert the invoice date column into year-month-date format.

Code:

```
df['InvoiceDateTruncated'] = df['InvoiceDate'].astype(str).apply(lambda x:x.split()[0])

df['InvoiceDateTruncated'] = df['InvoiceDateTruncated'].apply(lambda x:datetime.strptime(x,"%Y-%m-%d"))

df['InvoiceDateTruncated']
```

Output:

```
0         2010-12-01
1         2010-12-01
2         2010-12-01
3         2010-12-01
4         2010-12-01
             ...
541904    2011-12-09
541905    2011-12-09
541906    2011-12-09
541907    2011-12-09
541908    2011-12-09
Name: InvoiceDateTruncated, Length: 541909, dtype: datetime64[ns]
```

The data needs to be simplified further to demonstrate an effective visualization. Let us look at the number of records available in this data by Country.

Code:

```
df['Country'].value_counts().head(10)
```

Output:

```
United Kingdom    495478
Germany             9495
France              8557
EIRE                8196
Spain               2533
Netherlands         2371
Belgium             2069
Switzerland         2002
Portugal            1519
Australia           1259
Name: Country, dtype: int64
```

From these countries, let us consider four of the countries that can be compared in charts, and create a pivot that groups the data by the four shortlisted countries, four randomly shortlisted stock codes, and invoice dates.

Code:

```
df_pivot = df[df['Country'].isin(['Spain', 'Germany', 'France', 'EIRE']) &\
    df['StockCode'].isin(['POST', '22326', 'C2', '22423'])]\
.pivot_table(index = ['Country', 'StockCode', 'InvoiceDateTruncated'],\
            values = ['UnitPrice', 'Quantity'],\
            aggfunc = {'UnitPrice' : 'max', 'Quantity' : 'sum'})\
.reset_index()
df_pivot
```

Output:

	Country	StockCode	InvoiceDateTruncated	Quantity	UnitPrice
0	EIRE	C2	2010-12-01	1	50.0
1	EIRE	C2	2010-12-06	2	50.0
2	EIRE	C2	2010-12-17	2	50.0
3	EIRE	C2	2010-12-19	1	50.0
4	EIRE	C2	2010-12-23	1	50.0
...	...	...	...	...	...
503	Spain	POST	2011-11-17	2	28.0
504	Spain	POST	2011-11-20	4	28.0
505	Spain	POST	2011-11-21	3	28.0
506	Spain	POST	2011-11-24	1	28.0
507	Spain	POST	2011-12-06	1	28.0

508 rows × 5 columns

Figure 3.2: Simplified online retail data

Now that we have the data ready, let us look at how to use **seaborn** to visualize this data.

As a first step, let us set the chart background theme by setting the **style** as a **"dark grid"**.

Code:

sns.set_theme(style="darkgrid")

To conduct a comparison of four countries, let us add a relational plot with a facet grid and set the chart type as **line**, x- and y-axis as **Invoice Date** and **Quantity**, respectively, row as **Country**, size as **UnitPrice**, and hue and style as **StockCode**.

Code:

sns.relplot(

    data=df_pivot, kind="line",

    x="InvoiceDateTruncated", y="Quantity", row = "Country",

    hue="StockCode", size="UnitPrice", style="StockCode",

Visualization of Time Series Data

```
    height=5,
    facet_kws=dict(sharex=False),
    legend = False
)
```

Output:

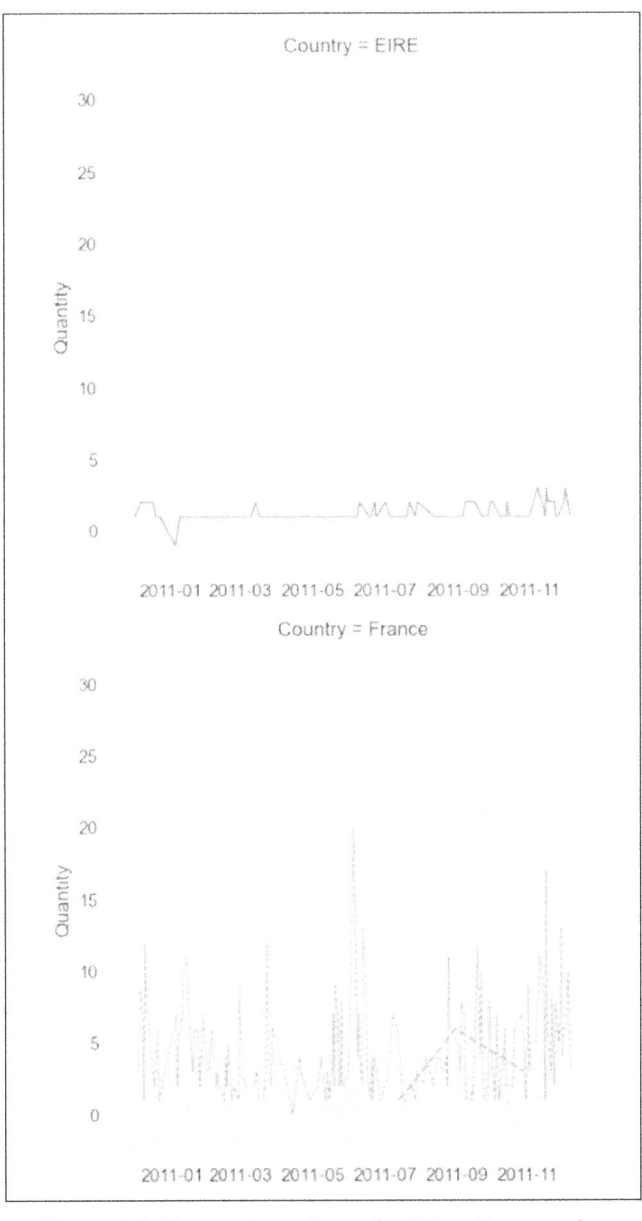

Figure 3.3: *Comparison chart of EIRE vs. France sales*

Similarly, let us also review the sales comparison charts for Germany and Spain.

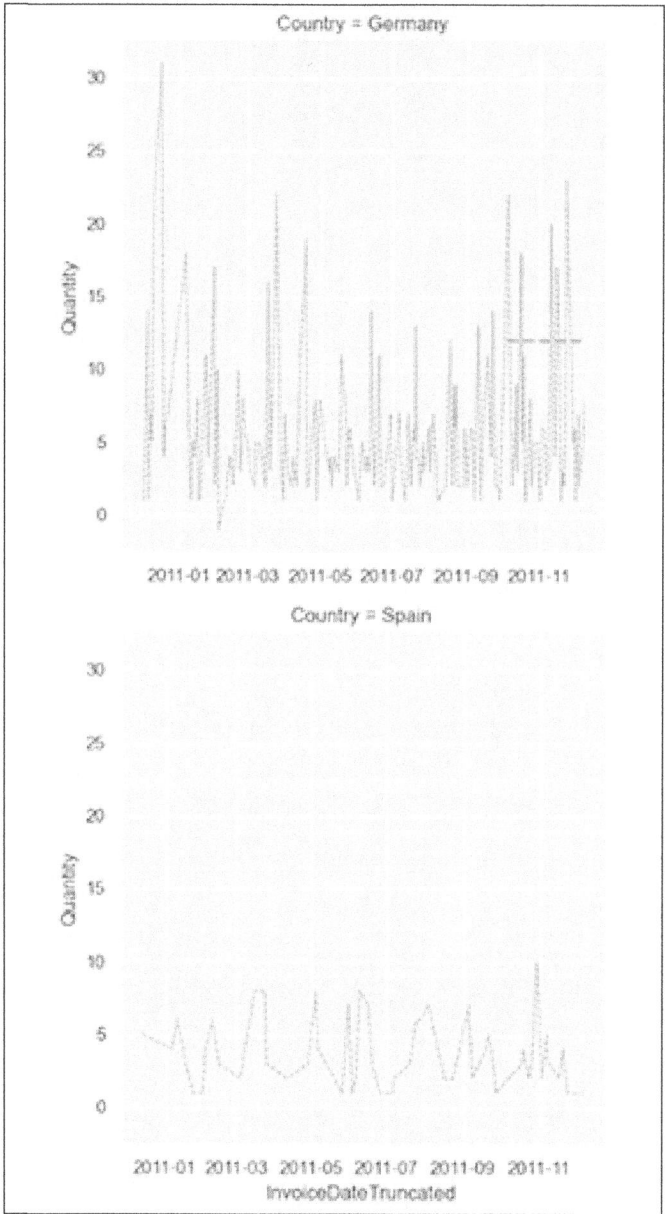

Figure 3.4: *Comparison chart of Germany vs. Spain sales*

This is one simple example of how to use the Seaborn library. In this chapter, we will explore various individual use cases and examples of using this library.

Visualization of Time Series Data

Now, let us look at another library named `Plotly` for time series visualization.

Exploring `Plotly` and Its Uses

Plotly is another important Python library for visualization of time series data or any other data. It provides an interactive interface for charts and graphs that makes it easy to perform exploratory data analysis.

Documentation

The documentation for this library is available at:

https://plotly.com/python/

Installation

`Plotly` can be installed for Python using the following command:

```
pip install plotly
```

Functionalities of `Plotly`

`Plotly` is an interactive visualization library that supports Python. It supports all the charts and graphs that can be designed using other visualization libraries, making them more usable because the charts can be drilled down to understand specifics.

To demonstrate an example of `Plotly`, let us bring back the Yahoo Finance dataset.

Code:

```
stocks = pd.read_excel('LNVGY.xlsx')

stocks
```

An example of daily stock market time series data for Lenevo Group Limited, sourced from https://finance.yahoo.com/, is represented in *Figure 3.5*.

Output:

	Date	Open	High	Low	Close	Adj Close	Volume
0	2022-03-23	21.150000	21.389999	21.139999	21.250000	20.413145	29400
1	2022-03-24	21.500000	21.799999	21.500000	21.790001	20.931879	16100
2	2022-03-25	21.600000	21.600000	21.320000	21.379999	20.538023	47200
3	2022-03-28	21.090000	21.660000	21.090000	21.660000	20.806997	78900
4	2022-03-29	22.620001	22.620001	21.690001	21.809999	20.951090	29500
...	...	...	...	...	...	...	...
247	2023-03-17	18.540001	19.290001	18.540001	18.830000	18.830000	32700
248	2023-03-20	18.540001	18.650000	18.490000	18.580000	18.580000	32500
249	2023-03-21	18.570000	18.620001	18.459999	18.570000	18.570000	10400
250	2023-03-22	18.600000	18.740000	18.559999	18.559999	18.559999	20600
251	2023-03-23	20.400000	20.809999	20.400000	20.600000	20.600000	92500

252 rows × 7 columns

Figure 3.5: Stocks data from Yahoo Finance

Let us now import the **Plotly** library and create an interactive line plot for the stocks data.

Code:

```
import plotly.express as px

fig = px.line(stocks, x='Date', y = 'High')

fig.update_layout(title='Lenovo Stock Prices', xaxis_title='Date', yaxis_title='Price')

fig.show()
```

Output:

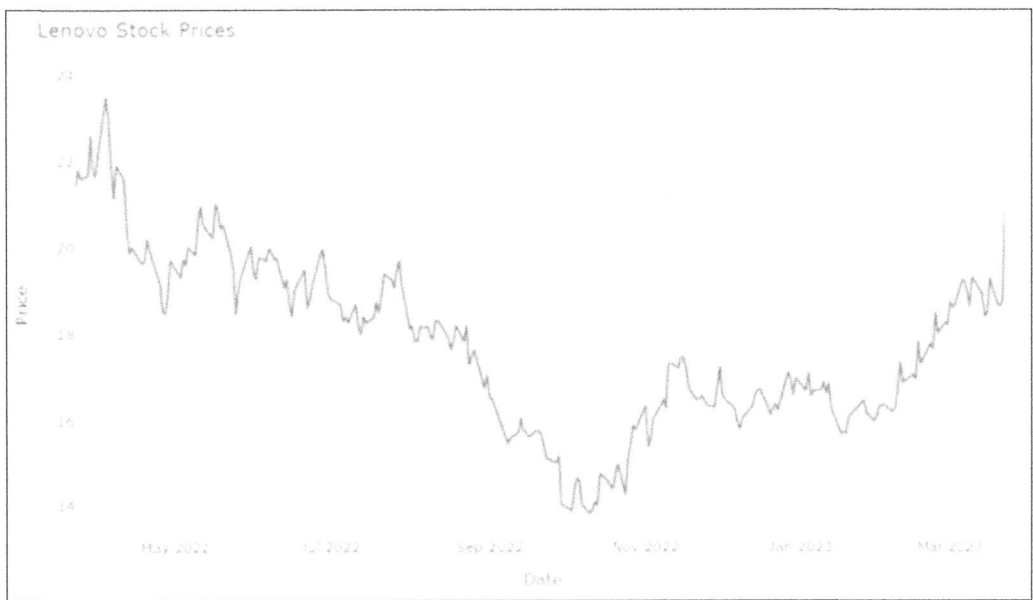

Figure 3.6: *Line chart of Yahoo Finance data using Plotly*

The line chart in *Figure* 3.6 can be expanded further by a single click, as shown in *Figure* 3.7. Let us look at the expanded view of the data for the month of October 2022:

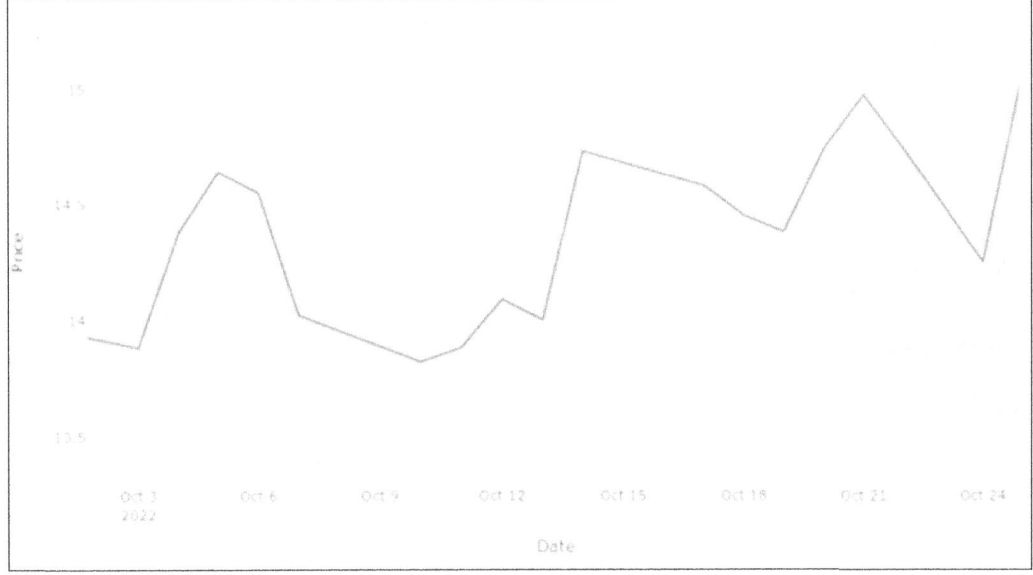

Figure 3.7: *Line chart of Yahoo Finance data using Plotly*

This is one simple example of how to use the Plotly library. In this chapter, we will discuss more individual use cases and examples of using this library.

With this understanding, let us now look at the basic time series plots that can be created using Matplotlib.

Basic Time Series Plots with Matplotlib

As Matplotlib is one of the first visualization libraries covered in this chapter, let us explore it further. In this section, we will cover the following basic time series plots using this library:

- Line plots
- Scatter plots
- Box plots
- Histograms

Line Plot

Line plot is used for a simple representation of time series data, depicting the trend of the date over time as a line. In this example, let us look at some of the features of Matplotlib to create a line plot.

We will start by defining the **x** and **y** variables that denote the data to be displayed in the x- and y-axis of the line plot. Let us continue using the Yahoo Finance dataset. The x-axis will be the **Date** column and the y-axis will be the **Low** column.

Code:

```
x = stocks['Date']
y = stocks['Low']
```

The following code defines a layout to create subplots, followed by a grid and parameters to create a line plot in green (**g**) color with a **grey** grid and red labels for the axes.

Code:

```
fig, ax = plt.subplots()
ax.plot(x, y, linestyle='-.', color = 'g')
ax.grid(True, linestyle=':', color = 'grey')
```

```
ax.tick_params(labelcolor='r', labelsize='medium', width=3)
plt.show()
```

Output:

Figure 3.8*: Line plot with Matplotlib*

This is an example of using various options available within Matplotlib to create a line plot. With this understanding, let us look further at an example of Scatter plot.

Scatter Plot

Scatter plots can also be used to represent time series data. It is usually created to understand the correlation between two variables.

In this example, let us create a scatter plot for the Yahoo Finance dataset. This plot will be created between two variables: **Date** and **Volume**. Let us start with defining the **x** and **y** variables for the plot.

Code:

```
x = stocks['Date']
y = stocks['Volume']
```

Let us then import NumPy to create random values that will help in various plot parameters for this example.

Code:

```
import numpy as np
```

To define the random value to color the data points, let us create a random seed and a **colors** variable.

Code:

```
np.random.seed(1234)
colors = np.random.rand(len(y))
colors
```

Output:

```
array([0.19151945, 0.62210877, 0.43772774, 0.78535858, 0.77997581,
       0.27259261, 0.27646426, 0.80187218, 0.95813935, 0.87593263,
       0.35781727, 0.50099513, 0.68346294, 0.71270203, 0.37025075,
       0.56119619, 0.50308317, 0.01376845, 0.77282662, 0.88264119,
       0.36488598, 0.61539618, 0.07538124, 0.36882401, 0.9331401 ,
       0.65137814, 0.39720258, 0.78873014, 0.31683612, 0.56809865,
       0.86912739, 0.43617342, 0.80214764, 0.14376682, 0.70426097,
       0.70458131, 0.21879211, 0.92486763, 0.44214076, 0.90931596,
       0.05980922, 0.18428708, 0.04735528, 0.67488094, 0.59462478,
       0.53331016, 0.04332406, 0.56143308, 0.32966845, 0.50296683,
       0.11189432, 0.60719371, 0.56594464, 0.00676406, 0.61744171,...]
```

These values will act as the colors for the data points in the scatter plot.

Let us also define the marker size for the data points as follows:

Code:

```
size = 200 * colors
size
```

Output:

```
array([ 38.30389008, 124.42175421,  87.5455478 , 157.07171674,
       155.99516162,  54.51852106,  55.29285103, 160.37443551,
       191.62787074, 175.18652695,  71.56345399, 100.1990251 ,
       136.69258703, 142.5404054 ,  74.05015096, 112.23923721,
       100.61663306,   2.75368992, 154.56532432, 176.52823813,
        72.97719678, 123.07923569,  15.07624833,  73.7648012 ,
       186.6280204 , 130.27562865,  79.44051555, 157.74602859,
        63.36722443, 113.61973053, 173.82547791,  87.23468478,
       160.42952842,  28.7533649 , 140.85219422, 140.91626164,
        43.75842113, 184.97352572,  88.42815108, 181.86319179,
        11.96184456,  36.85741676,   9.47105576, 134.97618872,
       118.92495599, 106.6620326 ,   8.66481254, 112.28661601,
        65.93368912, 100.59336662,  22.37886351, 121.43874124,
       113.18892861,   1.3528124 , 123.48834176, 182.42457729,
       158.10482661, 198.41629324, 191.76035243, 158.39282706,
        57.050192  , 124.98334106,  95.61875913,  39.13503573,
        76.46349041,  10.77473703,  90.32968165, 196.4009483 ,...]
```

The final step will be to plot the volume against date using the **scatter** method.

Code:

```
plt.scatter(x, y, s=size, c=colors, alpha=0.5)
plt.show()
```

Output:

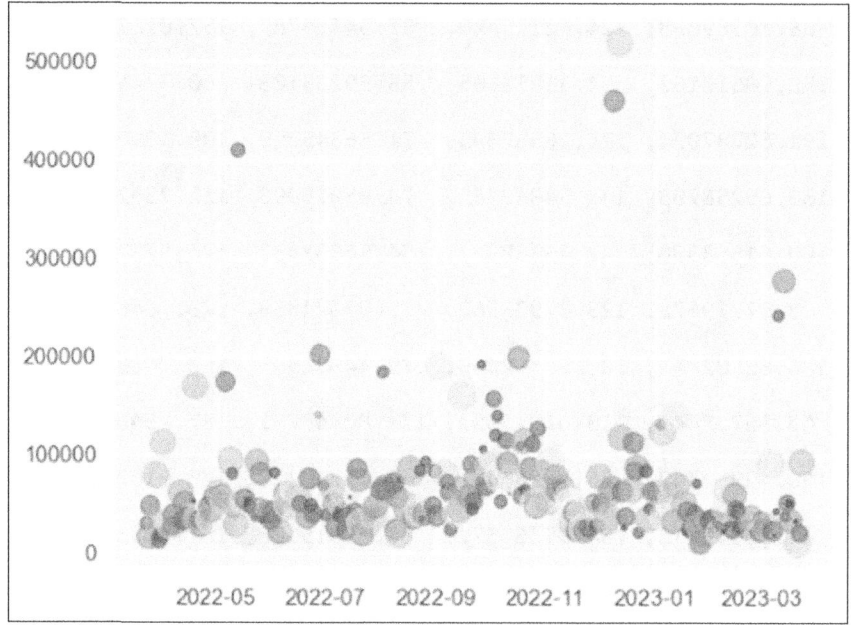

Figure 3.9: Scatter plot with Matplotlib

This is an example of using various options available within `Matplotlib` to create a scatter plot. Let us now delve into an example of a Box plot.

Box Plot

Box plot is used to understand the distribution of data by looking at its key statistical measures and possible outliers in the dataset. Let us look at an example of box plot using `Matplotlib` and review its elements.

Let us start by creating a layout for drawing two subplots for box plots. Box plots can be either rectangular or notched. In the notched plot, the notch represents the confidence intervals around the median.

Code:

fig, (ax1, ax2) = plt.subplots(nrows=2, ncols=1, figsize=(5, 10))

The first type of box plot in this example will be a rectangular box plot. This box plot will be plotted for three variables of the Yahoo Finance stock data: `Open`, `High`, and `Low`. Let us also set a title for the `rectangular box plot`.

Code:

```
rectangle = ax1.boxplot(stocks[['Open', 'High', 'Low']],
                        vert=True,
                        patch_artist=True,
                        labels=['Open', 'High', 'Low'])
ax1.set_title('Stock data outliers in rectangular box plot')
```

The second type of box plot in this example will be a notched box plot.

Code:

```
notch = ax2.boxplot(stocks[['Open', 'High', 'Low']],
                    notch=True,
                    vert=True,
                    patch_artist=True,
                    labels=['Open', 'High', 'Low'])
ax2.set_title('Stock data outliers in notched box plot')
```

We can set a uniform color code for the boxes in both box plots.

Code:

```
colors = ['lightgrey', 'lightyellow', 'skyblue']
for plot in (rectangle, notch):
    for param, color in zip(plot['boxes'], colors):
        param.set_facecolor(color)
```

In addition to that, we can also set uniform axes titles for both plots.

Code:

```
for ax in [ax1, ax2]:
    ax.set_xlabel('Stock Price Features')
    ax.set_ylabel('Stock Prices')
```

Let us finally display the plots.

Code:

plt.show()

Output:

The final output of the rectangular box plot is represented in *Figure 3.10*.

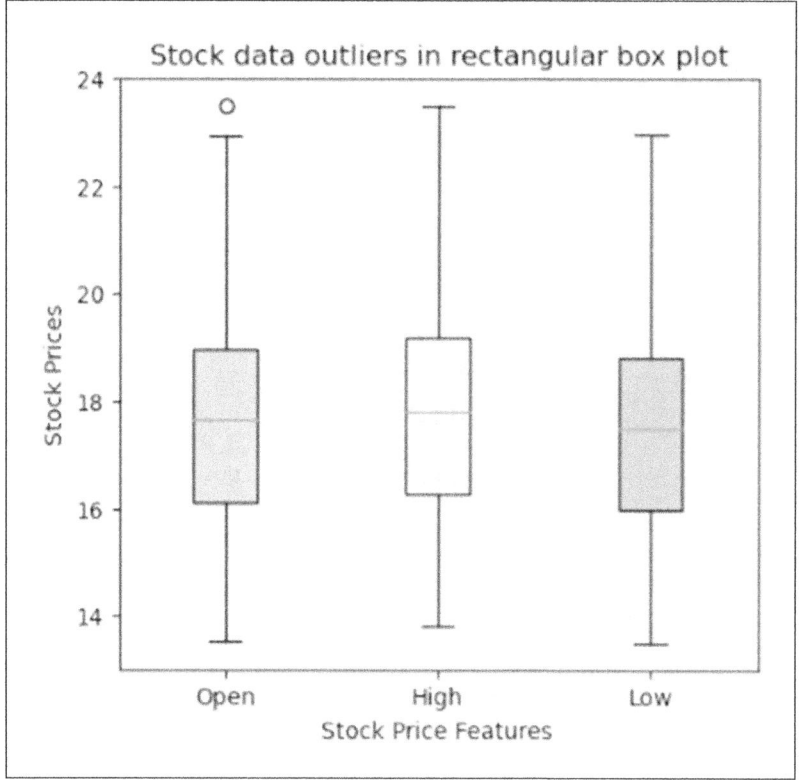

Figure 3.10: *Rectangular box plot example*

The final output of the notched box plot is represented in *Figure 3.11*:

Visualization of Time Series Data   81

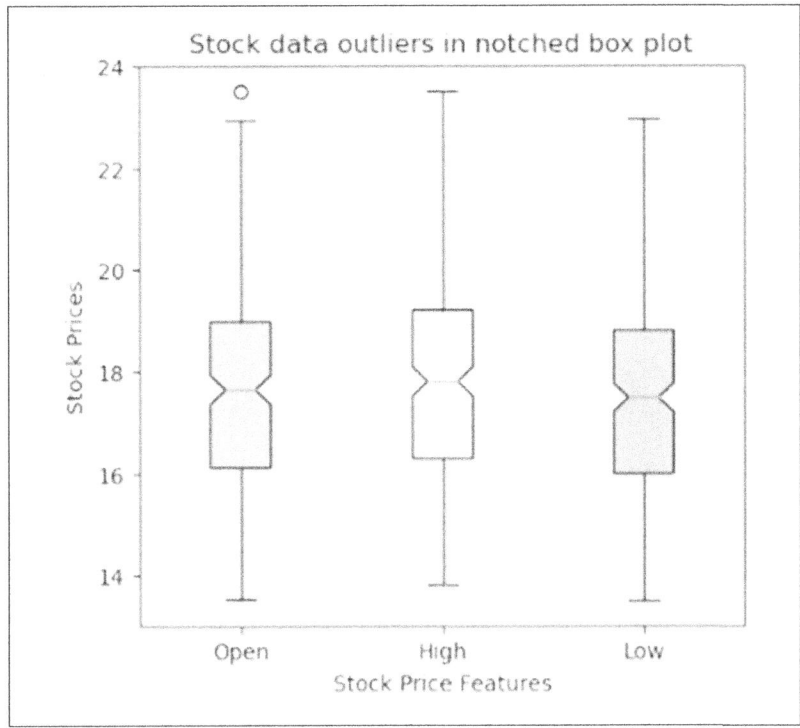

Figure 3.11: Notched box plot example

The box in the preceding box plots Figures 3.10 and 3.11 represents the interquartile range (IQR) of the data. The bottom line of the box is the first quartile or Q1, and the top line of the box is the third quartile or Q3. The line in the middle of the box is the median. The whiskers extending from the top and bottom of the box extend up to 1.5 times the IQR. The values in the data that lie beyond these whiskers on either the top or bottom are considered as outliers in the data.

With this understanding, let us look further at an example of a Histogram.

Histogram

Histogram can be used to visualize the distribution of a time series dataset similar to other datasets. It plots the frequency of observations in a time series dataset by grouping them into regular intervals called bins.

In this example, let us create a histogram for the traded volume of the stock in the Yahoo Finance dataset.

Let us create a variable named '**volume**' and assign the **Volume** column from **stocks** data.

Code:

volume = stocks['Volume']

volume

Output:

0   29400

1   16100

2   47200

3   78900

4   29500

...

247   32700

248   32500

249   10400

250   20600

251   92500

Name: Volume, Length: 252, dtype: int64

We will then plot the histogram using the **hist** method from Matplotlib by setting the volume as data, a bin size of 20, and the color as green. Let us also add the x and y labels along with the title.

Code:

plt.hist(volume, bins=20, color = 'green')

plt.xlabel('Volume Traded')

plt.ylabel('Frequency')

plt.title("Histogram of Lenovo's volume traded")

plt.show()

Output:

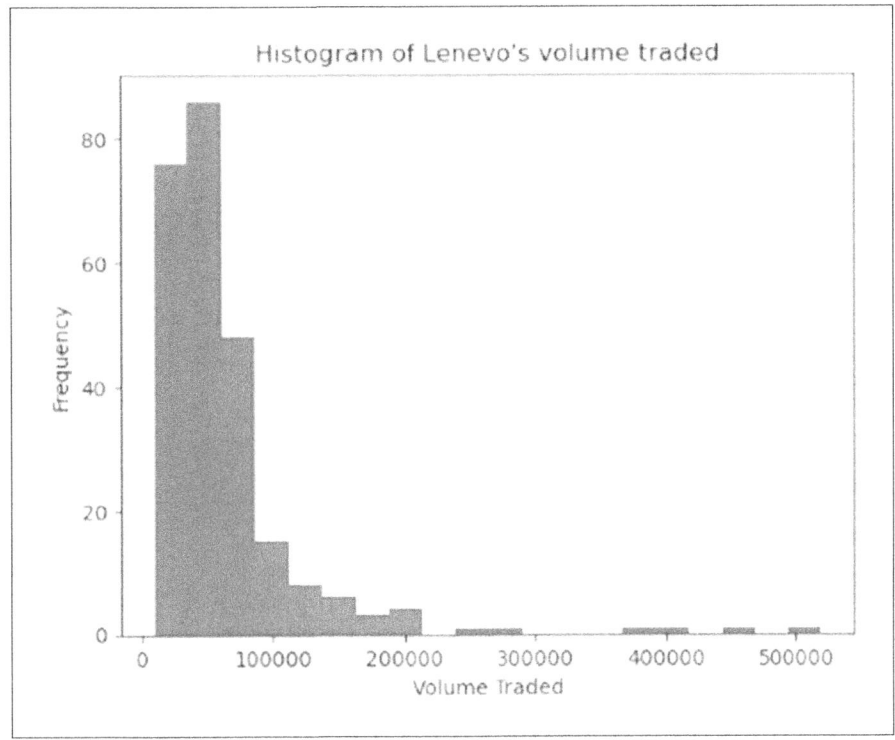

Figure 3.12: *An example of Histogram*

These are some of the basic time series plots that can be created using Matplotlib. These plots can be used to gain insights into the data, understand trends, and identify relationships in time series data.

Given this insight, let us move forward to more advanced time series visualizations using `seaborn`.

Advanced Time Series Visualization with Seaborn

Seaborn is the next important visualization library covered in this chapter. Let us delve further into it. In this section, we will cover the following advanced time series plots using this library:

- Heat maps
- Pair plots

Heat Map

A heat map is another graphical representation of data, which is used to visualize the correlation between variables and patterns in the data. A heat map is a tabular representation with colors that shows the intensity of the values or the relationship between variables.

For this example, let us download the gas sensor data from the UCI Machine Learning repository:

Gas sensor array temperature modulation - UCI Machine Learning Repository (https://archive.ics.uci.edu/dataset/487/gas+sensor+array+temperature+modulation).

Let us start this example by importing the following libraries:

1. Pandas
2. Seaborn
3. Matplotlib.pyplot
4. Cov from Numpy

Code:

import pandas as pd

import seaborn as sns

import matplotlib.pyplot as plt

from numpy import cov

Let us then load the gas sensor data downloaded from the UCI Machine Learning repository.

Code:

sensor_data = pd.read_csv("gas+sensor+array+temperature+modulation.csv", nrows = 365)

sensor_data.head(5).transpose()

Output:

	0	1	2	3	4
Time (s)	0.0000	0.3090	0.6180	0.9260	1.2340
CO (ppm)	0.0000	0.0000	0.0000	0.0000	0.0000
Humidity (%r.h.)	49.7534	55.8400	55.8400	55.8400	55.8400
Temperature (C)	23.7184	26.6200	26.6200	26.6200	26.6200
Flow rate (mL/min)	233.2737	241.6323	241.3888	241.1461	240.9121
Heater voltage (V)	0.8993	0.2112	0.2070	0.2042	0.2030
R1 (MOhm)	0.2231	2.1314	10.5318	29.5749	49.5111
R2 (MOhm)	0.6365	5.3552	22.5612	49.5111	67.0368
R3 (MOhm)	1.1493	9.7569	37.2635	65.6318	77.8317
R4 (MOhm)	0.8483	6.3188	17.7848	26.1447	27.9625
R5 (MOhm)	1.2534	9.4472	33.0704	58.3847	71.7732
R6 (MOhm)	1.4449	10.5769	36.3160	67.5130	79.9474
R7 (MOhm)	1.9906	13.6317	42.5746	68.0064	79.8631
R8 (MOhm)	1.3303	21.9829	49.7495	59.2824	62.5385
R9 (MOhm)	1.4480	16.1902	31.7533	36.7821	39.6271

Figure 3.13: *Gas sensor dataset*

The attributes of this dataset are as follows:

Code:

sensor_data.dtypes

Output:

```
Time (s)               float64
CO (ppm)                 int64
Humidity (%r.h.)       float64
Temperature (C)        float64
Flow rate (mL/min)     float64
Heater voltage (V)     float64
R1 (MOhm)              float64
R2 (MOhm)              float64
R3 (MOhm)              float64
R4 (MOhm)              float64
R5 (MOhm)              float64
R6 (MOhm)              float64
R7 (MOhm)              float64
R8 (MOhm)              float64
R9 (MOhm)              float64
R10 (MOhm)             float64
R11 (MOhm)             float64
R12 (MOhm)             float64
R13 (MOhm)             float64
R14 (MOhm)             float64
dtype: object
```

Figure 3.14: Attributes of gas sensor dataset

More detailed information on each individual gas sensor data attribute, such as temperature, humidity, CO, and more, is available in Burgus, Javier (2019).

In the next step, we will estimate a covariance matrix between two variables – `Humidity` and `Temperature`. A covariance matrix is a square matrix whose values represent the covariance between two variables.

Code:

```
covariance = cov(sensor_data[['Humidity (%r.h.)', 'Temperature (C)']])
covariance
```

Output:

```
array([[338.9106125, 380.37135  , 380.37135  , ..., 367.35385  ,
        367.35385  , 367.35385  ],
       [380.37135  , 426.9042   , 426.9042   , ..., 412.2942   ,
        412.2942   , 412.2942   ],
       [380.37135  , 426.9042   , 426.9042   , ..., 412.2942   ,
        412.2942   , 412.2942   ],
       ...,
       [367.35385  , 412.2942   , 412.2942   , ..., 398.1842   ,
        398.1842   , 398.1842   ],
       [367.35385  , 412.2942   , 412.2942   , ..., 398.1842   ,
        398.1842   , 398.1842   ],
       [367.35385  , 412.2942   , 412.2942   , ..., 398.1842   ,
        398.1842   , 398.1842   ]])
```

Now that the data is ready, we can proceed further with creating a heat map using **sns.heatmap** from the **seaborn** library.

Code:

```
sns.heatmap(covariance, cmap='RdYlBu_r')
plt.xlabel('Humidity')
plt.ylabel('Temperature ')
plt.title('Gas Sensor Data Heatmap')
plt.show()
```

Output:

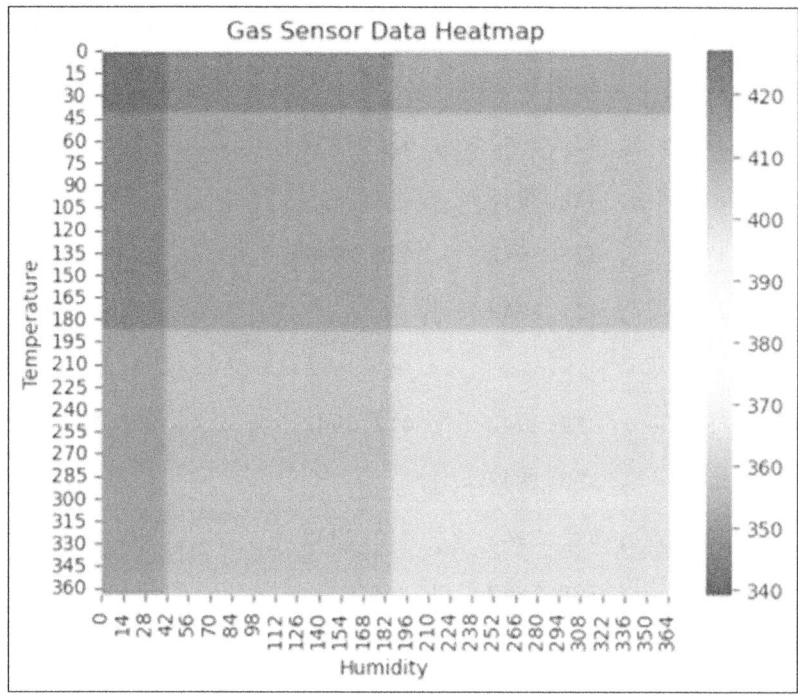

Figure 3.15: *Humidity vs. temperature – heatmap*

This is an example of using various options available within seaborn to create a heatmap. Let us now delve further at an example of Pair plots.

Pair Plots

Pair plots are a matrix of scatter plots that are created to analyze all the variables in a dataset and their pairwise relationship with other variables. In this example, we will use the pairplot function from the seaborn library to create plots that can be used to perform exploratory analysis on the variables of the gas sensor dataset.

Let us continue with the example dataset used for heat maps and call **sns.pairplot** on a subset of the data.

Code:

```
sns.pairplot(sensor_data[['CO (ppm)', 'Humidity (%r.h.)', 'Temperature (C)',
        'Flow rate (mL/min)', 'Heater voltage (V)']], diag_kind='kde')
```

Visualization of Time Series Data

```
plt.show()
```

Output:

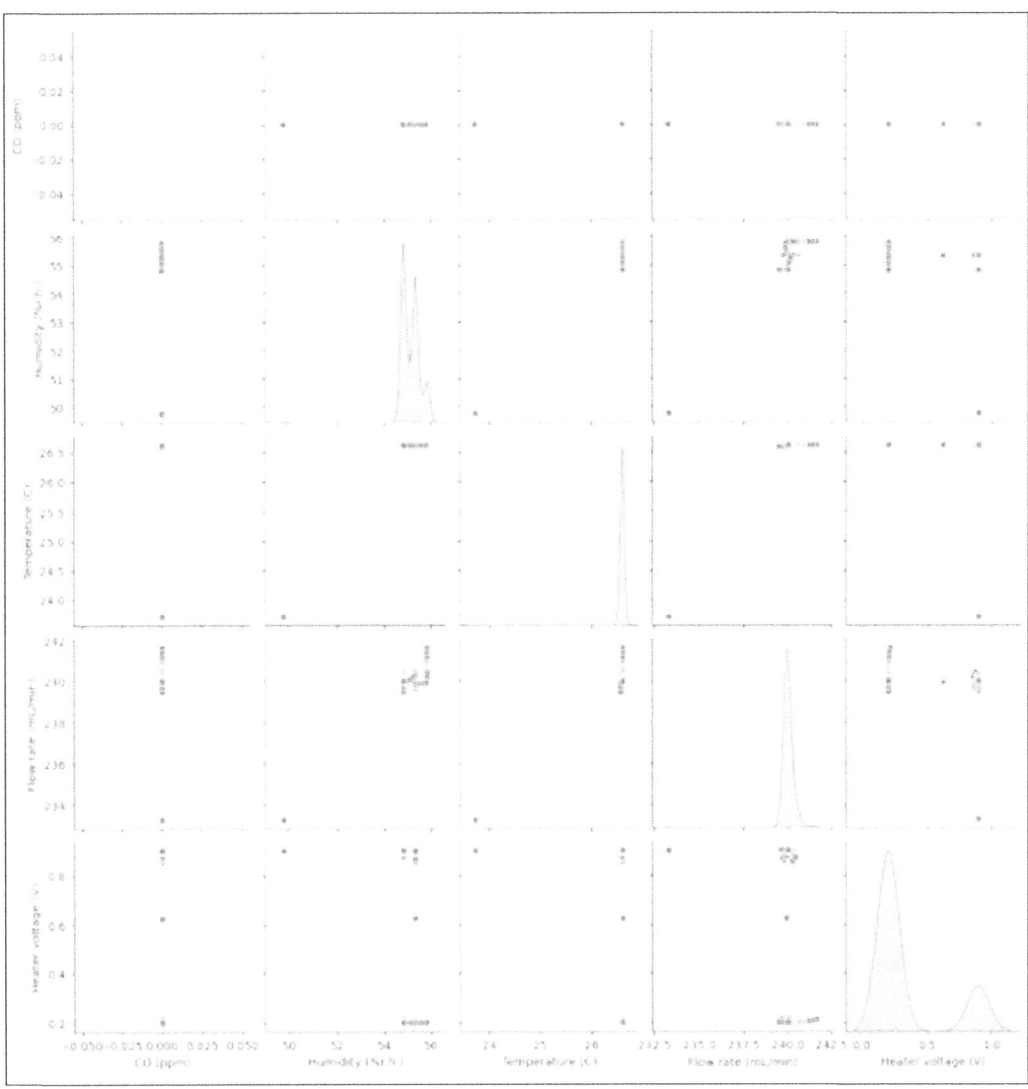

Figure 3.16: Pair plot of gas sensor data subset

In this example, as shown in *Figure* 3.16, we have created pair plots for **Carbon Monoxide**, **Humidity**, **Temperature**, **Flow rate,** and **Heater voltage** of gas sensor data. There is a positive correlation observed in the pair plot between Humidity, Temperature, and Flow Rate, whereas there is weak or no correlation between other variables. This observation can further be verified by creating a correlation matrix on this dataset as follows:

Code:

```
correlation_matrix = sensor_data[['CO (ppm)', 'Humidity (%r.h.)',
'Temperature (C)','Flow rate (mL/min)', 'Heater voltage (V)']].corr()

correlation_matrix
```

Output:

	CO (ppm)	Humidity (%r.h.)	Temperature (C)	Flow rate (mL/min)	Heater voltage (V)
CO (ppm)	NaN	NaN	NaN	NaN	NaN
Humidity (%r.h.)	NaN	1.000000	0.670983	0.744575	-0.161274
Temperature (C)	NaN	0.670983	1.000000	0.802698	-0.095393
Flow rate (mL/min)	NaN	0.744575	0.802698	1.000000	-0.134934
Heater voltage (V)	NaN	-0.161274	-0.095393	-0.134934	1.000000

Figure 3.17: Correlation matrix of gas sensor data subset

This is an example of using seaborn to create pairplots. Let us explore a few examples from another visualization library named Plotly.

Interactive Time Series Visualization with Plotly

At the beginning of this chapter, we looked at a brief introduction to Plotly with an example demonstrating how to create an interactive line plot using this library. In this section, we will examine two more examples:

- Area plot
- Candlestick plot

Area Plot

Interactive area plots can be created to show the distribution of data over a period of time. This plot is more effective for visualizing cumulative data or stacked data for various features.

To explore an example of an interactive area plot using Plotly, let us use the Yahoo Finance stocks dataset. For this example, we will be using two columns, **Date** and **Volume,** and examine the distribution of Volume by Date.

Visualization of Time Series Data

Let us begin by importing **plotly.express**.

Code:

```
import plotly.express as px
```

In the next step, let us make use of the **area** function to create an interactive area plot.

Code:

```
fig = px.area(stocks, x='Date', y='Volume')
fig.show()
```

Output:

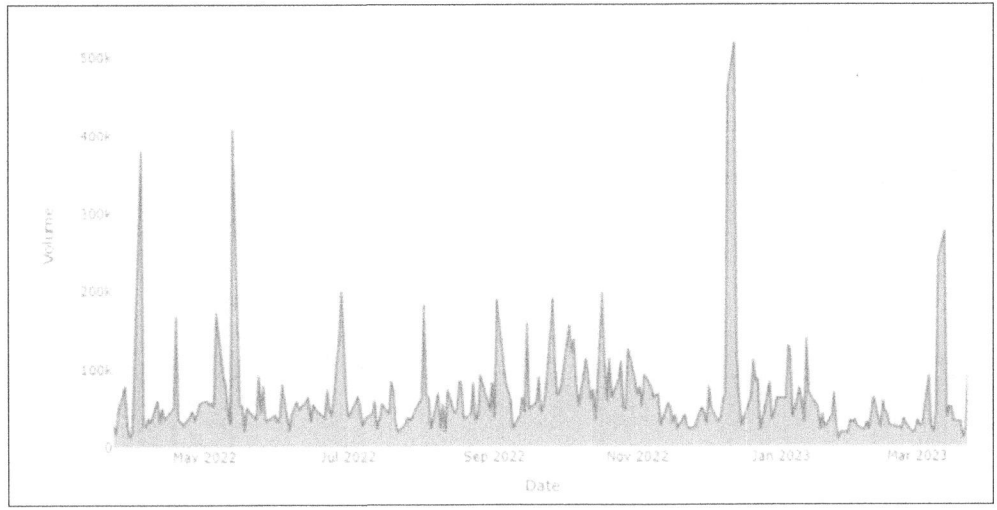

Figure 3.18: Interactive area plot of stocks data

This is an example of using a plot to create an area plot. Building on this understanding, let us look further at the last example of this section, which will be the candlestick plot.

Candlestick Plot

Candlestick plots are majorly used to understand the movement of stock prices in the domain of financial data analysis. In this example, let us continue using the stock market data.

We will begin by importing **plotly.graph_objects**.

In the next step, let us use the `go.Candlestick` function to create an interactive candlestick plot.

Code:

```
import plotly.graph_objects as go
fig = go.Figure(data=[go.Candlestick(x=stocks['Date'],
                open=stocks['Open'],
                high=stocks['High'],
                low=stocks['Low'],
                close=stocks['Close'])])
fig.show()
```

Output:

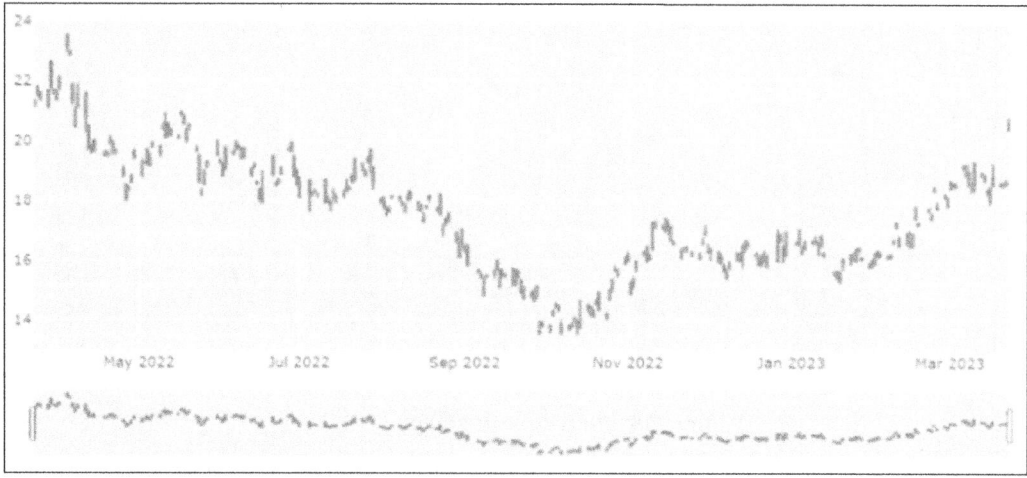

Figure 3.19: Interactive candlestick plot of stocks data

With this understanding, let's delve deeper into exploratory analysis of time series data in the upcoming chapter.

Conclusion

In this chapter, we have covered an introduction to time series visualization libraries in Python, including Matplotlib, Seaborn, and Plotly.

We also explored the basic time series plots using Matplotlib, followed by advanced time series visualizations using Seaborn, and interactive visualizations using Plotly.

In the next chapter, we will provide an overview of time series data visualizations in Python with examples and code.

References

- Visualization with Python (no date) Matplotlib. Available at: https://matplotlib.org/ (Accessed: 30 June 2023).
- Statistical Data Visualization (no date) Seaborn. Available at: https://seaborn.pydata.org/ (Accessed: 30 June 2023).
- Online retail (no date) UCI Machine Learning Repository. Available at: https://archive.ics.uci.edu/dataset/352/online+retail (Accessed: 30 June 2023).
- Plotly (no date) Plotly Python Graphing Library. Available at: https://plotly.com/python/ (Accessed: 30 June 2023).
- Yahoo Finance - Stock Market Live, quotes, Business & Finance News (no date) Yahoo! Finance. Available at: https://finance.yahoo.com/ (Accessed: 30 June 2023).
- Gas sensor array temperature modulation (no date) UCI Machine Learning Repository. Available at: https://archive.ics.uci.edu/dataset/487/gas+sensor+array+temperature+modulation (Accessed: 30 June 2023).
- Burgus, Javier (2019). Gas sensor array temperature modulation. UCI Machine Learning Repository. https://doi.org/10.24432/C5S302.

CHAPTER 4
Exploratory Analysis of Time Series Data

Exploratory analysis is an important process performed in data science to understand the data and its characteristics, to identify correlations, to extract patterns, and to prepare the data for further stages of analysis such as forecasting or prediction.

In this chapter, we will explore some of the techniques that can be applied to the time series data to perform exploratory data analysis. We will start by loading and inspecting the time series data followed by reviewing the descriptive statistics of time series data. We will then cover the concepts of time series decomposition followed by stationarity analysis. We will further look at autocorrelation and partial correlation of time series data followed by additional statistical analysis.

Structure

In this chapter, we will cover the following topics:
- Loading and Inspection of Time Series Data
- Understanding Descriptive Statistics
- Exploring Time Series Decomposition
- Performing Stationarity Analysis
- Reviewing Autocorrelation and Partial Autocorrelation
- Exploring Rolling Statistics

Loading and Inspection of Time Series Data

The first step in any exploratory data analysis process is to load the data and then review the properties of the data. Let us start this section by loading the time series data from the UCI Machine learning repository: https://archive.ics.uci.edu/dataset/791/metropt+3+dataset

The dataset used in this example is the operational data from a metro train. The attributes of this dataset are a combination of pressure values, temperature, oil levels, and so on, of various components. More details on the attributes are available in the attribute information section of the dataset source available at https://archive.ics.uci.edu/dataset/791/metropt+3+dataset.

Let us start by importing pandas so that we can make use of the methods available in this library to perform exploratory data analysis.

Code:

```
import pandas as pd
```

We will then load a sample of the metro train dataset.

Code:

```
metropt = pd.read_csv("metropt.csv")

metropt.columns
```

The data has the following columns:

Output:

```
Index(['timestamp', 'TP2', 'TP3', 'H1', 'DV_pressure', 'Reservoirs',
       'Oil_temperature', 'Motor_current', 'COMP', 'DV_eletric', 'Towers',
       'MPG', 'LPS', 'Pressure_switch', 'Oil_level', 'Caudal_impulses'],
      dtype='object')
```

Let us then look at the shape of the dataset using **pandas.shape**, which provides the total number of rows and columns.

Code:

```
metropt.shape
```

Output:

(1026, 16)

Since this is a sample of the metro train dataset and not the complete data itself, we have 1026 records in this data with all 16 columns.

Code:

pd.DataFrame(data = metropt.dtypes, columns = ['Data Type'])

The **dtypes** property provides the data types or the default schema of the data that is loaded. This property helps in understanding the current structure of the data so that required data type conversions can be performed on the data as needed.

Output:

	Data Type
timestamp	object
TP2	float64
TP3	float64
H1	float64
DV_pressure	float64
Reservoirs	float64
Oil_temperature	float64
Motor_current	float64
COMP	int64
DV_eletric	int64
Towers	int64
MPG	int64
LPS	int64
Pressure_switch	int64
Oil_level	int64
Caudal_impulses	int64

Figure 4.1: Data types of metro train data

The next step of exploratory analysis will be to convert the data into the data types as appropriate for each column. In this example, we have a **timestamp** as an object instead of a **datetime** attribute. We need to convert the timestamp into the correct data type so that this column can be used for time series analysis. To perform this type conversion, let us make use of **pandas.to_datetime** method.

Code:

```
metropt['timestamp'] = pd.to_datetime(metropt['timestamp'])
metropt['timestamp']
```

Output:

```
0       2020-01-02 00:00:00
1       2020-01-02 00:00:00
2       2020-01-02 00:00:00
3       2020-01-02 00:00:00
4       2020-01-02 00:00:00
                ...
1021    2020-01-02 02:48:00
1022    2020-01-02 02:48:00
1023    2020-01-02 02:48:00
1024    2020-01-02 02:49:00
1025    2020-01-02 02:49:00
Name: timestamp, Length: 1026, dtype: datetime64[ns]
```

Now that the schema is updated with the correct data types. The next step will be to take a look at the data and eyeball the information at a high level.

Code:

```
metropt.head(5).transpose()
```

Exploratory Analysis of Time Series Data

Output:

	0	1	2	3	4
timestamp	01-02-2020 00:00	01-02-2020 00:00	01-02-2020 00:00	01-02-2020 00:00	01-02-2020 00:00
TP2	-0.012	-0.014	-0.012	-0.012	-0.012
TP3	9.358	9.348	9.338	9.328	9.318
H1	9.34	9.332	9.322	9.312	9.302
DV_pressure	-0.024	-0.022	-0.022	-0.022	-0.022
Reservoirs	9.358	9.348	9.338	9.328	9.318
Oil_temperature	53.6	53.675	53.6	53.425	53.475
Motor_current	0.04	0.04	0.0425	0.04	0.04
COMP	1	1	1	1	1
DV_eletric	0	0	0	0	0
Towers	1	1	1	1	1
MPG	1	1	1	1	1
LPS	0	0	0	0	0
Pressure_switch	1	1	1	1	1
Oil_level	1	1	1	1	1
Caudal_impulses	1	1	1	1	1

Figure 4.2: Sample data from the metro train dataset

Figure 4.2 shows the first five records of the metro train dataset for all 16 attributes. This gives a high-level view of how the data looks like.

After loading the data and inspecting it, we can further perform more analysis on the time series data. In the upcoming section, we will explore at descriptive statistics in a bit more detail.

Understanding Descriptive Statistics

Descriptive statistics provides a numerical summary of the data to understand the characteristics of data and to provide insights. Basic statistics such as measures of central tendency, variability, range and quantiles can be understood from descriptive statistics. For this section, let us continue using the metro train dataset from the UCI machine learning repository.

Measures of central tendency are values such as mean, median and mode of the data. We can make use of the built-in functions available in Pandas to calculate these values.

Mean

The average value of each column can be calculated using Pandas `dataframe.mean()`.

Code:

pd.DataFrame(data = metropt.mean(numeric_only = True), columns = ['Mean'])

Output:

	Mean
TP2	0.436014
TP3	8.959480
H1	8.501996
DV_pressure	-0.023105
Reservoirs	8.959834
Oil_temperature	51.820200
Motor_current	1.126333
COMP	0.950292
DV_eletric	0.049708
Towers	0.973684
MPG	0.950292
LPS	0.000000
Pressure_switch	0.999025
Oil_level	1.000000
Caudal_impulses	1.000000

Figure 4.3: Mean value of time series data

The mean is calculated on columns with numerical data types.

Median

The median is calculated by finding the middle value of the time series data when sorted in ascending order. We will make use of Pandas `dataframe.median()` to identify the median.

Code:

```
pd.DataFrame(data = metropt.median(numeric_only = True), columns = ['Median'])
```

Output:

	Median
TP2	-0.0140
TP3	8.9330
H1	8.8640
DV_pressure	-0.0240
Reservoirs	8.9360
Oil_temperature	52.2625
Motor_current	0.0400
COMP	1.0000
DV_eletric	0.0000
Towers	1.0000
MPG	1.0000
LPS	0.0000
Pressure_switch	1.0000
Oil_level	1.0000
Caudal_impulses	1.0000

Figure 4.4: Median value of time series data

The median is calculated on columns with numerical data types.

Mode

Mode is the value that occurs most often and can be calculated using Pandas `dataframe.mode()`.

Code:

```
metropt.mode().head(1).transpose()
```

Output:

	0
timestamp	2020-01-02 00:00:00
TP2	-0.014
TP3	9.392
H1	-0.014
DV_pressure	-0.024
Reservoirs	8.548
Oil_temperature	52.725
Motor_current	0.04
COMP	1.0
DV_eletric	0.0
Towers	1.0
MPG	1.0
LPS	0.0
Pressure_switch	1.0
Oil_level	1.0
Caudal_impulses	1.0

Figure 4.5: Mode of the dataset

The mode is calculated on all columns of the time series dataset.

During the process of exploratory analysis, the data can further be reviewed for more information such as missing values, skewed data, and more.

In the next step, let us look at the basic statistical information of the data such as the total number of records in each column, mean, standard deviation, minimum value, 25th percentile, 50th percentile, 75th percentile, and maximum value in each column using Pandas `dataframe.describe()`.

Code:

```
metropt.describe().transpose()
```

Output:

	count	mean	std	min	25%	50%	75%	max
TP2	1026.0	0.436014	2.001841	-0.026	-0.014	-0.0140	-0.01200	10.4340
TP3	1026.0	8.959480	0.553638	8.066	8.472	8.9330	9.42350	10.0980
H1	1026.0	8.501996	2.002248	-0.028	8.384	8.8640	9.36750	10.1000
DV_pressure	1026.0	-0.023105	0.001037	-0.026	-0.024	-0.0240	-0.02200	-0.0140
Reservoirs	1026.0	8.959834	0.553394	8.064	8.471	8.9360	9.42550	10.0980
Oil_temperature	1026.0	51.820200	1.214192	49.225	50.825	52.2625	52.80000	53.8250
Motor_current	1026.0	1.126333	1.914070	0.035	0.040	0.0400	3.77875	6.3125
COMP	1026.0	0.950292	0.217446	0.000	1.000	1.0000	1.00000	1.0000
DV_eletric	1026.0	0.049708	0.217446	0.000	0.000	0.0000	0.00000	1.0000
Towers	1026.0	0.973684	0.160151	0.000	1.000	1.0000	1.00000	1.0000
MPG	1026.0	0.950292	0.217446	0.000	1.000	1.0000	1.00000	1.0000
LPS	1026.0	0.000000	0.000000	0.000	0.000	0.0000	0.00000	0.0000
Pressure_switch	1026.0	0.999025	0.031220	0.000	1.000	1.0000	1.00000	1.0000
Oil_level	1026.0	1.000000	0.000000	1.000	1.000	1.0000	1.00000	1.0000
Caudal_impulses	1026.0	1.000000	0.000000	1.000	1.000	1.0000	1.00000	1.0000

Figure 4.6: Descriptive statistics of metro train dataset

These descriptive statistics provide an overview of the time series data and help in performing further analysis. With this understanding, let us continue to look at time series decomposition.

Exploring Time Series Decomposition

Time series decomposition is the process of breaking down the time series data into trend, seasonality, level, and noise.

Trend

Trend denotes the direction of movement of the time series data. It is usually either upward or downward. For example, the price of a stock increasing on a daily basis or decreasing on a daily basis denotes its trend.

Seasonality

Seasonality denotes the repetition of a particular value, set of values, or a pattern over time. For example, the sales of gift articles increasing during the Christmas season every year denotes a seasonal pattern in the time series data.

Level

Level denotes the average behavior of the time series data. Level can be calculated after removing the influence of trend and seasonality from the data.

Noise

Noise is the irregularity or error in the time series data that stays after removing trend and seasonality from the data.

In this example, let us continue using the metro train dataset.

In the first step, let us consider two columns from the data: `timestamp` and `oil_temperature`. We will first set the `timestamp` as an index.

Code:

```
decomp_df = metropt.set_index('timestamp')[['Oil_temperature']]

decomp_df
```

Output:

timestamp	Oil_temperature
2020-01-02 00:00:00	53.600
2020-01-02 00:00:00	53.675
2020-01-02 00:00:00	53.600
2020-01-02 00:00:00	53.425
2020-01-02 00:00:00	53.475
...	...
2020-01-02 02:48:00	52.925
2020-01-02 02:48:00	52.900
2020-01-02 02:48:00	52.900
2020-01-02 02:49:00	52.900
2020-01-02 02:49:00	52.825

1026 rows × 1 columns

Figure 4.7: Metro train dataset with a timestamp as an index

Now that the dataset is ready, we can further look at time series decomposition on the data by applying **STL** (Season-Trend decomposition using LOESS) from

Exploratory Analysis of Time Series Data

statsmodels. More details on this library and **STL** are available at https://www.statsmodels.org/dev/generated/statsmodels.tsa.seasonal.STL.html.

Code:

```
from statsmodels.tsa.seasonal import STL

decomposition = STL(decomp_df, period = 60).fit()
```

In the preceding code, the time series data is provided as input, with the period set as 60 for illustration purposes. Once we fit **STL** on the data, we can look at the values set by **STL** for various time series components on the dataset.

The number of observations is stored in **nobs**.

Code:

```
decomposition.nobs
```

Output:

```
(1026, 1)
```

The observed data is stored in **observed**, and the output is the same as *Figure* 4.7.

Code:

```
decomposition.observed
```

The noise or residuals are estimated and stored in **resid**.

Code:

```
decomposition.resid
```

Output:

```
timestamp
2020-01-02 00:00:00    -0.116297
2020-01-02 00:00:00     0.016401
2020-01-02 00:00:00    -0.022917
2020-01-02 00:00:00    -0.125004
2020-01-02 00:00:00    -0.020982
                          ...
2020-01-02 02:48:00     0.133674
```

```
2020-01-02 02:48:00     0.136478
2020-01-02 02:48:00     0.050295
2020-01-02 02:49:00     0.030257
2020-01-02 02:49:00    -0.086469
Name: resid, Length: 1026, dtype: float64
```

The values for seasonality are estimated and stored in **seasonal**.

Code:

```
decomposition.seasonal
```

Output:

```
timestamp
2020-01-02 00:00:00    -0.098487
2020-01-02 00:00:00    -0.130924
2020-01-02 00:00:00    -0.141357
2020-01-02 00:00:00    -0.189032
2020-01-02 00:00:00    -0.217827
                          ...
2020-01-02 02:48:00    -1.193938
2020-01-02 02:48:00    -1.278085
2020-01-02 02:48:00    -1.248301
2020-01-02 02:49:00    -1.284715
2020-01-02 02:49:00    -1.299494
Name: season, Length: 1026, dtype: float64
```

The values for the trend of oil temperature are estimated and stored in **trend**.

Code:

```
decomposition.trend
```

Output:

```
timestamp
```

Exploratory Analysis of Time Series Data

```
2020-01-02 00:00:00    53.814783
2020-01-02 00:00:00    53.789524
2020-01-02 00:00:00    53.764274
2020-01-02 00:00:00    53.739036
2020-01-02 00:00:00    53.713810
                          ...
2020-01-02 02:48:00    53.985264
2020-01-02 02:48:00    54.041607
2020-01-02 02:48:00    54.098006
2020-01-02 02:49:00    54.154459
2020-01-02 02:49:00    54.210964
Name: trend, Length: 1026, dtype: float64
```

The weights used in the estimation are stored in `weights`.

Code:

```
decomposition.weights
```

Output:

```
timestamp
2020-01-02 00:00:00    1.0
2020-01-02 00:00:00    1.0
2020-01-02 00:00:00    1.0
2020-01-02 00:00:00    1.0
2020-01-02 00:00:00    1.0
                       ...
2020-01-02 02:48:00    1.0
2020-01-02 02:48:00    1.0
2020-01-02 02:48:00    1.0
2020-01-02 02:49:00    1.0
```

```
2020-01-02 02:49:00    1.0
Name: robust_weight, Length: 1026, dtype: float64
```

We can further visualize the time series decomposition by importing **Matplotlib**.

Code:

```
import matplotlib.pyplot as plt

decomposition.plot()

plt.show()
```

Output:

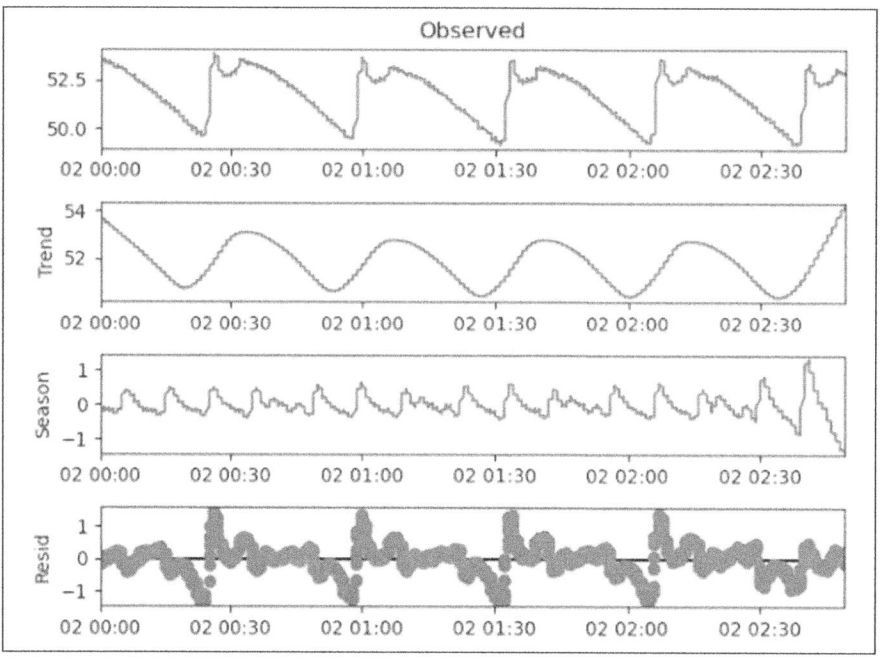

Figure 4.8: Time series decomposition

Having understood time series decomposition, let us now explore at how to perform stationarity analysis on the time series data.

Performing Stationarity Analysis

In this section, let us look at the next topic of time series exploratory data analysis, which is known as stationarity analysis. Stationarity analysis is used to understand the nature of time series data, whether it is stationary or non-stationary. A stationary time series data becomes easier to predict or forecast since it would usually have constant features or values over time, such as mean, variance and covariance. Comparatively, non-stationary data is more complex in nature and will have variations in the statistical properties and will also have characteristics such as trend and seasonality in the data.

In this section, let us make use of `statsmodels` in Python to check the stationarity of the data. More details of this library can be found at https://www.statsmodels.org/.

Augmented Dickey-Fuller Test

ADF Test (Dickey and Fuller, 1979) is a unit root test performed on time series data to identify if the series is stationary. The null hypothesis of the test is that a unit root is present in the time series data, while the alternate hypothesis is that the time series is stationary.

Python implementation of ADF is available in `statsmodel` and can be referred to in the following link:

https://www.statsmodels.org/dev/examples/notebooks/generated/stationarity_detrending_adf_kpss.html

Let us continue to use the `decomp_df` data frame, which is a time series sample of the oil temperature data frame from the previous section.

In this example, we will be importing `adfuller` from `statsmodel`.

Code:

```
from statsmodels.tsa.stattools import adfuller
```

In the next step, let us perform `adfuller` test on the `decomp_df` data frame.

Code:

```
adf_test = adfuller(decomp_df)
adf_test
```

The `adf_test` returns the following values.
1. First value: A test statistic of the `adf` test
2. Second value: P-value based on MacKinnon's approximation from MacKinnon (1994, 2010)
3. Third value: The number of lags used
4. Fourth value: Number of observations from the data

5. Fifth-set of values: Critical values for the test statistic
6. Sixth value: The maximized information criterion

Detailed implementation of ADF test from **statsmodels** can be referred to in the following documentation:

https://www.statsmodels.org/dev/_modules/statsmodels/tsa/stattools.html

Output:

(-3.8866094307664327,

 0.002135634506558302,

 14,

 1011,

 {'1%': -3.436834649927693,

  '5%': -2.864403033735098,

  '10%': -2.568294409927983},

 -1819.906554013356)

The output is then converted into a data frame for better interpretation.

Code:

df_adf = pd.DataFrame([[adf_test[0], adf_test[1], adf_test[2], adf_test[3], adf_test[4]['1%'],adf_test[4]['5%'],adf_test[4]['10%'], adf_test[5]]])

df_adf.columns = ['ADF Test Statistic', 'PValue', 'Used Lag', 'No. of observations', 'Critical Value 1%', 'Critical Value 5%', 'Critical Value 10%', 'ICBest']

df_adf.transpose()

Output:

	0
ADF Test Statistic	-3.886609
PValue	0.002136
Used Lag	14.000000
No. of observations	1011.000000
Critical Value 1%	-3.436835
Critical Value 5%	-2.864403
Critical Value 10%	-2.568294
ICBest	-1819.906554

Figure 4.9: Augmented Dickey-Fuller Test

From the ADF test results, let us check if the time series is stationary. To test it, we can define a function with a significance level of 0.05.

Code:

```
def check_stationary(pval):
    if (pval) > 0.05:
        print ('Time series is non-stationary')
    else:
        print ('Time series is stationary')
check_stationary(adf_test[1])
```

Output:

```
Time series is stationary
```

The time series of the oil temperature column is stationary and does not have a unit root.

With this understanding, let us look at another statistical test named KPSS.

Kwiatkowski-Phillips-Schmidt-Shin (KPSS) Test

KPSS tests are also used to test the stationarity of the time series data, similar to ADF tests. The null hypothesis of the test is that the time series is stationary, while the alternate hypothesis is that a unit root is present in the time series data. Similar to the ADF test, the KPSS test also returns a p-value. In this case, if the p-value is greater than the significance level (let us consider 0.05), then the time series can be considered to be stationary.

Python implementation of KPSS is available in **statsmodel** and can be referred to in the following link:

https://www.statsmodels.org/dev/examples/notebooks/generated/stationarity_detrending_adf_kpss.html

Let us continue to use the **decomp_df** data frame, which is a time series sample of the oil temperature data frame from the previous section.

In this example, we will be importing **kpss** from **statsmodel**.

Code:

```
from statsmodels.tsa.stattools import kpss
```

In the next step, let us perform the **kpss** test on the **decomp_df** data frame.

Code:

```
kpss_test = kpss(decomp_df)
kpss_test
```

The KPSS test returns the following values.

1. First value: A test statistic of the kpss test
2. Second value: P-value interpolated from Table 1 in Kwiatkowski et al. (1992)
3. Third value: The number of lags used
4. Fourth-set of values: Critical values for the test statistic
5. Fifth value: The maximized information criterion

Detailed implementation of ADF test from statsmodels can be referred to in the following documentation:

https://www.statsmodels.org/dev/_modules/statsmodels/tsa/stattools.html

Output:

(0.17862977185661982,

 0.1,

 19,

 {'10%': 0.347, '5%': 0.463, '2.5%': 0.574, '1%': 0.739})

The output is then converted into a data frame for better interpretation.

Code:

df_kpss = pd.DataFrame([[kpss_test[0], kpss_test[1], kpss_test[2], kpss_test[3]['10%'], kpss_test[3]['5%'],kpss_test[3]['2.5%'], kpss_test[3]['1%']]])

df_kpss.columns = ['KPSS Test Statistic', 'PValue', 'Lags', 'Critical Value 10%', 'Critical Value 5%', 'Critical Value 2.5%', 'Critical Value 1%']

df_kpss.transpose()

Output:

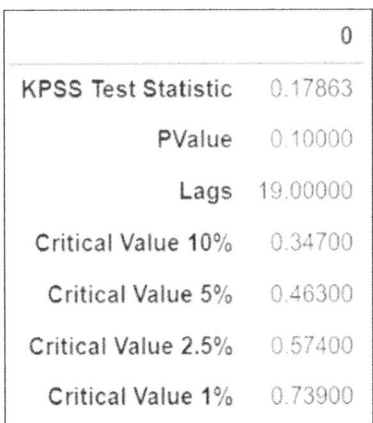

Figure 4.10: KPSS Test

From the KPSS test results, let us check if the time series is stationary. To test it, we can define a function with a significance level of 0.05.

Code:

```
def check_stationary_kpss(pval):
    if (pval) > 0.05:
        print ('Time series is stationary')
    else:
        print ('Time series is non-stationary')
check_stationary_kpss(kpss_test[1])
```

Output:

```
Time series is stationary
```

The time series of the oil temperature column is stationary and does not have a unit root.

Let us now explore another topic: autocorrelation and partial autocorrelation.

Reviewing Autocorrelation and Partial Autocorrelation

Autocorrelation and partial autocorrelation are used to identify the presence of correlation between observations in time series data at different lags. These two methods will help us understand the temporal relationships between time series data points. This is important for choosing the suitable prediction or forecasting models on time series data. There are libraries available in Python that can be used to identify and visualize autocorrelation and partial autocorrelation. Let us look at them with examples in this section.

Autocorrelation

We can calculate the autocorrelation of a time series data by calculating the correlation between a time series and its lag. Let us look at an example by calculating the autocorrelation of `decomp_df` using `plot_acf` from `statsmodels` and then plotting the values using `Matplotlib`.

Exploratory Analysis of Time Series Data

Code:

```
from statsmodels.graphics.tsaplots import plot_acf

plot_acf(decomp_df, lags = 1000)

plt.show()
```

Let us look at the `acf` by calculating 1000 lags in this output, since the lag size can be lesser than the sample size, which is 1026 for the `decomp_df` dataset.

Output:

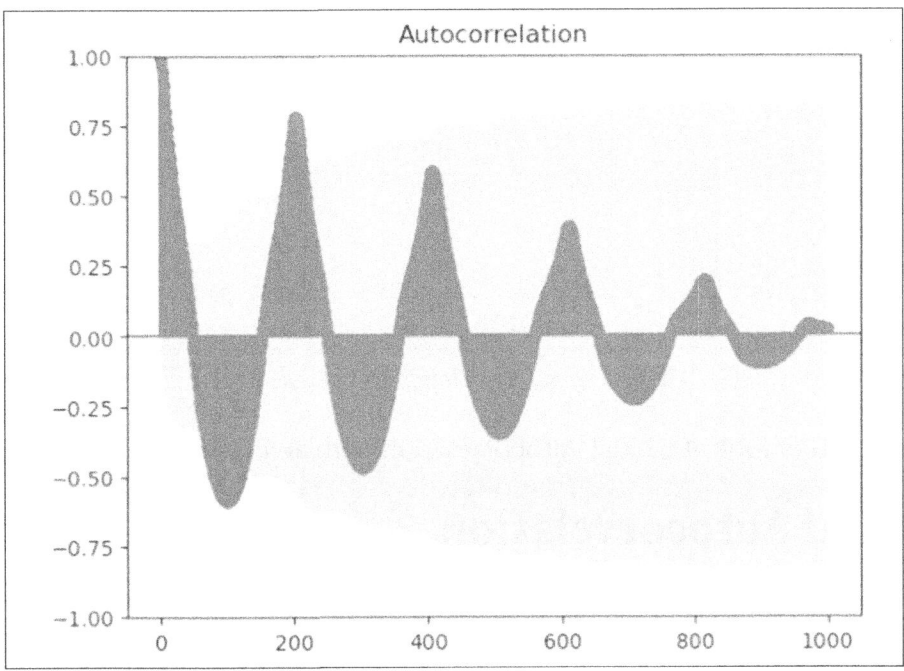

Figure 4.11: Autocorrelation plot with lags = 1000

We can look at the plot with a simplified view by bringing down the number of lags to 30.

Code:

```
plot_acf(decomp_df, lags = 30)

plt.show()
```

Output:

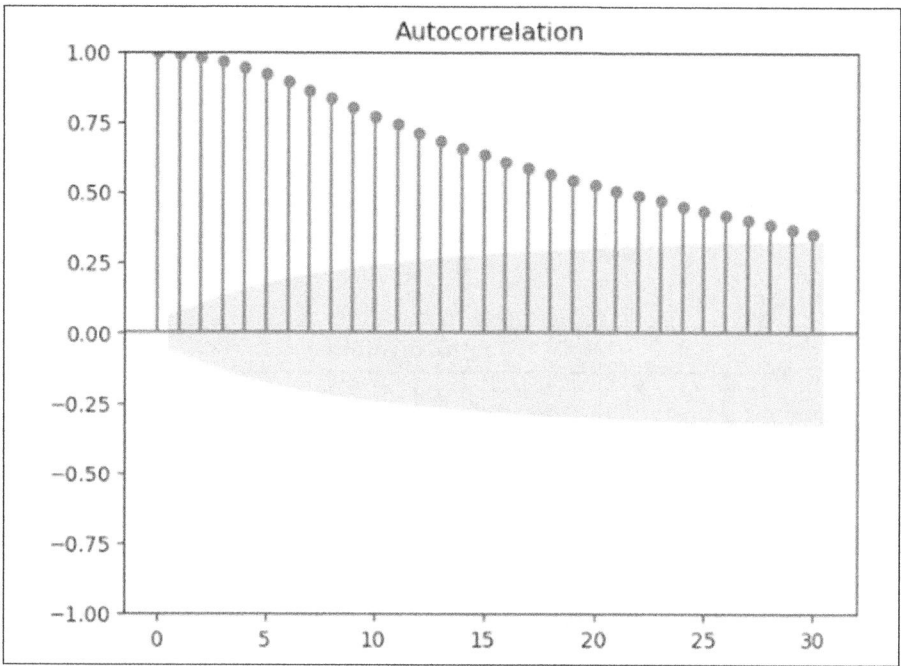

Figure 4.12: *Autocorrelation plot with lags = 30*

Let us further look at partial autocorrelation with an example.

Partial Autocorrelation

Partial autocorrelation can be used to calculate the correlation of a time series and its lag after removing the effect of intermediate lags. Let us look at an example by calculating the autocorrelation of `decomp_df` using `plot_pacf` from `statsmodels` and then plotting the values using `Matplotlib`.

Code:

```
from statsmodels.graphics.tsaplots import plot_pacf

plot_pacf(decomp_df, lags = 500)

plt.show()
```

Let us look at the **pacf** by calculating 500 lags in this output, since the lags can be 50% or less of the sample size in the case of **pacf**.

Output:

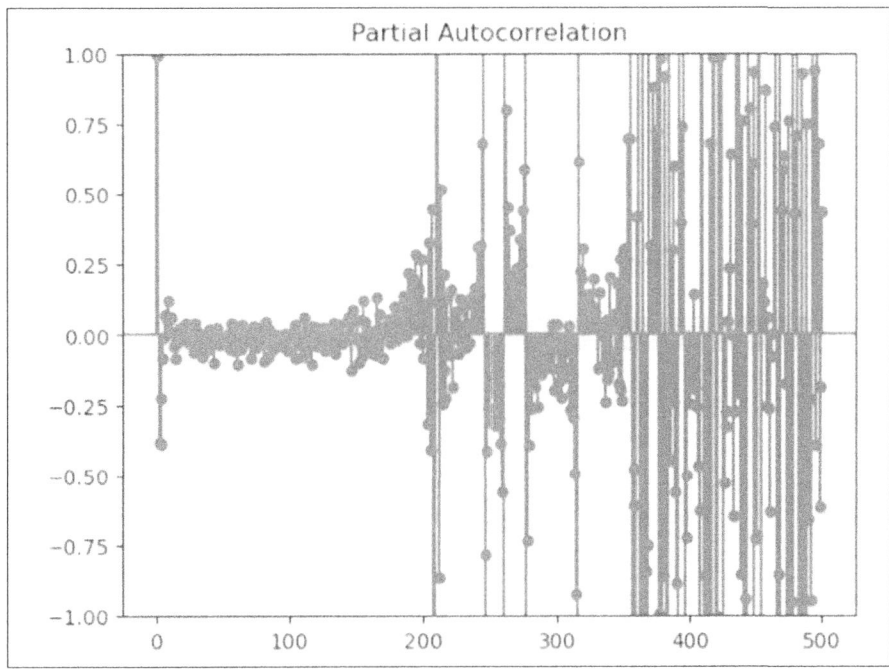

Figure 4.13: Partial autocorrelation plot with lags = 500

We can look at the plot with a simplified view by bringing down the number of lags to 30.

Code:

plot_pacf(decomp_df, lags = 30)

plt.show()

Output:

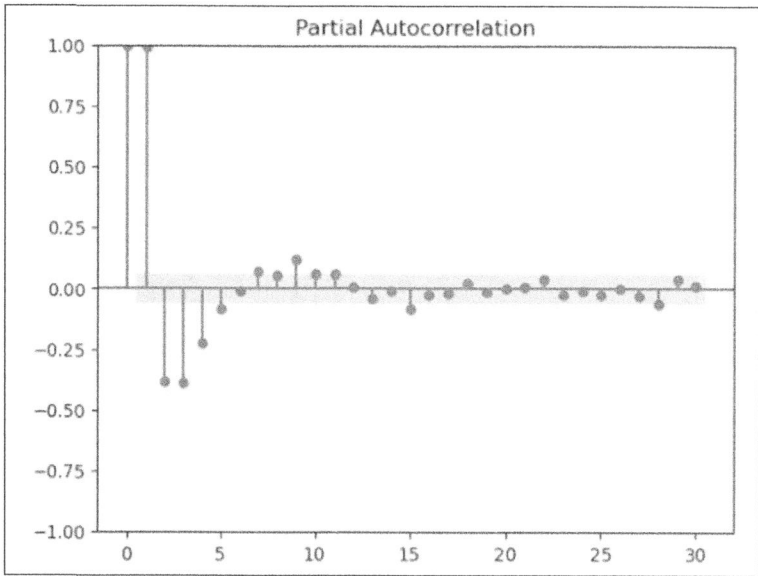

Figure 4.14: *Partial autocorrelation plot with lags = 30*

Exploring Rolling Statistics

Rolling statistics and moving averages are measures that can be calculated on the time series data to understand the movement of data over a specific window after noise smoothening. These measures will help in studying the underlying patterns and trends in the data.

The summary statistics of a time series data such as mean, median or standard deviation can be calculated for specific windows of data points as it moves through the time series. We can look at examples of rolling statistics by continuing with the `decomp_df` data frame.

Let us set a window size of 60 and calculate the rolling statistics of oil temperature in the `decomp_df` dataset.

Code:

```
window = 60
```

We will look at the rolling standard deviation by using the `rolling.std()` method in pandas.

Code:

Exploratory Analysis of Time Series Data

```
rolling_std = decomp_df.rolling(window=window).std()
```

We will then plot the rolling standard deviation using **Matplotlib**.

Code:

```
plt.figure(figsize=(12, 6))
plt.plot(decomp_df, label='Observed Time Series', color='blue')
plt.plot(rolling_std, label='Rolling Standard Deviation', color='red')
plt.xlabel('Date Time')
plt.ylabel('Oil Temperature')
plt.title('Time Series with Rolling Standard Deviation')
plt.legend()
plt.show()
```

Output:

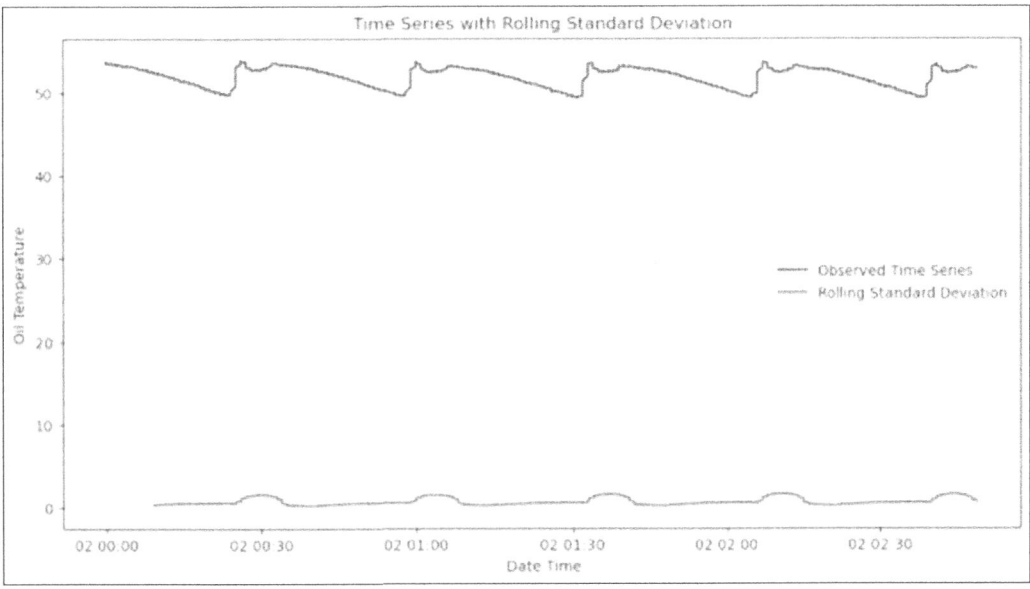

Figure 4.15: Rolling standard deviation

The plot in *Figure* 4.15 shows the observed time series data in comparison to the rolling standard deviation.

We will further look at the rolling median by using the **rolling.median()** method in pandas.

Code:

```
rolling_median = decomp_df.rolling(window=window).median()
```

We will then plot the rolling median using **Matplotlib**.

Code:

```
plt.figure(figsize=(12, 6))

plt.plot(decomp_df, label='Observed Time Series', color='blue')

plt.plot(rolling_median, label='Rolling Median', color='red')

plt.xlabel('Date Time')

plt.ylabel('Oil Temperature')

plt.title('Time Series with Rolling Median')

plt.legend()

plt.show()
```

Output:

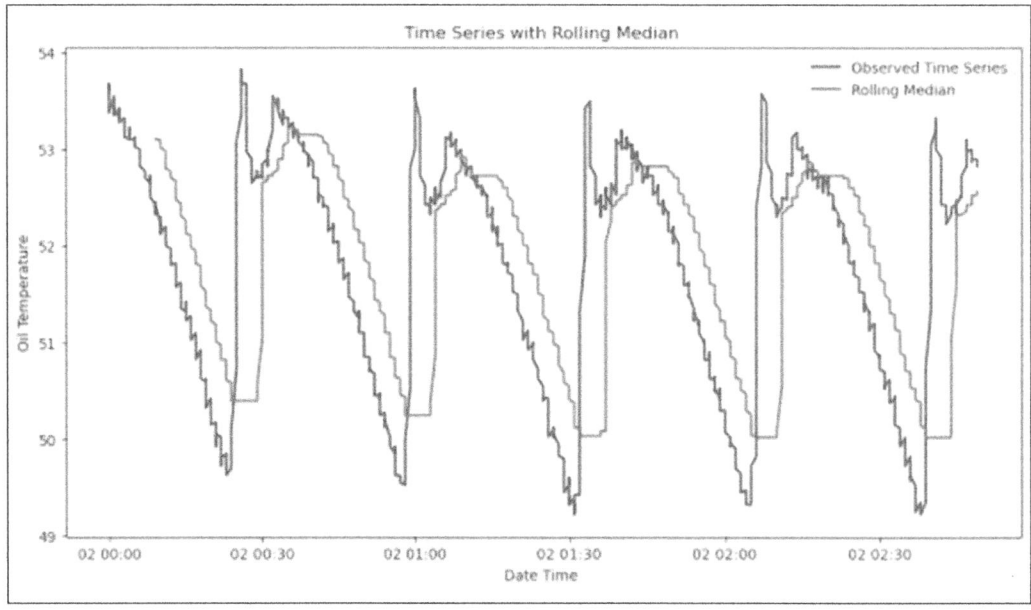

Figure 4.16: Rolling median

The plot in *Figure* 4.16 shows the observed time series data in comparison to the rolling median.

Exploratory Analysis of Time Series Data

We will further look at the rolling mean by using the **rolling.mean()** method in pandas. This method can be used to calculate simple moving averages of the time series data.

Code:

```
rolling_mean = decomp_df.rolling(window=window).mean()
```

We will then plot the rolling mean using **Matplotlib**

Code:

```
plt.figure(figsize=(12, 6))
plt.plot(decomp_df, label='Observed Time Series', color='blue')
plt.plot(rolling_mean, label='Rolling Mean', color='red')
plt.xlabel('Date Time')
plt.ylabel('Oil Temperature')
plt.title('Time Series with Rolling Mean')
plt.legend()
plt.show()
```

Output:

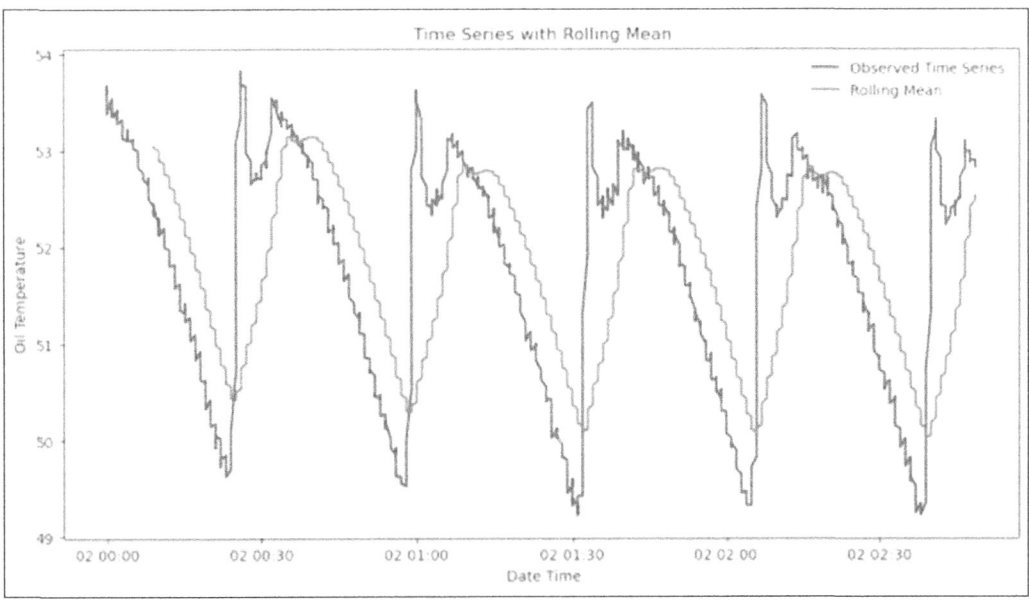

Figure 4.17: *Rolling mean*

The plot in *Figure 4.17* shows the observed time series data in comparison to the rolling mean or simple moving average.

These rolling statistics will help us identify trends and patterns in the time series while reducing noise and fluctuations. This will make it easier to interpret the data and detect underlying patterns or changes.

With this understanding, let us explore further the feature engineering of time series data in the upcoming chapter, which will also be an extension of this chapter.

Conclusion

In this chapter, we have learned about the loading and inspection of time series data using the libraries in Python.

We also looked at the basic descriptive statistics of the data. We further explored the decomposition of time series data followed by stationarity analysis. We then reviewed the concepts of autocorrelation and partial autocorrelation.

We then learned about the various rolling statistics on the time series data and visualized the values against the original data.

In the next chapter, we will look at feature engineering of time series data in Python with examples and code.

References

- Davari, Narjes, Veloso, Bruno, Ribeiro, Rita, and Gama, Joao. (2023). MetroPT-3 Dataset. UCI Machine Learning Repository. https://doi.org/10.24432/C5VW3R.
- Dickey, D.A. and Fuller, W.A. (1979) 'Distribution of the estimators for autoregressive time series with a unit root', Journal of the American Statistical Association, 74(366a), pp. 427–431. doi:10.1080/01621459.1979.10482531.
- METROPT-3 Dataset (no date) UCI Machine Learning Repository. Available at: https://archive.ics.uci.edu/dataset/791/metropt+3+dataset (Accessed: 20 August 2023).
- Statsmodels.tsa.seasonal.STL (no date) statsmodels.tsa.seasonal.STL - statsmodels 0.15.0 (+49). Available at: https://www.statsmodels.org/dev/generated/statsmodels.tsa.seasonal.STL.html (Accessed: 20 August 2023).

- Statsmodels.org (no date). Available at: https://www.statsmodels.org/ (Accessed: 20 August 2023).
- Stationarity and detrending (ADF/KPSS) (no date) Stationarity and detrending (ADF/KPSS) - statsmodels 0.15.0 (+49). Available at: https://www.statsmodels.org/dev/examples/notebooks/generated/stationarity_detrending_adf_kpss.html (Accessed: 20 August 2023).
- Source code for statsmodels.tsa.stattools (no date) statsmodels.tsa.stattools - statsmodels 0.15.0 (+49). Available at: https://www.statsmodels.org/dev/_modules/statsmodels/tsa/stattools.html (Accessed: 20 August 2023).
- Kwiatkowski, D. et al. (1992) 'Testing the null hypothesis of stationarity against the alternative of a unit root', Journal of Econometrics, 54(1–3), pp. 159–178. doi:10.1016/0304-4076(92)90104-y.
- Visualization with Python (no date) Matplotlib. Available at: https://matplotlib.org/ (Accessed: 20 August 2023).
- Pandas.dataframe.rolling (no date) pandas.DataFrame.rolling - pandas 2.0.3 documentation. Available at: https://pandas.pydata.org/docs/reference/api/pandas.DataFrame.rolling.html (Accessed: 20 August 2023).

CHAPTER 5
Feature Engineering on Time Series

Feature Engineering, in this context, is the process of preparing input variables or features necessary for machine learning models to predict or forecast based on time series data. This is an important step in time series modeling because the better the quality of the input features, the better the predictive power of the models will be. Feature engineering of time series data involves creating features that capture patterns, trends, and relationships present in the data. It plays a vital role in extracting meaningful information from raw time series data. Performing feature engineering on the data is a creative and insightful process that needs both technical skills and domain knowledge.

In this chapter, we will explore some of the techniques that can be applied to time series data to perform feature engineering. We will start by looking at various techniques involved in feature engineering of univariate time series data. Then, we will cover the feature engineering techniques of multivariate time series data.

Structure

In this chapter, the following topics will be covered:
- Univariate Feature Engineering
    - Creating Lag-Based Univariate Features
    - Calculating Rolling Statistics
    - Computing Expanding Window Statistics

- - Calculating Exponential Moving Averages
- Multivariate Feature Engineering
  - Creating Lag-Based Multivariate Features
  - Creating Interaction Terms-Based Features
  - Creating Aggregated Features

Univariate Feature Engineering

Univariate time series data consists of a single variable time series, which can be provided as input for forecasting future values. Univariate feature engineering involves deriving features from a single variable to identify patterns, trends, or seasonality in the data. In this section, we will look at some of the techniques that can be used to perform univariate feature engineering.

For the examples in univariate feature engineering, let us make use of a sample from the UCI Machine Learning dataset (Tan, James) available at:

https://archive.ics.uci.edu/dataset/396/sales+transactions+dataset+weekly.

Creating Lag-Based Univariate Features

Lag-based features are created from the target variables of the single-variable time series data. The historical observations of target variables are used to calculate the time lag of the variable and create new features out of them. For example, the lag feature for an observation at time T can be created using the value at time T-1 or T-2, and so on. These features can be used to identify correlations and patterns in data, thereby increasing the forecasting accuracy of the data.

The summary of steps to be followed is as follows:
1. Decide and set the lag values based on the problem, dataset, and domain.
2. Create new columns by shifting the time series variable for the chosen lag value.
3. Review the newly created features.

Let us begin the feature engineering by importing the dataset into a data frame.

Code:

```
import pandas as pd

sales_df = pd.read_csv("SalesTransactions.csv")
```

Feature Engineering on Time Series

```
sales_df.head(5)
```

Output:

	Week	Purchase Quantity
0	W0	11
1	W1	12
2	W2	10
3	W3	8
4	W4	13

Figure 5.1: Sales transaction data

We will then set **Week** as the index of the data.

Code:

```
sales_df.set_index('Week', inplace = True)
sales_df.head(5)
```

The next step is to create a variable named **lag** and add the list of lags that need to be created as new features.

Code:

```
lag = [1,2,3]
```

In the next step, let us add new variables by shifting the existing **purchase quantity** using the **lag** values.

Code:

```
for value in lag:
    sales_df[f'Purchase Quantity {value}'] = sales_df['Purchase Quantity'].shift(value)
```

Let us further fill **Null** values with **0s**.

Code:

```
sales_df.fillna(0, inplace = True)
sales_df.head(10)
```

Output:

Week	Purchase Quantity	Purchase Quantity 1	Purchase Quantity 2	Purchase Quantity 3
W0	11	0.0	0.0	0.0
W1	12	11.0	0.0	0.0
W2	10	12.0	11.0	0.0
W3	8	10.0	12.0	11.0
W4	13	8.0	10.0	12.0
W5	12	13.0	8.0	10.0
W6	14	12.0	13.0	8.0
W7	21	14.0	12.0	13.0
W8	6	21.0	14.0	12.0
W9	14	6.0	21.0	14.0

Figure 5.2: Lag features of Purchase quantity

In the next step, let us review the newly created features in comparison to the existing time series variable by plotting them using `matplotlib`.

Here are the steps to visualize:
1. Import Matplotlib.
2. Set the date column as the x-axis.
3. Set the time series variable column and its corresponding lag values as the line parameters that will be plotted on the y-axis.
4. Visualize the existing variable against the newly created variables in a line graph to gain further understanding.

Code:

```
import matplotlib.pyplot as plt

date = sales_df.index

variable = sales_df['Purchase Quantity']

lag1 = sales_df['Purchase Quantity 1']

lag2 = sales_df['Purchase Quantity 2']

lag3 = sales_df['Purchase Quantity 3']
```

```
fig, ax = plt.subplots()
ax.plot(date, variable, linestyle='-.', color = 'green')
ax.plot(date, lag1, linestyle='-.', color = 'red')
ax.plot(date, lag2, linestyle='-.', color = 'blue')
ax.plot(date, lag3, linestyle='-.', color = 'grey')

ax.grid(True, linestyle=':', color = 'grey')
ax.tick_params(labelcolor='r', labelsize='medium', width=5)
ax.set_xticks([])

plt.show()
```

Output:

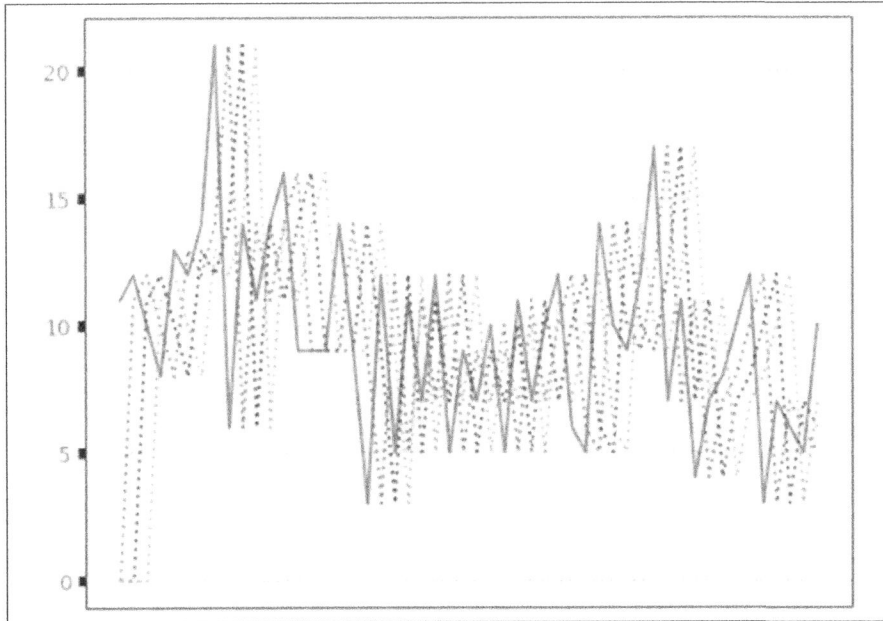

Figure 5.3: *Visualization of Lag features*

Visualizing the new variables gives further opportunities to make domain-specific decisions on the relevance of the newly created variables and to decide if they can be further used for predictions. This is one method of creating time series features.

With this understanding, let us proceed to the next method in univariate feature creation.

Calculating Rolling Statistics

Rolling statistics are created to understand the behavior of the time series data over a rolling window. The statistical parameters such as mean, median, or standard deviation over a sliding window can be calculated as features.

Let us start the feature engineering by continuing with the **Sales Transaction** dataset. In this example, we can create rolling mean and rolling standard deviation as new time series features for the sales transactions data using the **rolling** method in **pandas**.

The summary of steps to be followed is as follows:
1. Select the rolling window size and set it as a variable.
2. Decide the statistics that need to be calculated on the data, for example, Mean.
3. Calculate the statistics as a new column by sliding the window for the selected size across the time series variable.
4. Review the newly created features.

The first step is to set the window size and then create two columns to calculate the rolling mean and rolling standard deviation.

Code:

```
window = 3
sales_df['rolling_mean'] = sales_df['Purchase Quantity'].rolling(window=window).mean()
sales_df['rolling_std'] = sales_df['Purchase Quantity'].rolling(window=window).std()
sales_df.fillna(0, inplace = True)
sales_df.head(10)
```

Feature Engineering on Time Series

Output:

Week	Purchase Quantity	Purchase Quantity 1	Purchase Quantity 2	Purchase Quantity 3	rolling_mean	rolling_std
W0	11	0.0	0.0	0.0	0.000000	0.000000
W1	12	11.0	0.0	0.0	0.000000	0.000000
W2	10	12.0	11.0	0.0	11.000000	1.000000
W3	8	10.0	12.0	11.0	10.000000	2.000000
W4	13	8.0	10.0	12.0	10.333333	2.516611
W5	12	13.0	8.0	10.0	11.000000	2.645751
W6	14	12.0	13.0	8.0	13.000000	1.000000
W7	21	14.0	12.0	13.0	15.666667	4.725816
W8	6	21.0	14.0	12.0	13.666667	7.505553
W9	14	6.0	21.0	14.0	13.666667	7.505553

Figure 5.4: Rolling Statistics features of Purchase quantity

In the next step, let us review the newly created features in comparison to the existing time series variable by plotting them using **matplotlib**.

Here are the steps to visualize:

1. Import **matplotlib**.
2. Set the date column as the x-axis.
3. Set the time series variable column and its corresponding rolling statistics values as the line parameters that will be plotted on the y-axis.
4. Visualize the existing variable against the newly created variables in a line graph to gain further understanding.

Code:

```
date = sales_df.index
variable = sales_df['Purchase Quantity']
mean = sales_df['rolling_mean']
std = sales_df['rolling_std']


fig, ax = plt.subplots()
ax.plot(date, variable, linestyle='-.', color = 'green')
```

```
ax.plot(date, mean, linestyle='--', color = 'red')
ax.plot(date, std, linestyle=':', color = 'blue')


ax.grid(True, linestyle=':', color = 'grey')
ax.tick_params(labelcolor='r', labelsize='medium', width=5)
ax.set_xticks([])


plt.show()
```

Output:

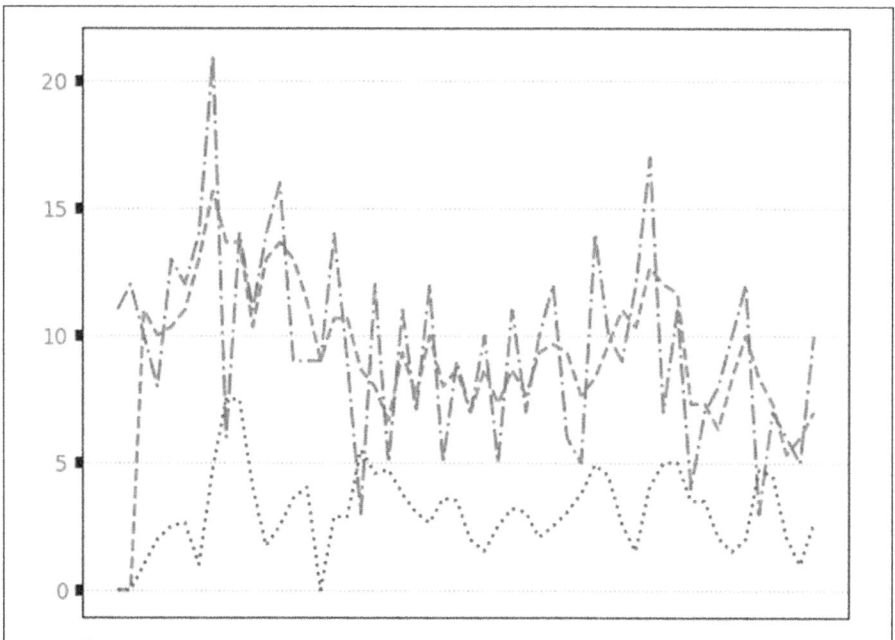

Figure 5.5: *Visualization of Rolling Statistics features of Purchase quantity*

Visualizing the new variables opens up further opportunities to make domain-specific decisions regarding their relevance of the newly created variables and to decide if they can be used further for predictions.

This is another method of creating time series features. Let us now explore the next method in univariate feature creation.

Computing Expanding Window Statistics

Expanding window statistical features are an extension of rolling window statistical features. In rolling window features, we created rolling average and rolling standard deviation for a single fixed window of time period, whereas in expanding window, we will be creating features over an increasing number of historical time periods. These features would help in capturing patterns or trends over changing time periods in a time series data.

The summary of steps to be followed is as follows:

1. Decide the start and end values for the expanding windows.
2. Set two variables with minimum and maximum window sizes.
3. Decide the expanding statistics that need to be calculated as new features, for example, Mean.
4. Calculate the statistics with the sliding window for all window sizes between the minimum and maximum values.
5. Store the results in new columns within the time series dataset.
6. Review the newly created features.

For this example, let us continue using the `sales_df` dataset. In the first step, we need to create two variables to set the minimum and maximum window sizes for expanding statistics calculation.

Code:

```
window_min = 3
window_max = 10
```

In the next step, let us define a `loop` to calculate expanding statistics for the time periods between the minimum and maximum windows.

Code:

```
for window in range(window_min, window_max + 1):
    sales_df[f'Expanding_Mean_{window}'] = sales_df['Purchase Quantity'].expanding(window).mean()
    sales_df[f'Expanding_Std_{window}'] = sales_df['Purchase Quantity'].expanding(window).std()
```

```
sales_df.fillna(0, inplace = True)
sales_df.columns
```

Output:

```
Index(['Purchase Quantity', 'Purchase Quantity 1', 'Purchase Quantity 2',
       'Purchase Quantity 3', 'rolling_mean', 'rolling_std',
       'Expanding_Mean_3', 'Expanding_Std_3', 'Expanding_Mean_4',
       'Expanding_Std_4', 'Expanding_Mean_5', 'Expanding_Std_5',
       'Expanding_Mean_6', 'Expanding_Std_6', 'Expanding_Mean_7',
       'Expanding_Std_7', 'Expanding_Mean_8', 'Expanding_Std_8',
       'Expanding_Mean_9', 'Expanding_Std_9', 'Expanding_Mean_10',
       'Expanding_Std_10'],
      dtype='object')
```

In the preceding output, eight new features were created for each mean and standard deviation of purchase quantity for the time periods between 3 and 10.

Code:

```
sales_df[['Expanding_Mean_3', 'Expanding_Std_3', 'Expanding_Mean_4',
          'Expanding_Std_4', 'Expanding_Mean_5', 'Expanding_Std_5',
          'Expanding_Mean_6', 'Expanding_Std_6', 'Expanding_Mean_7',
          'Expanding_Std_7', 'Expanding_Mean_8', 'Expanding_Std_8',
          'Expanding_Mean_9', 'Expanding_Std_9', 'Expanding_Mean_10',
          'Expanding_Std_10']].head(5).transpose()
```

The data for the expanding statistics appears as follows:

Output:

Feature Engineering on Time Series

Week	W0	W1	W2	W3	W4
Expanding_Mean_3	0.0	0.0	11.0	10.250000	10.800000
Expanding_Std_3	0.0	0.0	1.0	1.707825	1.923538
Expanding_Mean_4	0.0	0.0	0.0	10.250000	10.800000
Expanding_Std_4	0.0	0.0	0.0	1.707825	1.923538
Expanding_Mean_5	0.0	0.0	0.0	0.000000	10.800000
Expanding_Std_5	0.0	0.0	0.0	0.000000	1.923538
Expanding_Mean_6	0.0	0.0	0.0	0.000000	0.000000
Expanding_Std_6	0.0	0.0	0.0	0.000000	0.000000
Expanding_Mean_7	0.0	0.0	0.0	0.000000	0.000000
Expanding_Std_7	0.0	0.0	0.0	0.000000	0.000000
Expanding_Mean_8	0.0	0.0	0.0	0.000000	0.000000
Expanding_Std_8	0.0	0.0	0.0	0.000000	0.000000
Expanding_Mean_9	0.0	0.0	0.0	0.000000	0.000000
Expanding_Std_9	0.0	0.0	0.0	0.000000	0.000000
Expanding_Mean_10	0.0	0.0	0.0	0.000000	0.000000
Expanding_Std_10	0.0	0.0	0.0	0.000000	0.000000

Figure 5.6: Expanding Statistics features of Purchase quantity

In the next step, let us review the newly created features in comparison to the existing time series variable by plotting them using Matplotlib.

Here are the steps to visualize:
1. Import Matplotlib.
2. Set the date column as the x-axis.
3. Set the time series variable column and its corresponding expanding window statistics values as the line parameters that will be plotted on the y-axis.
4. Visualize the existing variables against the newly created variables in a line graph to gain further understanding.

Code:
```
date = sales_df.index
variable = sales_df['Purchase Quantity']
```

```python
exp1 = sales_df['Expanding_Mean_3']
exp2 = sales_df['Expanding_Mean_4']
exp3 = sales_df['Expanding_Mean_5']
exp4 = sales_df['Expanding_Mean_6']
exp5 = sales_df['Expanding_Mean_7']
exp6 = sales_df['Expanding_Mean_8']
exp7 = sales_df['Expanding_Mean_9']
exp8 = sales_df['Expanding_Mean_10']


fig, ax = plt.subplots()
ax.plot(date, variable, linestyle='-.', color = 'green')
ax.plot(date, exp1, linestyle='--', color = 'paleturquoise')
ax.plot(date, exp2, linestyle=':', color = 'lightseagreen')
ax.plot(date, exp3, linestyle='--', color = 'turquoise')
ax.plot(date, exp4, linestyle=':', color = 'darkslategrey')
ax.plot(date, exp5, linestyle='--', color = 'teal')
ax.plot(date, exp6, linestyle=':', color = 'aqua')
ax.plot(date, exp7, linestyle='--', color = 'lightskyblue')
ax.plot(date, exp8, linestyle=':', color = 'dodgerblue')

ax.grid(True, linestyle=':', color = 'grey')
ax.tick_params(labelcolor='r', labelsize='medium', width=5)
ax.set_xticks([])


plt.show()
```

The output for this code is the comparison of expanding window mean values against the time series variable.

Output:

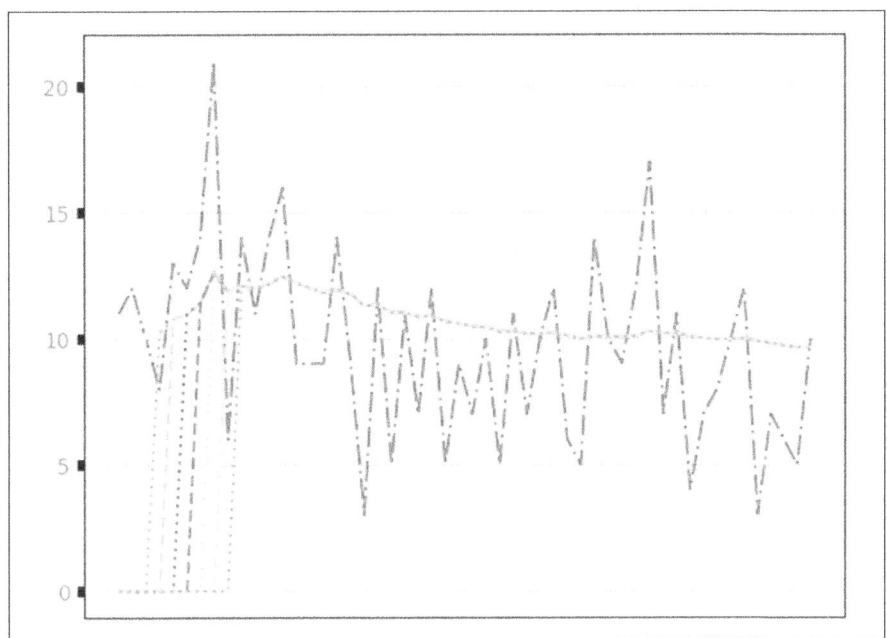

Figure 5.7: Visualization of Expanding Window features of Mean

Similarly, we can plot the expanding statistics for standard deviation as well.

Code:

```
date = sales_df.index
variable = sales_df['Purchase Quantity']
exp1 = sales_df['Expanding_Std_3']
exp2 = sales_df['Expanding_Std_4']
exp3 = sales_df['Expanding_Std_5']
exp4 = sales_df['Expanding_Std_6']
exp5 = sales_df['Expanding_Std_7']
exp6 = sales_df['Expanding_Std_8']
```

```
exp7 = sales_df['Expanding_Std_9']
exp8 = sales_df['Expanding_Std_10']


fig, ax = plt.subplots()
ax.plot(date, variable, linestyle='-.', color = 'green')
ax.plot(date, exp1, linestyle='--', color = 'paleturquoise')
ax.plot(date, exp2, linestyle=':', color = 'lightseagreen')
ax.plot(date, exp3, linestyle='--', color = 'turquoise')
ax.plot(date, exp4, linestyle=':', color = 'darkslategrey')
ax.plot(date, exp5, linestyle='--', color = 'teal')
ax.plot(date, exp6, linestyle=':', color = 'aqua')
ax.plot(date, exp7, linestyle='--', color = 'lightskyblue')
ax.plot(date, exp8, linestyle=':', color = 'dodgerblue')

ax.grid(True, linestyle=':', color = 'grey')
ax.tick_params(labelcolor='r', labelsize='medium', width=5)
ax.set_xticks([])


plt.show()
```

The output for this code is the comparison of expanding window standard deviation values against the time series variable.

Output:

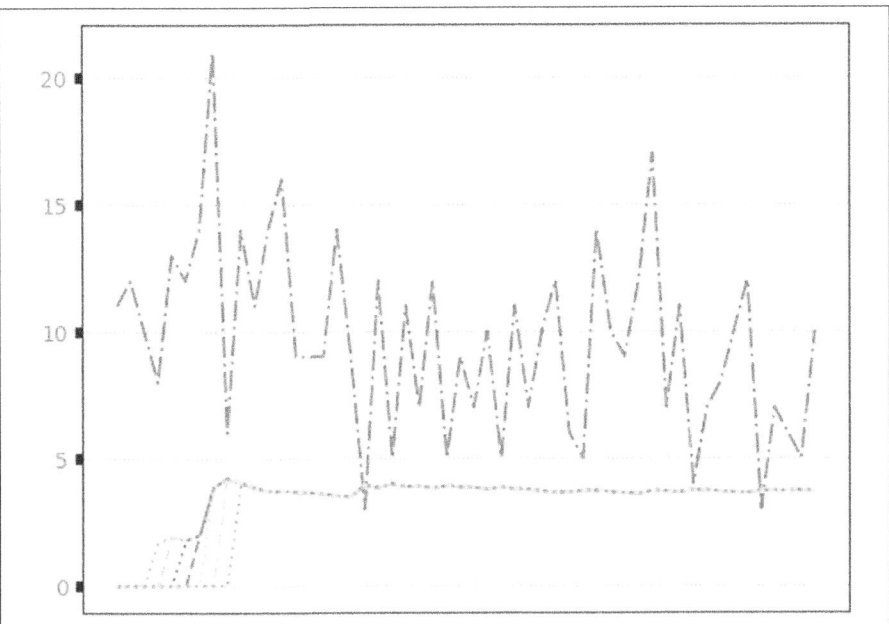

Figure 5.8: Visualization of Expanding Window features of Standard deviation

Visualizing the new variables offers further opportunities to make domain-specific decisions on the relevance of the newly created variables and whether they can be utilized for future predictions.

With this understanding, let us look at the next section, which covers calculating exponential moving averages.

Calculating Exponential Moving Averages

Exponential moving averages are another method of creating time series features by calculating weighted averages over a period of time. In this method, more weightage is given to the recent observations compared to the older ones, thus giving an advantage to the recent observations, which are more relevant to understand the data. This method helps in smoothing the data from noise and any other fluctuations in the data over time. It also helps in identifying short-term trends in the data.

The summary of steps to be followed is as follows:
1. Select the smoothing factor denoted by alpha as a value between 0 and 1.
2. Define a function to calculate the exponential moving averages.
3. Provide alpha, data frame, and time series variables as input parameters.
4. Define a list to capture the exponential moving averages (EMA).
5. Initialize the EMA list with the first observation of the time series variable.
6. EMA at the time (t) is calculated by the formula: EMA(t) = alpha * Current Observation + (1-alpha) * Previous EMA
7. Append the EMA calculated at every time point into the EMA list.
8. Create a new column in the time series dataset and assign the values from the EMA list into the column.

Let us start the feature creation by defining a function named **calc_exp_mov_avgs** and providing the following input parameters: **alpha**, **dataset**, and **inputvariable**.

Code:

```
def calc_exp_mov_avgs(alpha, dataset, inputvariable):
    ema_list = [dataset[inputvariable].iloc[0]]
    for i in range(1, len(dataset)):
        ema = alpha*dataset[inputvariable].iloc[i] + (1-alpha) * ema_list[-1]
        ema_list.append(ema)
    dataset['EMA'] = ema_list
    return dataset[[inputvariable, 'EMA']].head(10)

calc_exp_mov_avgs(0.3, sales_df, 'Purchase Quantity')
```

The output of this code displays the first 10 records of sales transactions data frame, limited to two columns: **Purchase Quantity** and **EMA**, which has been calculated.

Feature Engineering on Time Series

Output:

	Purchase Quantity	EMA
Week		
W0	11	11.000000
W1	12	11.300000
W2	10	10.910000
W3	8	10.037000
W4	13	10.925900
W5	12	11.248130
W6	14	12.073691
W7	21	14.751584
W8	6	12.126109
W9	14	12.688276

Figure 5.9: Exponential moving averages

In the next step, let us review the newly created features in comparison to the existing time series variable by plotting them using `Matplotlib`.

Here are the steps to visualize:

1. Import `Matplotlib`.
2. Set the date column as the x-axis.
3. Set the time series variable column and its corresponding exponential moving average values as the line parameters that will be plotted on the y-axis.
4. Visualize the existing variable against the newly created variables in a line graph to gain further understanding.

Code:

```
date = sales_df.index
variable = sales_df['Purchase Quantity']
ema = sales_df['EMA']
```

```
fig, ax = plt.subplots()
ax.plot(date, variable, linestyle='-.', color = 'green')
ax.plot(date, ema, linestyle='--', color = 'red')

ax.grid(True, linestyle=':', color = 'grey')
ax.tick_params(labelcolor='r', labelsize='medium', width=5)
ax.set_xticks([])


plt.show()
```

The output for this code is the comparison of exponential moving average values against the time series variable.

Output:

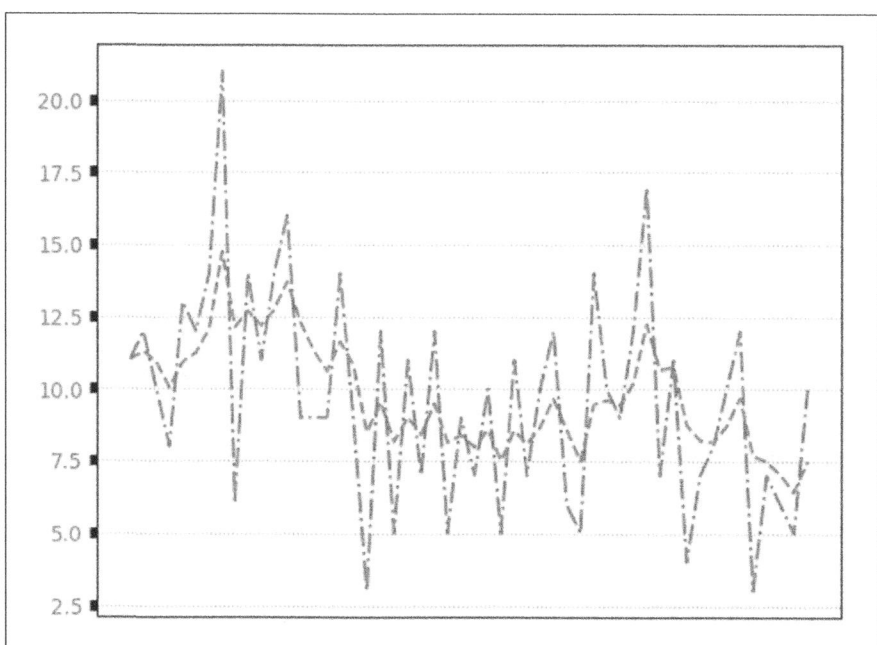

Figure 5.10: *Visualization of Exponential moving averages*

Visualizing the new variables gives further opportunities to make domain-specific decisions on the relevance of the newly created variables and to decide if they can be used further for predictions.

Lets explore the various methods for creating features on multivariate time series data.

Multivariate Feature Engineering

Multivariate time series data consists of multiple variable time series data, which can be provided as input for forecasting future values. Multivariate feature engineering involves deriving features from more than one variable to identify patterns, trends, or seasonality in the data. In this section, we will look at some of the techniques that can be used to perform multivariate feature engineering.

For the examples in multivariate feature engineering, let us make use of a sample from the UCI Machine Learning dataset, **Productivity Prediction of Garment Employees**, available at https://archive.ics.uci.edu/dataset/597/productivity+prediction+of+garment+employees.

This dataset consists of the following columns, and the explanations are from the UCI Machine Learning dataset.

Column	Description
date	Date in MM-DD-YYYY
day	Day of the Week
quarter	A portion of the month. A month was divided into four quarters
department	Associated department with the instance
team_no	Associated team number with the instance
no_of_workers	Number of workers in each team
no_of_style_change	Number of changes in the style of a particular product
targeted_productivity	Targeted productivity set by the Authority for each team for each day.
smv	Standard Minute Value, it is the allocated time for a task
wip	Work in progress. Includes the number of unfinished items for products
over_time	Represents the amount of overtime by each team in minutes
incentive	Represents the amount of financial incentive (in BDT) that enables or motivates a particular course of action.
idle_time	The amount of time when the production was interrupted due to several reasons
idle_men	The number of workers who were idle due to production interruption
actual_productivity	The actual % of productivity that was delivered by the workers. It ranges from 0-1.

Figure 5.11: Columns in Productivity Prediction of Garment Employees

In this section, let us further explore creating new features from some of the variables present in this dataset.

Let us prepare the data for feature engineering before applying the feature creation methods.

Code:

garment_df = pd.read_csv('garments_worker_productivity.csv')

garment_df.head(10).transpose()

Output:

	0	1	2	3	4	5	6	7	8	9
date	1/1/2015	1/1/2015	1/1/2015	1/1/2015	1/1/2015	1/1/2015	1/1/2015	1/1/2015	1/1/2015	1/1/2015
quarter	Quarter1	Quarter1	Quarter1	Quarter1	Quarter1	Quarter1	Quarter1	Quarter1	Quarter1	Quarter1
department	sweing	finishing	sweing	sweing	sweing	sweing	finishing	sweing	sweing	sweing
day	Thursday	Thursday	Thursday	Thursday	Thursday	Thursday	Thursday	Thursday	Thursday	Thursday
team	8	1	11	12	6	7	2	3	2	1
targeted_productivity	0.8	0.75	0.8	0.8	0.8	0.8	0.75	0.75	0.75	0.75
smv	26.16	3.94	11.41	11.41	25.9	25.9	3.94	28.08	19.87	28.08
wip	1108.0	NaN	968.0	968.0	1170.0	984.0	NaN	795.0	733.0	681.0
over_time	7080	960	3660	3660	1920	6720	960	6900	6000	6900
incentive	98	0	50	50	50	38	0	45	34	45
idle_time	0.0	0.0	0.0	0.0	0.0	0.0	0.0	0.0	0.0	0.0
idle_men	0	0	0	0	0	0	0	0	0	0
no_of_style_change	0	0	0	0	0	0	0	0	0	0
no_of_workers	59.0	8.0	30.5	30.5	56.0	56.0	8.0	57.5	55.0	57.5
actual_productivity	0.940725	0.8865	0.80057	0.80057	0.800382	0.800125	0.755167	0.753683	0.753098	0.750428

Figure 5.12: Sample data from Productivity Prediction of Garment Employees

In the next step, let us review the data types of the data.

Code:

garment_df.dtypes

Output:

date	object
quarter	object
department	object
day	object
team	int64
targeted_productivity	float64
smv	float64
wip	float64
over_time	int64

Feature Engineering on Time Series

```
incentive                  int64
idle_time                  float64
idle_men                   int64
no_of_style_change         int64
no_of_workers              float64
actual_productivity        float64
dtype: object
```

Update the data type of column **date** into date time.

Code:

garment_df['date'] = pd.to_datetime(garment_df['date'])

garment_df['date']

Output:

```
0       2015-01-01
1       2015-01-01
2       2015-01-01
3       2015-01-01
4       2015-01-01
           ...
1192    2015-03-11
1193    2015-03-11
1194    2015-03-11
1195    2015-03-11
1196    2015-03-11
Name: date, Length: 1197, dtype: datetime64[ns]
```

Let us now sort the **date** column and filter the **team** column with **team = 1**. Reset the index and review the data.

Code:

```
garment_df = garment_df.sort_values(by='date')

garment_df_team1 = garment_df[garment_df['team']==1]

garment_df_team1.reset_index(inplace = True, drop = True)

garment_df_team1.head(5).transpose()
```

Output:

	0	1	2	3	4
date	2015-01-01 00:00:00	2015-01-01 00:00:00	2015-01-03 00:00:00	2015-01-03 00:00:00	2015-01-04 00:00:00
quarter	Quarter1	Quarter1	Quarter1	Quarter1	Quarter1
department	finishing	sweing	sweing	finishing	finishing
day	Thursday	Thursday	Saturday	Saturday	Sunday
team	1	1	1	1	1
targeted_productivity	0.75	0.75	0.8	0.8	0.8
smv	3.94	28.08	28.08	3.94	3.94
wip	NaN	681.0	772.0	NaN	NaN
over_time	960	6900	6300	960	960
incentive	0	45	50	0	0
idle_time	0.0	0.0	0.0	0.0	0.0
idle_men	0	0	0	0	0
no_of_style_change	0	0	0	0	0
no_of_workers	8.0	57.5	56.5	8.0	8.0
actual_productivity	0.8865	0.750428	0.800725	0.902917	0.915229

Figure 5.13: Team 1 data

In the next step, let us look at the data description for **smv**, **wip**, and **incentive** to understand if there are any outliers.

Code:

```
garment_df_team1[['smv', 'wip', 'incentive']].describe(percentiles = [0.25, 0.5, 0.75, 0.98])
```

Feature Engineering on Time Series

Output:

	smv	wip	incentive
count	105.000000	56.000000	105.000000
mean	15.370857	1609.196429	46.600000
std	11.336076	2105.399150	98.837824
min	3.940000	171.000000	0.000000
25%	3.940000	1185.000000	0.000000
50%	22.520000	1418.000000	30.000000
75%	26.160000	1537.000000	75.000000
98%	28.080000	1870.700000	113.000000
max	49.100000	16882.000000	960.000000

Figure 5.14: Team 1 data with Describe

From *Figure 5.14*, it appears that the difference between the 98th percentile and the maximum is comparatively large for the **wip** and **incentive** columns, denoting the presence of outliers in the data.

In the next step, let us define a function to cap the values at the 98th percentile, so that **outliers** in the data are handled.

Code:

```
def treat_outlier(dataset, variable, x):
    cap = dataset[variable].describe(percentiles =[0.98])['98%']
    if (x>cap):
        return cap
    else:
        return x
garment_df_team1['wip'] = garment_df_team1['wip'].apply(lambda x: treat_outlier(garment_df_team1, 'wip', x))
garment_df_team1['incentive'] = garment_df_team1['wip'].apply(lambda x: treat_outlier(garment_df_team1, 'incentive', x))
garment_df_team1[['smv', 'wip', 'incentive']].describe()
```

Output:

	smv	wip	incentive
count	105.000000	105.000000	105.000000
mean	15.370857	715.270476	60.266667
std	11.336076	717.827721	56.644687
min	3.940000	0.000000	0.000000
25%	3.940000	0.000000	0.000000
50%	22.520000	708.000000	113.000000
75%	26.160000	1422.000000	113.000000
max	49.100000	1870.700000	113.000000

Figure 5.15: Team 1 data with Describe after outlier treatment

Now that the data is ready, it can be used for multivariate feature engineering.

Creating Lag-Based Multivariate Features

In multivariate analysis, lag-based features are created from multiple independent variables present in the time series data. The historical observations of all or a subset of variables are used to calculate the time lag of the variables and to create new features out of them. For example, the lag feature for an observation at time T can be created using the value at time T-1 or T-2, and so on. These features can be used to identify correlations and patterns in the data and increase the forecasting accuracy of the data.

Let us start by setting the lag order and applying a range of lags for the variables – **smv**, **wip**, and **incentive**.

Code:

```
lag_order = 2

for variable in ['smv', 'wip', 'incentive']:
    for lag in range(1, lag_order + 1):
        col_name = f'{variable}_Lag{lag}'
        garment_df_team1[col_name] = garment_df_team1[variable].shift(lag)
```

```
garment_df_team1 = garment_df_team1.fillna(0)
garment_df_team1[['smv', 'smv_Lag1', 'smv_Lag2', 'wip', 'wip_Lag1', 'wip_Lag2', 'incentive', 'incentive_Lag1', 'incentive_Lag2']]
```

Output:

	smv	smv_Lag1	smv_Lag2	wip	wip_Lag1	wip_Lag2	incentive	incentive_Lag1	incentive_Lag2
0	3.94	0.00	0.00	0.0	0.0	0.0	0.0	0.0	0.0
1	28.08	3.94	0.00	681.0	0.0	0.0	113.0	0.0	0.0
2	28.08	28.08	3.94	772.0	681.0	0.0	113.0	113.0	0.0
3	3.94	28.08	28.08	0.0	772.0	681.0	0.0	113.0	113.0
4	3.94	3.94	28.08	0.0	0.0	772.0	0.0	0.0	113.0
...	...	...	...	...	...	...	...	...	...
100	26.82	3.94	3.94	1322.0	0.0	0.0	113.0	0.0	0.0
101	3.94	26.82	3.94	0.0	1322.0	0.0	0.0	113.0	0.0
102	26.82	3.94	26.82	1574.0	0.0	1322.0	113.0	0.0	113.0
103	26.82	26.82	3.94	1322.0	1574.0	0.0	113.0	113.0	0.0
104	3.94	26.82	26.82	0.0	1322.0	1574.0	0.0	113.0	113.0

105 rows × 9 columns

Figure 5.16: Team 1 data with lag features

The lag features in multivariate time series data are created similarly to the lag features in univariate data. In the next section, let us look at creating interaction terms-based features.

Creating Interaction Terms-Based Features

Interaction terms are the features that can be created by blending or merging one or more features of a multivariate time series dataset. These are the features that can capture correlation between features and provide a new insight into the data that was not previously available while the variables were separate.

The summary of steps to be followed is as follows:
1. Identify the variables that can be blended.
2. Apply the right interaction calculation to merge the variables.
3. Create a new column and save the derived new feature.

Let us review the columns in the dataset and choose the relevant variables to create interaction features.

Code:

```
garment_df_team1.columns
```

Output:

```
Index(['date', 'quarter', 'department', 'day', 'team', 'targeted_productivity',
       'smv', 'wip', 'over_time', 'incentive', 'idle_time', 'idle_men',
       'no_of_style_change', 'no_of_workers', 'actual_productivity',
       'smv_Lag1', 'smv_Lag2', 'wip_Lag1', 'wip_Lag2', 'incentive_Lag1',
       'incentive_Lag2'],
      dtype='object')
```

We can calculate actual and targeted individual productivity values and the gap in individual production from the following variables: **targeted_productivity**, **actual_productivity**, and **no_of_workers**.

Code:

```
garment_df_team1['targeted_individual_productivity'] = garment_df_team1['targeted_productivity']/garment_df_team1['no_of_workers']

garment_df_team1['actual_individual_productivity'] = garment_df_team1['actual_productivity']/garment_df_team1['no_of_workers']

garment_df_team1['individual_productivity_gap'] = garment_df_team1['targeted_individual_productivity'] - garment_df_team1['actual_individual_productivity']

garment_df_team1[['date', 'targeted_productivity', 'actual_productivity',
'targeted_individual_productivity', 'actual_individual_productivity',
          'individual_productivity_gap']].head(10)
```

The interaction features are provided in the following output:

Output:

	date	targeted_productivity	actual_productivity	targeted_individual_productivity	actual_individual_productivity	individual_productivity_gap
0	2015-01-01	0.75	0.886500	0.093750	0.110812	-0.017062
1	2015-01-01	0.75	0.750428	0.013043	0.013051	-0.000007
2	2015-01-03	0.80	0.800725	0.014159	0.014172	-0.000013
3	2015-01-03	0.80	0.902917	0.100000	0.112865	-0.012865
4	2015-01-04	0.80	0.915229	0.100000	0.114404	-0.014404
5	2015-01-04	0.80	0.800319	0.013559	0.013565	-0.000005
6	2015-01-05	0.80	0.800319	0.013559	0.013565	-0.000005
7	2015-01-05	0.80	0.961059	0.100000	0.120132	-0.020132
8	2015-01-06	0.80	0.850502	0.013559	0.014415	-0.000856
9	2015-01-06	0.80	0.936496	0.100000	0.117062	-0.017062

Figure 5.17: Interaction features

In the next step, let us review the newly created features in comparison to the existing time series variable by plotting them using Matplotlib.

Here are the steps to visualize:

1. Import Matplotlib.
2. Set the date column as the x-axis.
3. Set the interaction features as the line parameters that will be plotted on the y-axis.
4. Visualize the newly created variables in a line graph to gain further understanding.

Code:

```
date = garment_df_team1['date']

tgt = garment_df_team1['targeted_individual_productivity']

act = garment_df_team1['actual_individual_productivity']

gap = garment_df_team1['individual_productivity_gap']


fig, ax = plt.subplots()

ax.plot(date, tgt, linestyle='-.', color = 'red')

ax.plot(date, act, linestyle='--', color = 'green')

ax.plot(date, gap, linestyle=':', color = 'blue')
```

```
ax.grid(True, linestyle=':', color = 'grey')
ax.tick_params(labelcolor='r', labelsize='medium', width=5)
```

```
plt.show()
```

The output for this code is the comparison of newly created interaction features.

Output:

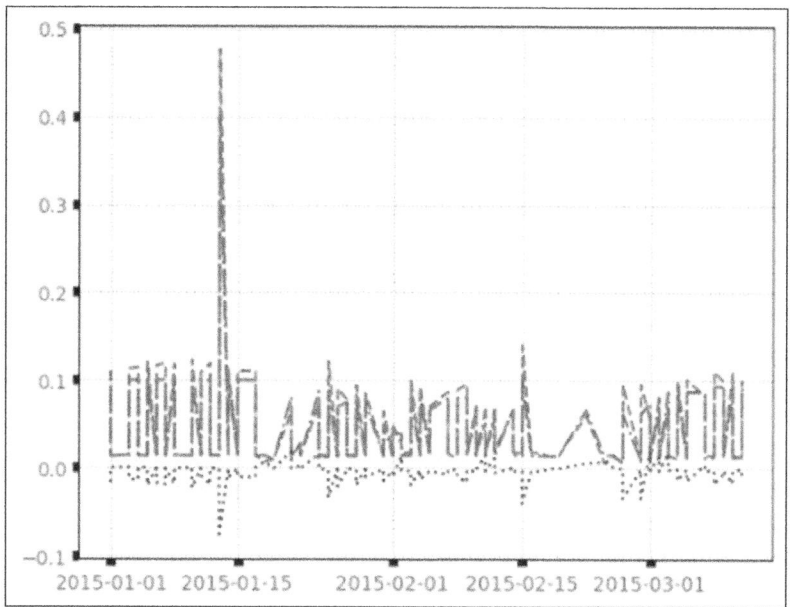

Figure 5.18: *Visualization of Interaction features*

Visualizing the new variables provides further opportunities to make domain-specific decisions on the relevance of the newly created variables and potential for further use in predictions.

With this understanding, let us look at the last topic for this chapter, which will be the creation of aggregated features.

Creating Aggregated Features

Aggregated features are created by aggregating or summarizing the variables from multiple time steps to form combined features that are simplified. When the data size is large and the information is too granular, aggregating the features will provide more of a consolidated view of the data.

Feature Engineering on Time Series

The summary of steps to be followed is as follows:
1. Choose the aggregation window by reviewing the date time parameters of the dataset.
2. Copy the variables to be used for aggregation into a new data frame.
3. For all the variables, create aggregate features using the chosen aggregation window and a rolling statistical metric.
4. Drop the original variables of the new dataset and keep only aggregated features.
5. Drop all the initial rows that have null values for rolling and aggregated features.
6. Review the newly created aggregated features.

Let us start the feature creation by reviewing the data day parameter in **garment_df_team1** data frame.

Code:
```
garment_df_team1['day'].unique()
```

Output:
```
array(['Thursday', 'Saturday', 'Sunday', 'Monday', 'Tuesday', 'Wednesday'],
      dtype=object)
```

The data has six working days excluding Fridays. This means that we can have a rolling window size of 6 to create new features. Let us then create a new data frame with the variables that are available in the original garments dataset.

Code:
```
garment_df_team1_agg = garment_df_team1[['date','targeted_productivity',
    'smv', 'wip', 'over_time', 'incentive', 'idle_time', 'idle_men',
    'no_of_style_change', 'no_of_workers', 'actual_productivity']]
```

In the next step, let us set the window size as 6 and create a list of columns for which aggregate features need to be created.

Code:
```
window = 6
columns = ['targeted_productivity', 'smv', 'wip', 'over_time', 'incentive',
'idle_time', 'idle_men', 'no_of_style_change', 'no_of_workers', 'actual_
```

productivity']

Let us now create the aggregate features as rolling mean of the existing variables for a window size of 6.

Code:

```
for col in columns:
    garment_df_team1_agg[f'Aggregate_{col}'] = garment_df_team1_
    agg[col].rolling(window).mean()
```

In the next step, we will drop the columns from the original data and keep only the aggregated features. We will also remove the null value records from aggregated features.

Code:

```
garment_df_team1_agg.drop(columns = columns, inplace = True)

garment_df_team1_agg.dropna(inplace = True)

garment_df_team1_agg.head(5).transpose()
```

The aggregated features dataset is now available for further analysis and processing.

Output:

	5	6	7	8	9
date	2015-01-04 00:00:00	2015-01-05 00:00:00	2015-01-05 00:00:00	2015-01-06 00:00:00	2015-01-06 00:00:00
Aggregate_targeted_productivity	0.783333	0.791667	0.8	0.8	0.8
Aggregate_smv	15.68	19.393333	15.37	15.06	15.05
Aggregate_wip	414.333333	604.0	490.5	559.666667	559.666667
Aggregate_over_time	3860.0	4860.0	4050.0	4770.0	4850.0
Aggregate_incentive	56.5	75.333333	56.5	56.5	56.5
Aggregate_idle_time	0.0	0.0	0.0	0.0	0.0
Aggregate_idle_men	0.0	0.0	0.0	0.0	0.0
Aggregate_no_of_style_change	0.0	0.0	0.0	0.0	0.0
Aggregate_no_of_workers	32.833333	41.333333	33.083333	33.5	33.5
Aggregate_actual_productivity	0.842686	0.828323	0.863428	0.871724	0.877321

Figure 5.19: Aggregated features

These are some of the methods that can be applied to the time series data to create new features.

Conclusion

In this chapter, we have learned about the univariate and multivariate feature engineering techniques that can be applied to the time series data to create new features.

In the univariate feature engineering, we learned how to create lag-based features, and then we explored the concept of rolling statistics-based feature engineering. We also reviewed expanding window statistics and exponential moving averages.

We then learned about the various methods that can be applied in multivariate feature engineering, such as the creation of lag-based features, feature engineering of interaction terms, and aggregated terms.

In the next chapter, we will look at machine learning on time series data in Python with examples and code.

References

- Tan, James. (2017). Sales_Transactions_Dataset_Weekly. UCI Machine Learning Repository. https://doi.org/10.24432/C5XS4Q.
- Productivity Prediction of Garment Employees. (2020). UCI Machine Learning Repository. https://doi.org/10.24432/C51S6D.
- Pandas.dataframe.rolling (no date) pandas.DataFrame.rolling - pandas 2.0.3 documentation. Available at: https://pandas.pydata.org/docs/reference/api/pandas.DataFrame.rolling.html (Accessed: 20 August 2023).

Chapter 6
Time Series Forecasting – ML Approach Part 1

Introduction

Time series data is the sequential data collected over time in a specific domain or to solve a specific business problem. When data is collected over a period of time, the primary purpose is to understand future trends from history by forecasting data for either the short term or the long term. There are various methods for forecasting data in the field of artificial intelligence. Both machine learning and deep learning algorithms can be used for this purpose. In this chapter, we will explore forecasting time series data with some of the time series-based machine learning algorithms.

Structure

In this chapter, the following topics will be covered:
- Understanding Autoregressive Integrated Moving Average (ARIMA)
- Seasonal Decomposition of Time Series (STL)
- Exponential Smoothing Models
- Facebook Prophet

Data Introduction

Throughout this chapter, we will be using one dataset, focusing on a single variable from the dataset to forecast future values based on various machine learning algorithms that support time series data. The dataset used for this section is synthetically generated data to illustrate the examples in this chapter, and the data is available in the GitHub repository: https://github.com/OrangeAVA/Time-Series-Analysis-and-Forecasting-with-Python/blob/main/ProductSalesData.csv.

The dataset has the following variables:
- **Date:** Date of Sales
- **Units Sold**: Number of units of a product sold in a day. Values ranging between `1` and `1000`
- **Stock Level**: Number of units stocked in the inventory. Values ranging between `1000` and `5000`
- **Discount**: Percentage of discount provided on the product each day. Values ranging between `5` and `10%`
- **Promotion**: Value denoting if there was a promotion on the product on a particular day. Values are `'Yes'` or `'No'`

Given various attributes in this dataset, the two variables of interest for this chapter will be `Date` and `Units Sold`.

Understanding Autoregressive Integrated Moving Average (ARIMA)

In this section, let us explore the ARIMA model and its application on time series data. ARIMA, which stands for Autoregressive Integrated Moving Average, is applied to time series data to forecast future values based on historical data. ARIMA will be used for univariate time series forecasting. There are three components in ARIMA model that are defined to perform time series forecasting. These components are as follows:
- **Autoregressive (AR):** The linear dependency between the current value of the time series and the historical data is captured by this component.
- **Integrated (I):** The non-stationarity of data is handled in this component of ARIMA. A time series data is defined as non-stationary when the

statistical properties of the data such as mean and variance are changing over a period of time in the data. Converting the non-stationary data to stationary data is handled in the integrated (I) component.

- **Moving Average (MA):** The moving average (MA) is the component that handles the impact of errors that are caused in the previous forecasts of the historical time series data while performing predictions using the current data.

Model Documentation

The first conceptualization of the ARIMA model is explained in its introductory paper, *Time Series Analysis: Forecasting and Control* by George E. P. Box and Gwilym M. Jenkins (Box and Jenkins, 1976). The concept is further elaborated in multiple revisions of the book, with the latest version published in 2015 (Box et al., 2015).

The paper and book (Box et al., 2015) propose a four-step approach to ARIMA model building as follows:

1. **Identification**

    In this step, the time series data is analyzed to understand its parameters and their order by studying the autocorrelation plots (ACF) and partial autocorrelation plots (PACF). The three components are the parameters of ARIMA and are denoted as follows:

    - Autoregressive (AR) as p
    - Integrated (I) as d
    - Moving Average (MA) as q

2. **Estimation**

    In this step, the parameters are estimated to minimize the forecasting error. One of the error metrics used in time series forecasting is the mean squared error (MSE), and the values of p, d, and q are determined using statistical methods to minimize MSE.

3. **Diagnostic Checking**

    In this step, the residuals of the model are reviewed after fitting the model in the data. Residuals are the difference between the predicted values and the actual or observed values of the time series data.

4. **Forecasting**

   In this step, the validated model will be used for forecasting future values. The model parameters from estimation will be used for predicting future values.

   ARIMA models are simple and effective in forecasting time series data in a variety of applications.

Library Introduction

The `statsmodels` library in Python is most commonly used to implement the ARIMA model in various time series applications.

The detailed documentation of the ARIMA model can be found at:

https://www.statsmodels.org/stable/generated/statsmodels.tsa.arima.model.ARIMA.html#statsmodels.tsa.arima.model.ARIMA

The ARIMA model in `statsmodels` has the following class structure and parameters:

```
class statsmodels.tsa.arima.model.ARIMA(
    endog,
    exog=None,
    order=(0, 0, 0),
    seasonal_order=(0, 0, 0, 0),
    trend=None,
    enforce_stationarity=True,
    enforce_invertibility=True,
    concentrate_scale=False,
    trend_offset=1,
    dates=None,
    freq=None,
    missing='none',
    validate_specification=True)
```

Let us understand every parameter of this model before it is applied to time series data:

- **endog**: The endogenous variable. This is the time series data that is provided as input to the model or predict.
- **exog**: Exogenous variables are external variables that are optional. These variables are not within the time series dataset but might have an impact on the data.
- **order**: The (p, d, q) tuple of the model.
- **seasonal_order**: The (p, d, q, s) tuple for the seasonal component of the model.
- **trend**: This parameter specifies a trend to be included in the model. Examples include n for none, c for constant, and t for linear trend.
- **enforce_stationarity**: A Boolean value to include stationarity to the time series data by transforming the model's AR parameters.
- **enforce_invertibility**: A Boolean value to include invertibility to the time series data by transforming the model's MA parameters.
- **concentrate_scale**: A Boolean value; when set to True, the scale is set to concentrate the scale (variance of the error term) out of the likelihood.
- **trend_offset**: The offset at which to start time trend values. This is an optional parameter and is set to a default value.
- **dates**: An optional array of datetime objects.
- **freq**: The frequency of the time series. It is used for prediction if the endog is not a Pandas object.
- **missing**: Decision on how to handle missing data.
- **validate_specification**: A Boolean value to decide if ARIMA model specification needs to be validated before fitting the model.

Let us now proceed with the implementation of ARIMA on time series data.

Application of ARIMA on Time Series Data

In this example, we will look at forecasting the `Units Sold` variable from `ProductSalesData`.

Let us start by importing the relevant libraries:

Code:

```
import pandas as pd
from statsmodels.tsa.arima.model import ARIMA
from statsmodels.tsa.stattools import adfuller
from sklearn.metrics import mean_squared_error, mean_absolute_error
import numpy as np
import matplotlib.pyplot as plt
```

In the next step, let us load the dataset and remove the unnamed column:

Code:

```
df = pd.read_csv('ProductSalesData.csv')
df.drop(columns = ['Unnamed: 0'], inplace = True)
df.head(5)
```

In this step, let us review a sample of the dataset:

	Date	Stock Level	Discount	Promotion	Units Sold
0	2010-01-01	2381.0	8.506768	Yes	59.0
1	2010-01-02	3252.0	9.283937	No	203.0
2	2010-01-03	2883.0	9.548446	No	33.0
3	2010-01-04	3586.0	9.660054	Yes	117.0
4	2010-01-05	3578.0	9.086065	No	71.0

Figure 6.1: Product Sales data sample

The variable of focus for this example will be the **Date** and **Units Sold** from *Figure 6.1*.

Let us set the **Date** variable as the index for the data:

Code:

```
df['Date'] = pd.to_datetime(df['Date'])
df.set_index('Date', inplace=True)
```

In the next step, the first 80% of the records will be split as train data and the remaining 20% as test data:

Code:

```
train_size = int(len(df) * 0.8)
train, test = df[0:train_size], df[train_size:len(df)]
```

Now, let us check the stationarity of the data using the Augmented Dickey-Fuller test.

In this step, let us perform an ADF test on the `Units Sold` column of the train dataset. This test is performed to check the presence of the unit root in this dataset. This will help to determine if the `Units Sold` is stationary or not:

Code:

```
adf_test = adfuller(train['Units Sold'].dropna())
print('ADF Statistic:', adf_test[0])
print('p-value:', adf_test[1])
if adf_test[1] > 0.05:
    train['Units Sold'] = train['Units Sold'].diff().dropna()
```

The ADF test is performed on the data after dropping Null values from the train dataset if any. We are then examining the results of the test by reviewing the ADF test statistic and the p-value.

Output:

```
ADF Statistic: -2.972627780063655
```

We have obtained a negative value for the ADF test statistic, which implies there is a stronger rejection of the hypothesis that there is a unit root. This means that the data is non-stationary.

Output:

```
p-value: 0.037530900423791626
```

The usual threshold set for p-value tests would be 0.05. Hence, we are setting 0.05 to check the p-value of this dataset. The null hypothesis in this case is that the time series is non-stationary. The p-value here indicates the probability of observing the data if the null hypothesis is true. If the p-value of the test is greater than 0.05, then the null hypothesis of the ADF test cannot be rejected, indicating that the series might be non-stationary. To address this, let us calculate the first difference of the **Units Sold** series and update the **Units Sold** column with these differenced values, again dropping any NaNs that might result from differencing.

The ADF Statistic is −2.972, and the p-value is 0.037. This indicates that the null hypothesis of the ADF test can be rejected at a 5% level of significance. Therefore, there is statistical evidence that the **Units Sold** time series is stationary. Since the p-value is less than 0.05, the conditional statement that checks if the p-value is greater than 0.05 is not executed for this data, and the **Units Sold** is not modified with its differencing.

Now that the dataset is analyzed for its stationarity, let us move further to apply the ARIMA model to the data:

Code:

```
model = ARIMA(train['Units Sold'], order=(2, 2, 1), freq = 'D')
model_fit = model.fit()
```

The preceding code creates an instance of ARIMA model with the following parameters:

1. The train data for **Units Sold**.
2. The order of p, d, and q parameters.
3. The frequency of the time series, which is 'D', indicating the day for the dataset.

The **fit** method is then applied to the model to estimate the model parameters. This fitted model will then be used to forecast future values of **Units Sold**. The model efficiency for forecasting is defined by the values chosen for p, d, and q parameters.

Code:

```
forecast = model_fit.forecast(steps=len(test))
```

The preceding code generates future predictions or forecasts based on the model that was fitted to the training dataset:

Code:

```
mse = mean_squared_error(test['Units Sold'], forecast)

rmse = np.sqrt(mse)

mae = mean_absolute_error(test['Units Sold'], forecast)
```

```
print('Mean Squared Error:', mse)

print('Root Mean Squared Error:', rmse)

print('Mean Absolute Error:', mae)
```

Output:

```
Mean Squared Error: 27270.8772884412

Root Mean Squared Error: 165.13896356838745

Mean Absolute Error: 135.30488599374993
```

The preceding code is used to calculate three common error metrics: Mean Squared Error (MSE), Root Mean Squared Error (RMSE), and Mean Absolute Error (MAE):

- MSE is computed as the average squared difference between the estimated values and the actual value. A lower MSE indicates a model with better accuracy.
- RMSE is computed as the difference between values predicted by the model and the values observed. Like MSE, a lower RMSE value indicates better model performance.
- MAE is computed as the average of the absolute errors between the predicted and the actual values. A lower MAE value also indicates a better model fit.

In the next step, let us plot the actual data and compare it against the predicted data.

Code:

```
plt.figure(figsize=(10,6))

plt.plot(train['Units Sold'], label='Training Data')

plt.plot(test['Units Sold'], label='Actual Data', color='green')

plt.title('Units Sold Actual')

plt.legend()

plt.show()

plt.figure(figsize=(10,6))
```

```
plt.plot(train['Units Sold'], label='Training Data')
plt.plot(test.index, forecast, label='Forecast', color='red')
plt.title('Units Sold Forecast')
plt.legend()
plt.show()
```

The output is displayed as follows:

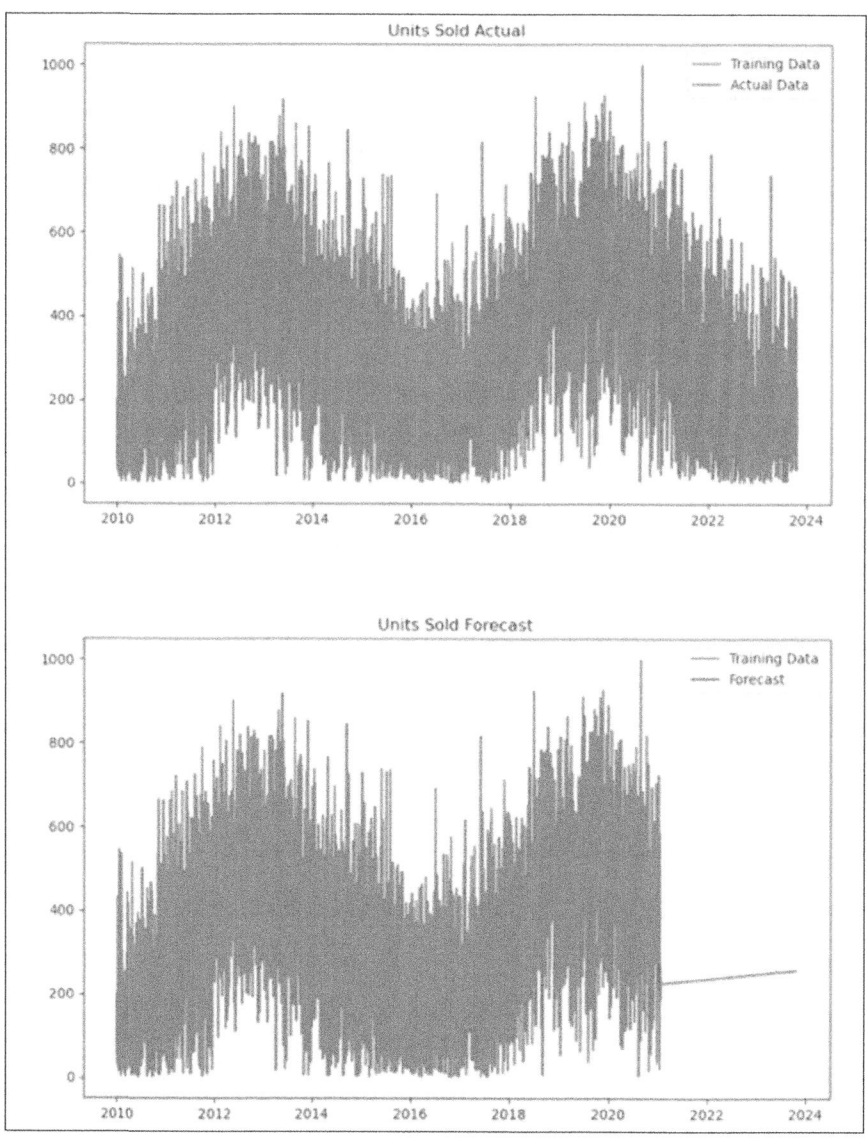

Figure 6.2: Predicted vs. Actual - ARIMA

The actual data in the plot in *Figure 6.2* shows a downward trend, while the predicted data shows an upward trend. Additionally, the error metrics of `MSE` with `27270.87`, `RMSE` with `165.13`, and `MAE` with `135.30` also indicate a greater scope to fine-tune the model parameters or use another model on the data to get better predictions. This example illustrates the method of applying ARIMA to time series data for forecasting future values, and these steps can be followed to apply this algorithm to any other datasets.

With this understanding, let us proceed further to look at examples of Exponential Smoothing models.

Illustrating Exponential Smoothing Models

In this section, let us explore exponential smoothing models, which are also widely used for forecasting time series data. This section will cover three types of exponential smoothing models with examples: simple exponential smoothing, double exponential smoothing, and triple exponential smoothing. All these models are defined in such a way that they apply exponentially decreasing weights to past observations and apply more weight to recent observations to predict future values.

Model Documentation

The exponential smoothing models were initially introduced in the 1950s, and they were expanded further within the same decade through various research papers written on the subject. The three papers where these models were proposed and derived are Brown (1956), Holt (1957), and Winters (1960).

Simple Exponential Smoothing

Simple exponential smoothing is the simplest form of exponential smoothing models and is used to forecast future values of time series data by using the level of data as the component for prediction.

The level of a time series is the baseline or average value of the time series in a dataset where the other components of the data are not present or smoothened out.

Library Introduction

The Python class for simple exponential smoothing and its corresponding documentation are available at https://www.statsmodels.org/dev/generated/statsmodels.tsa.holtwinters.SimpleExpSmoothing.html.

Simple exponential smoothing model in statsmodels has the following class structure and parameters:

```
class statsmodels.tsa.holtwinters.SimpleExpSmoothing
(
    endog,
    initialization_method=None,
    initial_level=None
)
```

Let us understand every parameter of this model before it is applied to time series data:

- **endog**: The endogenous variable. This is the time series data that is provided as input to the model or predict.
- **initialization_method**: This is an optional parameter that defines the method for initializing recursions for the model. The values can be `None`, `estimated`, `heuristic`, `legacy-heuristic`, or `known`.
- **Initial_level**: This is an optional parameter where the initial level component can be provided. This becomes a required parameter when the estimation method is set to `known`. It can also be used for other methods such as `estimated` or `heuristic`.

Let us now proceed with the implementation of this algorithm on the Product Sales dataset.

Application of Simple Exponential Smoothing on Time Series Data

In this example, we will look at forecasting the `Units Sold` variable from `ProductSalesData`.

Let us start by importing the relevant libraries.

Time Series Forecasting – ML Approach Part 1

Code:

```
import pandas as pd
from statsmodels.tsa.holtwinters import SimpleExpSmoothing
from sklearn.metrics import mean_squared_error, mean_absolute_error
import numpy as np
import matplotlib.pyplot as plt
```

In the preceding code, we have imported the libraries needed for data processing, forecasting, error calculation, and visualization.

Let us now read the data.

In the next step, let us load the dataset and remove the **unnamed** column:

Code:

```
df = pd.read_csv('ProductSalesData.csv')
df.drop(columns = ['Unnamed: 0'], inplace = True)
```

Let us set the **Date** variable as index for the data:

Code:

```
df['Date'] = pd.to_datetime(df['Date'])
df.set_index('Date', inplace=True)
```

In the next step, the first 80% of the records will be split as **train** data and the remaining 20% as **test** data:

Code:

```
train_size = int(len(df) * 0.8)
train, test = df[0:train_size], df[train_size:len(df)]
```

Let us proceed further with the model.

Code:

```
model = SimpleExpSmoothing(train['Units Sold'])
model_fit = model.fit()
```

The preceding code creates an instance of Simple Exponential Smoothing model, and it initializes the model to be used for forecasting. The model was applied to the train data of **Units Sold**. The **fit** method is then applied to the model to estimate the model parameters. This fitted model will then be used to forecast future values of Units Sold.

Code:

```
forecast = model_fit.forecast(steps=len(test))
```

The preceding code generates future predictions or forecasts based on the model that was fitted to the training dataset.

Code:

```
mse = mean_squared_error(test['Units Sold'], forecast)
rmse = np.sqrt(mse)
mae = mean_absolute_error(test['Units Sold'], forecast)


print('Mean Squared Error:', mse)
print('Root Mean Squared Error:', rmse)
print('Mean Absolute Error:', mae)
```

Output:

Mean Squared Error: 51464.902909250384

Root Mean Squared Error: 226.85877304889573

Mean Absolute Error: 196.7100853862921

The preceding code is used to calculate three common error metrics: Mean Squared Error (MSE), Root Mean Squared Error (RMSE), and Mean Absolute Error (MAE).

In the next step, let us plot the actual data and compare it against the predicted data.

Code:

```
plt.figure(figsize=(10,6))
plt.plot(train['Units Sold'], label='Training Data')
plt.plot(test['Units Sold'], label='Actual Data', color='green')
plt.title('Units Sold Actual')
```

```
plt.legend()
plt.show()
plt.figure(figsize=(10,6))
plt.plot(train['Units Sold'], label='Training Data')
plt.plot(test.index, forecast, label='Forecast', color='red')
plt.title('Units Sold Forecast')
plt.legend()
plt.show()
```

The output is displayed as follows:

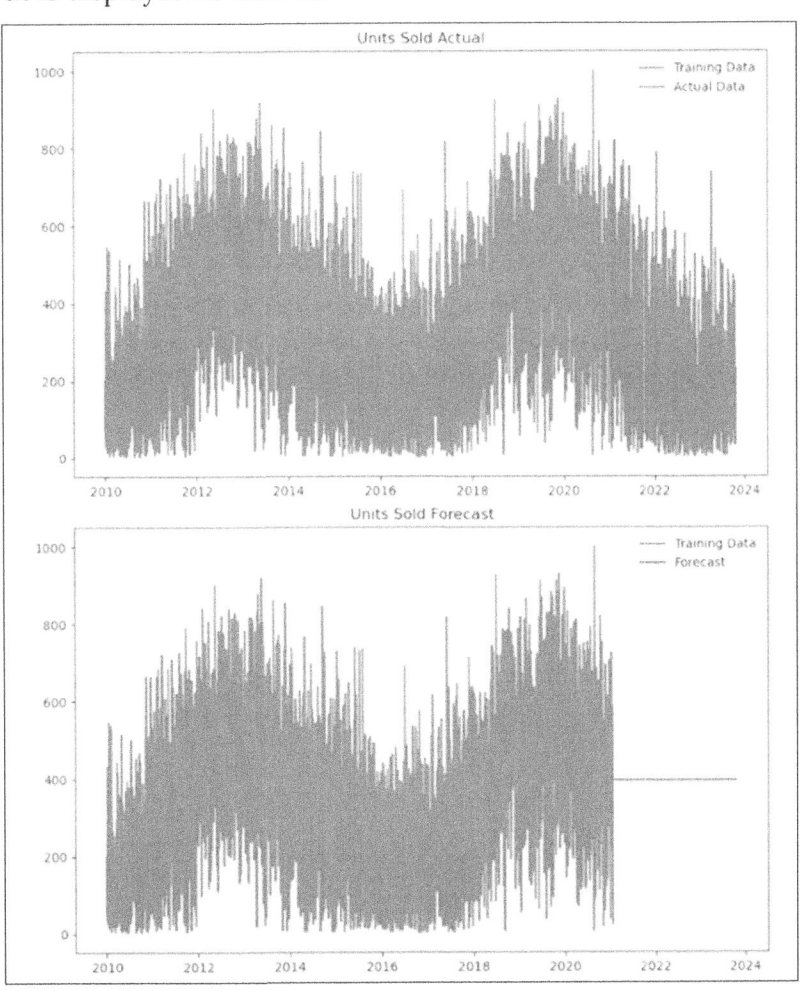

Figure 6.3: *Predicted vs. Actual – Simple Exponential Smoothing*

The actual data in the plot in *Figure* 6.3 shows a downward, while the predicted data shows a flat trend in a horizontal direction. The error metrics of MSE with 51464.90, RMSE with 226.85, and MAE with 196.71 also indicate a greater scope to fine-tune the model parameters or use another model on the data to get better predictions. The error values look to be greater than the values for the same metrics from ARIMA.

This example illustrates the method for applying Simple Exponential Smoothing to time series data for forecasting future values, and these steps can be followed to apply this algorithm to any other datasets.

Let us proceed further to look at an example of the Double Exponential Smoothing model.

Double Exponential Smoothing

Double exponential smoothing is an extension of simple exponential smoothing. In simple exponential smoothing, the component used for forecasting time series was the level, while in double exponential smoothing, trend is added as the second component. Hence, the forecasting happens on both the level and trend together.

Trend is defined as the direction in which the data changes over time. The data can be decreasing or increasing over time and the data can exhibit an upward, a downward trend, or a stable trend.

Library Introduction

The Python class for exponential smoothing and its corresponding documentation are available at https://www.statsmodels.org/dev/generated/statsmodels.tsa.holtwinters.ExponentialSmoothing.html.

Exponential smoothing model in `statsmodels` has the following class structure and parameters:

```
class statsmodels.tsa.holtwinters.ExponentialSmoothing
(
    endog,
    trend=None,
    damped_trend=False,
    seasonal=None,
```

```
    *,
    seasonal_periods=None,
    initialization_method='estimated',
    initial_level=None,
    initial_trend=None,
    initial_seasonal=None,
    use_boxcox=False,
    bounds=None,
    dates=None,
    freq=None,
    missing='none'
)
```

Let us understand every parameter of this model before it is applied to time series data:

- **endog**: The endogenous variable. This is the time series data that is provided as input to the model or predict.
- **trend**: This is an optional parameter indicating the calculation method for the trend. It can be either additive or multiplicative.
- **damped_trend**: This is an optional Boolean parameter indicating if the trend should be damped.
- **seasonal**: This is an optional parameter indicating the calculation method for the seasonality. It can be either additive or multiplicative.
- **seasonal_periods**: This parameter defines the seasonality of the dataset used for forecasting. If the data is daily, then the seasonal period will be 7. If the data is quarterly, then it would be 4, and if monthly, it would be 12, and so forth.
- **initialization_method**: This is an optional parameter that defines the method for initializing recursions for the model. The values can be None, estimated, heuristic, legacy-heuristic, or known.
- **initial_level**: This is an optional parameter where the initial level component can be provided. This becomes a required parameter when

the estimation method is set to known. It can also be used for other methods such as estimated or heuristic.

- **initial_trend**: This is an optional parameter where the initial trend component can be provided. This becomes a required parameter when the estimation method is set to known. It can also be used for other methods such as estimated or heuristic.
- **initial_seasonal**: This is an optional parameter where the initial seasonal component can be provided. This becomes a required parameter when the estimation method is set to known. It can also be used for other methods such as estimated or heuristic.
- **use_boxcox**: This is an optional parameter that accepts True, False, 'log', or float as input. This parameter is used to decide the type of transformation to be applied to the data such as box-cox, log, or float.
- **boundsdict**: This is a dictionary where bounds for various parameters of the data can be provided, such as for smoothing level, initial slope, initial seasonal, and more.
- **dates**: This is an array input that accepts the datetime objects of the time series data, such as the date index of the data.
- **freqstr**: This is an optional parameter indicating the frequency of the time series, such as 'D' for data, 'M' for month, and so forth.
- **missingstr**: This parameter determines the method of handling missing values in the data. Set this as 'drop' if the missing entries need to be dropped. Set as 'none' if no action is required, and set as 'raise' if an error needs to be raised.

Let us now proceed with the implementation of this algorithm on the Product Sales dataset.

Application of Double Exponential Smoothing on Time Series Data

In this example, we will look at forecasting the **Units Sold** variable from **ProductSalesData**.

Let us start by importing the relevant libraries.

Code:

```
import pandas as pd
```

Time Series Forecasting – ML Approach Part 1

```
from statsmodels.tsa.holtwinters import ExponentialSmoothing

from sklearn.metrics import mean_squared_error, mean_absolute_error

import numpy as np

import matplotlib.pyplot as plt
```

In the preceding code, we have imported the libraries needed for data processing, forecasting, error calculation, and visualization.

Let us now read the data.

In the next step, let us load the dataset and remove the unnamed column:

Code:

```
df = pd.read_csv('ProductSalesData.csv')

df.drop(columns = ['Unnamed: 0'], inplace = True)
```

Let us set the **Date** variable as index for the data.

Code:

```
df['Date'] = pd.to_datetime(df['Date'])

df.set_index('Date', inplace=True)
```

In the next step, the first 80% of the records will be split as train data and the remaining 20% as test data:

Code:

```
train_size = int(len(df) * 0.8)

train, test = df[0:train_size], df[train_size:len(df)]
```

Let us proceed further with the model.

Code:

```
model = ExponentialSmoothing(train['Units Sold'], trend='add')

model_fit = model.fit()
```

The preceding code creates an instance of **Exponential Smoothing** model and initializes the model to be used for forecasting. The model was applied on the train data of **Units Sold** and the **trend** parameter for the model is set to **additive**. The fit method is then applied to the model to estimate the model parameters. This fitted model will then be used to forecast future values of **Units Sold**.

Code:

```
forecast = model_fit.forecast(steps=len(test))
```

The preceding code generates future predictions or forecasts based on the double exponential smoothing model that was fitted to the training dataset.

Let us now calculate the error metrics for the model:

Code:

```
mse = mean_squared_error(test['Units Sold'], forecast)
rmse = np.sqrt(mse)
mae = mean_absolute_error(test['Units Sold'], forecast)


print('Mean Squared Error:', mse)
print('Root Mean Squared Error:', rmse)
print('Mean Absolute Error:', mae)
```

Output:

```
Mean Squared Error: 24895.570206366523
Root Mean Squared Error: 157.78330141800976
Mean Absolute Error: 126.78737056967982
```

The preceding code calculates three common error metrics, such as Mean Squared Error (MSE), Root Mean Squared Error (RMSE), and Mean Absolute Error (MAE).

In the next step, let us plot the actual data and compare it against the predicted data:

Code:

```
plt.figure(figsize=(10,6))
plt.plot(train['Units Sold'], label='Training Data')
plt.plot(test['Units Sold'], label='Actual Data', color='green')
plt.title('Units Sold Actual')
plt.legend()
```

```
plt.show()


plt.figure(figsize=(10,6))
plt.plot(train['Units Sold'], label='Training Data')
plt.plot(test.index, forecast, label='Forecast', color='red')
plt.title('Units Sold Forecast')
plt.legend()
plt.show()
```

The output is displayed as follows.

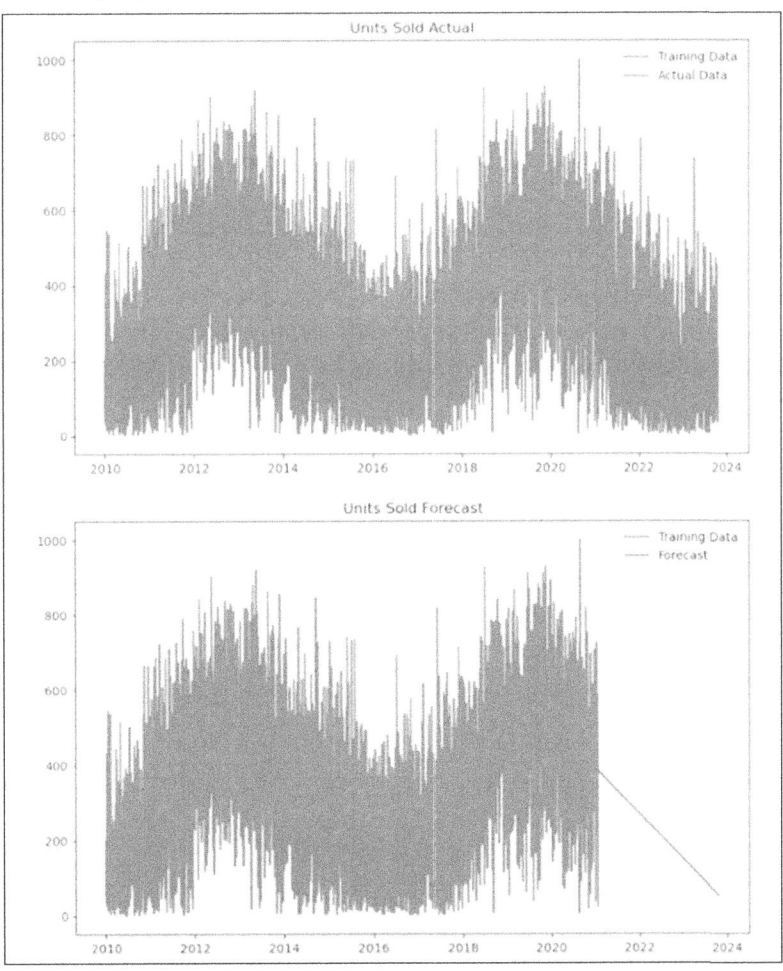

Figure 6.4: Predicted vs. Actual – Double Exponential Smoothing

The actual data in the plot in *Figure* 6.4 shows a downward, while the predicted data also shows a downward trend. The error metrics of MSE with 24895.57, RMSE with 157.78, and MAE with 126.78 also indicate a greater scope to fine-tune the model parameters or use another model on the data to get better predictions.

This example illustrates the method for applying Double Exponential Smoothing on time series data for forecasting future values, and these steps can be followed to apply this algorithm to any other datasets.

With this insight, let us proceed further to look at an example of the Triple Exponential Smoothing model.

Triple Exponential Smoothing

Triple exponential smoothing is a further extension of double exponential smoothing. This model is also known as Holt-Winters Exponential Smoothing. In this method, three components are used for time series forecasting: level, trend, and seasonality. Let us recall the level and trend from simple exponential smoothing and double exponential smoothing models. Level is the baseline or average value of the time series in a dataset, while trend is the direction in which the data changes over time. The third component of the model is seasonality.

Seasonality is defined as the repetition of a pattern over a short-term periodic cycle in the data. A time series has seasonality if the pattern occurs over a regular interval, such as every week, every month, or every summer, for instance.

Library Introduction

The Python class for exponential smoothing, which was applied for double exponential smoothing, is the same class used for applying triple exponential smoothing as well.

The exponential smoothing class, its parameters, and its corresponding documentation are available at https://www.statsmodels.org/dev/generated/statsmodels.tsa.holtwinters.ExponentialSmoothing.html

Let us now directly proceed with the implementation of this algorithm on the Product Sales dataset since the parameter descriptions have already been covered in the Double Exponential Smoothing section.

Application of Triple Exponential Smoothing on Time Series Data

In this example, we will look at forecasting the Units Sold variable from ProductSalesData.

Let us start by importing the relevant libraries.

Code:

```
import pandas as pd

from statsmodels.tsa.holtwinters import ExponentialSmoothing

from sklearn.metrics import mean_squared_error, mean_absolute_error

import numpy as np

import matplotlib.pyplot as plt
```

In the preceding code, we have imported the libraries needed for data processing, forecasting, error calculation, and visualization.

Let us now read the data.

In the next step, let us load the dataset and remove the unnamed column:

Code:

```
df = pd.read_csv('ProductSalesData.csv')

df.drop(columns = ['Unnamed: 0'], inplace = True)
```

Let us set the **Date** variable as index for the data:

Code:

```
df['Date'] = pd.to_datetime(df['Date'])

df.set_index('Date', inplace=True)
```

In the next step, the first 80% of the records will be split as train data and the remaining 20% as test data:

Code:

```
train_size = int(len(df) * 0.8)

train, test = df[0:train_size], df[train_size:len(df)]
```

Let us proceed further with the model.

Code:

```
model = ExponentialSmoothing(train['Units Sold'], trend='add', seasonal='add', seasonal_periods=12)

model_fit = model.fit()
```

The preceding code creates an instance of the **Exponential Smoothing** model and initializes the model for forecasting. The model was applied to the train data of **Units Sold,** with the **trend** and **seasonal** parameters for the model set to additive. The fit method is then applied to the model to estimate the model parameters. This fitted model will then be used to forecast future values of **Units Sold**.

Code:

```
forecast = model_fit.forecast(steps=len(test))
```

The preceding code generates future predictions or forecasts based on the triple exponential smoothing model that was fitted to the training dataset.

Let us now calculate the error metrics for the model:

Code:

```
mse = mean_squared_error(test['Units Sold'], forecast)

rmse = np.sqrt(mse)

mae = mean_absolute_error(test['Units Sold'], forecast)

print('Mean Squared Error:', mse)

print('Root Mean Squared Error:', rmse)

print('Mean Absolute Error:', mae)
```

Output:

```
Mean Squared Error: 27021.940978946146

Root Mean Squared Error: 164.38351796620654

Mean Absolute Error: 130.89085365672972
```

The preceding code is used for calculating three common error metrics: Mean Squared Error (MSE), Root Mean Squared Error (RMSE), and Mean Absolute Error (MAE).

In the next step, let us plot the actual data and compare it against the predicted data:

Code:

```
plt.figure(figsize=(10,6))
plt.plot(train['Units Sold'], label='Training Data')
plt.plot(test['Units Sold'], label='Actual Data', color='green')
plt.title('Units Sold Actual')
plt.legend()
plt.show()
plt.figure(figsize=(10,6))
plt.plot(train['Units Sold'], label='Training Data')
plt.plot(test.index, forecast, label='Forecast', color='red')
plt.title('Units Sold Forecast vs Actual')
plt.legend()
plt.show()
```

The output is displayed as follows:

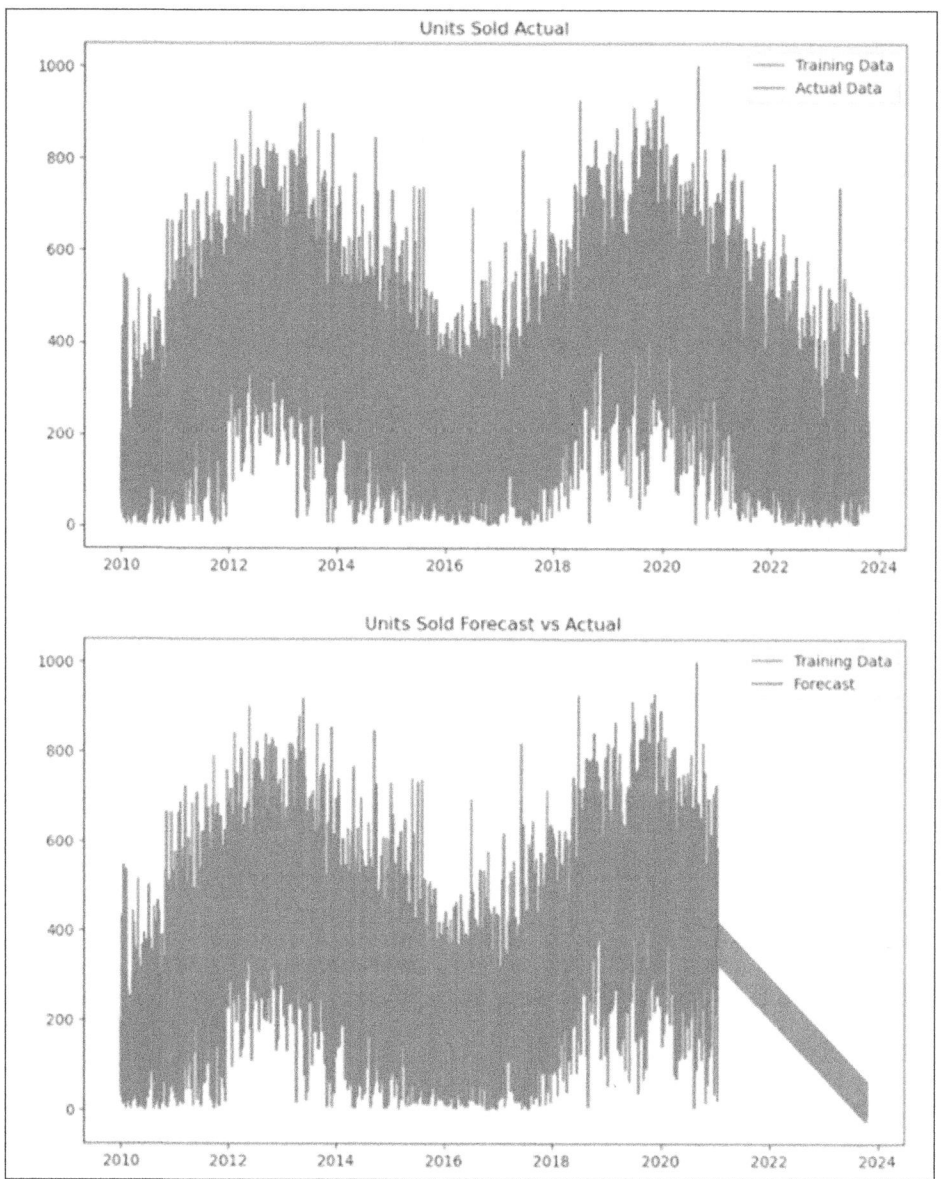

Figure 6.5: *Predicted vs. Actual – Triple Exponential Smoothing*

The actual data in the plot in Figure 6.5 shows a downward, while the predicted data also shows a downward trend. The error metrics of MSE with 27021.94, RMSE with 164.38, and MAE with 130.89 also indicate a greater scope to fine-tune the model parameters or use another model on the data to get better predictions.

This example illustrates the method for applying Triple Exponential Smoothing on time series data for forecasting future values, and these steps can be followed to apply this algorithm to any other datasets.

Let's now move forward to look at an example of the Prophet model.

Exploring the Prophet Algorithm

In this section, let us look at another time series forecasting algorithm called Prophet. This algorithm was developed by Facebook and is an open-source algorithm with multiple options to forecast time series data effectively. Prophet follows the scikit-learn API, and the steps involved in model training, fitting, and predicting are similar to the sklearn API. Prophet is an additive method-based algorithm that is effective in forecasting highly seasonal datasets.

Library Documentation

The Prophet library was introduced in the research paper by Taylor and Letham (2017), and the detailed documentation of the library is available at https://facebook.github.io/prophet/docs/quick_start.html.

Let us now proceed with the implementation of this algorithm on the Product Sales dataset.

The Python class for Prophet and its corresponding documentation are available at https://github.com/facebook/prophet/blob/main/python/prophet/forecaster.py

```
Prophet(
    growth='linear',
    changepoints=None,
    n_changepoints=25,
    changepoint_range=0.8,
    yearly_seasonality='auto',
    weekly_seasonality='auto',
    daily_seasonality='auto',
    holidays=None,
```

```
    seasonality_mode='additive',
    seasonality_prior_scale=10.0,
    holidays_prior_scale=10.0,
    changepoint_prior_scale=0.05,
    mcmc_samples=0,
    interval_width=0.8,
    uncertainty_samples=1000,
    stan_backend=None,
)
```

Let us now proceed with the implementation of this algorithm on the Product Sales dataset.

Application of Prophet on Time Series Data

In this example, we will look at forecasting the **Units Sold** variable from **ProductSalesData** using the Prophet library.

Let us start by importing the relevant libraries.

Code:

```
import pandas as pd
from prophet import Prophet
from sklearn.metrics import mean_squared_error, mean_absolute_error
import numpy as np
import matplotlib.pyplot as plt
```

In the preceding code, we have imported the libraries needed for data processing, forecasting - Prophet, error calculation, and visualization.

Let us now read the data.

In the next step, let us load the dataset and remove the unnamed column:

Code:

```
df = pd.read_csv('ProductSalesData.csv')
```

Time Series Forecasting – ML Approach Part 1

```
df.drop(columns = ['Unnamed: 0'], inplace = True)
```

Let us now create the data frame, which has two columns – 'ds' and 'y', since this is the expected data frame structure for Prophet Library:

Code:

```
df = df.rename(columns={'Date': 'ds', 'Units Sold': 'y'})

df['ds'] = pd.to_datetime(df['ds'])

df.drop(columns = ['Stock Level', 'Discount', 'Promotion'], inplace = True)

df.head(5)
```

The input data frame for Prophet is as follows:

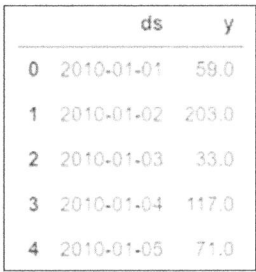

Figure 6.6: *Input data for Prophet*

Let us proceed further with the model.

Code:

```
model = Prophet()

model.fit(df)
```

Output:

```
00:07:58 - cmdstanpy - INFO - Chain [1] start processing
00:07:59 - cmdstanpy - INFO - Chain [1] done processing
<prophet.forecaster.Prophet at 0x1f77fe699c0>
```

The preceding code creates an instance of the Prophet model. The model was applied to the data of **Units Sold**. The fit method is applied to the model to estimate the model parameters.

The default parameters of the model are as follows:

`growth='linear'`,

`changepoints=None`,

`n_changepoints=25`,

`changepoint_range=0.8`,

`yearly_seasonality='auto'`,

`weekly_seasonality='auto'`,

`daily_seasonality='auto'`,

`holidays=None`,

`seasonality_mode='additive'`,

`seasonality_prior_scale=10.0`,

`holidays_prior_scale=10.0`,

`changepoint_prior_scale=0.05`,

`mcmc_samples=0`,

`interval_width=0.8`,

`uncertainty_samples=1000`,

`stan_backend=None`

In the next step, let us create a `dataframe` to capture future values for 60 time points.

Code:

```
df_future = model.make_future_dataframe(periods=60)
df_future.head(5)
```

Time Series Forecasting – ML Approach Part 1

The output dataframe is displayed as follows:

	ds
0	2010-01-01
1	2010-01-02
2	2010-01-03
3	2010-01-04
4	2010-01-05

Figure 6.7: Future dataframe for prediction

Code:

```
forecast = model.predict(df_future)
forecast.tail(5).transpose()
```

The preceding code generates future predictions or forecasts based on the Prophet model that was fitted to the training dataset.

The forecasted dataframe is displayed as follows with predicted and actual observations:

	5096	5097	5098	5099	5100
ds	2023-12-15 00:00:00	2023-12-16 00:00:00	2023-12-17 00:00:00	2023-12-18 00:00:00	2023-12-19 00:00:00
trend	102.720858	102.466673	102.212487	101.958302	101.704116
yhat_lower	-105.967161	-119.720642	-98.261123	-110.831618	-119.658134
yhat_upper	263.431706	285.090725	302.281509	282.585194	281.495735
trend_lower	102.620013	102.312277	102.045603	101.784907	101.468827
trend_upper	103.032697	102.864158	102.647503	102.461575	102.221372
additive_terms	-16.716775	-18.668605	-9.491732	-16.401619	-9.319596
additive_terms_lower	-16.716775	-18.668605	-9.491732	-16.401619	-9.319596
additive_terms_upper	-16.716775	-18.668605	-9.491732	-16.401619	-9.319596
weekly	1.156592	-1.510991	6.746250	-1.263714	4.565318
weekly_lower	1.156592	-1.510991	6.746250	-1.263714	4.565318
weekly_upper	1.156592	-1.510991	6.746250	-1.263714	4.565318
yearly	-17.873367	-17.157614	-16.237982	-15.137905	-13.884914
yearly_lower	-17.873367	-17.157614	-16.237982	-15.137905	-13.884914
yearly_upper	-17.873367	-17.157614	-16.237982	-15.137905	-13.884914
multiplicative_terms	0.0	0.0	0.0	0.0	0.0
multiplicative_terms_lower	0.0	0.0	0.0	0.0	0.0
multiplicative_terms_upper	0.0	0.0	0.0	0.0	0.0
yhat	86.004083	83.798067	92.720755	85.556683	92.384521

Figure 6.8: Forecasted dataframe from Prophet

Since we are predicting for 60 future time points, let us remove the last 60 time points from the time series data so that it can be used to calculate the accuracy of the model.

Code:

```
y_pred = forecast['yhat'][-60:]

y_true = df['y'][-60:]
```

Let us now calculate the error metrics for the model:

Code:

```
mse = mean_squared_error(y_true, y_pred)

rmse = np.sqrt(mse)

mae = mean_absolute_error(y_true, y_pred)


print('Mean Squared Error:', mse)

print('Root Mean Squared Error:', rmse)

print('Mean Absolute Error:', mae)
```

Output:

Mean Squared Error: 25448.002456842965

Root Mean Squared Error: 159.5243005214032

Mean Absolute Error: 124.81341133445848

The preceding code is used to calculate three common error metrics, including Squared Error (MSE), Root Mean Squared Error (RMSE), and Mean Absolute Error (MAE).

In the next step, let us plot the actual data and compare it against the predicted data.

Code:

```
fig = model.plot(forecast)

plt.title('Units Sold Forecast with Prophet')

plt.show()
```

The output is displayed as follows:

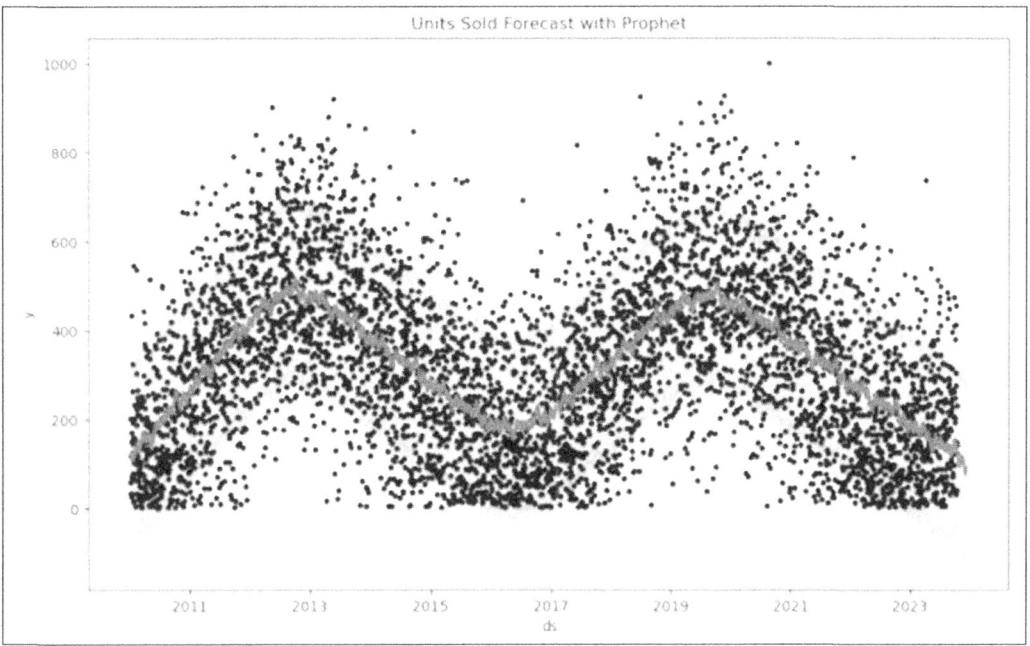

Figure 6.9: *Predicted vs. Actual – Prophet*

The trend of actual as well as predicted values in the plot in *Figure* 6.9 looks to be in the same direction, and the error metrics of MSE with 25448.00, RMSE with 159.52, and MAE with 124.81 also indicate a greater scope to fine-tune this model parameters or use another model on the data to get better predictions.

This example illustrates the method for applying Prophet with a linear model and additive method on time series data for forecasting future values, and these steps can be followed to apply this algorithm on any other datasets using Prophet.

These are some of the forecasting algorithms that can be used to predict future values of univariate time series data.

Conclusion

In this chapter, we have learned about various time series algorithms that can be used for forecasting future data.

We also explored the parameters, documentation, and examples of the Autoregressive Integrated Moving Average (ARIMA) model.

We then learned about the variations of Exponential Smoothing models, along with examples for each. Additionally, we explored Facebook's Prophet Model for predicting time series data.

In the next chapter, we will examine the application of several more machine learning algorithms to forecast future values.

References

- Box, G.E.P. and Jenkins, G. (1976) Time Series Analysis: Forecasting and Control. San Francisco: Holden Day
- Box, G.E.P. et al. (2015) Time Series Analysis: Forecasting and Control. Hoboken, NJ: John Wiley & Sons, Inc.
- Statsmodels.tsa.arima.model.ARIMA (no date) statsmodels.tsa.arima.model.ARIMA - statsmodels 0.14.0. Available at: https://www.statsmodels.org/stable/generated/statsmodels.tsa.arima.model.ARIMA.html#statsmodels.tsa.arima.model.ARIMA (Accessed: 02 December 2023).
- Statsmodels.tsa.holtwinters.simpleexpsmoothing (no date) statsmodels.tsa.holtwinters.SimpleExpSmoothing - statsmodels 0.15.0 (+76). Available at: https://www.statsmodels.org/dev/generated/statsmodels.tsa.holtwinters.SimpleExpSmoothing.html (Accessed: 02 December 2023).
- Statsmodels.tsa.holtwinters.ExponentialSmoothing (no date) statsmodels.tsa.holtwinters.ExponentialSmoothing - statsmodels 0.15.0 (+76). Available at: https://www.statsmodels.org/dev/generated/statsmodels.tsa.holtwinters.ExponentialSmoothing.html (Accessed: 02 December 2023).
- Forecasting: Principles and practice (2nd ed) (no date) Chapter 7 Exponential smoothing. Available at: https://otexts.com/fpp2/expsmooth.html (Accessed: 02 December 2023).
- Brown, R.G. (1956) Exponential smoothing for predicting demand, Cambridge.
- Holt, C.C. (1957) 'Forecasting seasonals and trends by exponentially weighted moving averages', International Journal of Forecasting, 20(1), pp. 5–10. doi:10.1016/j.ijforecast.2003.09.015.
- Winters, P.R. (1960) 'Forecasting sales by exponentially weighted moving averages', Management Science, 6(3), pp. 324–342. doi:10.1287/mnsc.6.3.324.
- Taylor, S.J. and Letham, B. (2017) Forecasting at scale [Preprint]. doi:10.7287/peerj.preprints.3190v2.

CHAPTER 7
Time Series Forecasting – ML Approach Part 2

Introduction

In this chapter, we delve into the next set of time series forecasting approaches, exploring advanced statistical and machine learning techniques, including Hidden Markov Models (HMMs), Gaussian Processes (GPs), Support Vector Machines (SVMs), K-Nearest Neighbors (KNN), Random Forest, and Gradient Boosting.

Each of these models is built on unique approaches in forecasting or predicting data. These models can be used for predicting regression data as well as time series data after performing relevant feature engineering on the data. Let us explore each of these algorithms with suitable time series-based examples throughout this chapter.

Structure

In this chapter, the following topics will be covered:
- Applying Hidden Markov Models (HMM)
- Understanding Gaussian Process

- Developing a Machine Learning-Based Approach for Time Series Forecasting
- Applying Support Vector Machine (SVM)
- Applying K-Nearest Neighbor (KNN)
- Implementing with Random Forest
- Implementing with Gradient Boosting

Data Introduction

Throughout this chapter, we will be using one dataset, focusing on a single variable from the dataset to forecast future values based on various machine learning algorithms that support time series data. The dataset used for this section is synthetically generated data developed to illustrate the examples in this chapter, and the data is available in the GitHub repository: https://github.com/OrangeAVA/Mastering Time Series Analysis and Forecasting with Python

The variables of interest from this dataset for this chapter are as follows:
- **Date:** Date of Sales
- **Units Sold:** Number of units of a product sold in a day. Values ranging between 1 and 1000

Applying Hidden Markov Models (HMM)

Hidden Markov Models were originally proposed in the research paper titled 'An Inequality and Associated Maximization Technique in Statistical Estimation for Probabilistic Functions of Markov Processes' by Leonard E. Baum et al. This paper (Baum, 1972) laid the foundation for the fundamental concept of HMM.

In a Markov model, the future state depends on the current state and not on the events that were preceded by it. This is also known as Markov property. In the Hidden Markov Model, the states of these processes cannot be directly observed and are therefore considered to be hidden. While the states are hidden, each state produces an output that can be observed. The probability of this output depends on the current hidden state of the system.

The fundamental concept of Hidden Markov Models, as defined by Baum in his research, is a statistical model for sequences where underlying states affect the sequence, but these states are not directly observable. Instead, we observe a series of outputs, also known as emissions, that are probabilistically related

Time Series Forecasting – ML Approach Part 2

to these hidden states. The HMM provides a framework for modeling such sequences and making inferences about the hidden states and their dynamics.

Library Documentation

The model documentation and its parameter information are available in the HMM documentation at:

https://hmmlearn.readthedocs.io/en/latest/api.html

HMM with Gaussian emissions is the default model used in this library.

The parameters of the model as described in the library are as follows:

- `n_components`: This parameter is to input the number of states.
- `covariance_type`: This parameter is to input the type of covariance parameters to use in the model.
- `min_covar`: This is an optional input parameter.
- `startprob_prior`: This is an optional input parameter for the Dirichlet prior distribution.
- `transmat_prior`: This is an optional input parameter for the transition probabilities.
- `means_prior, means_weight`: These are optional input arrays for the precision of normal prior distributions.
- `covars_prior, covars_weight`: These are optional input arrays for the covariance matrix.
- `algorithm`: This is an optional input parameter denoting the decoder algorithm to be used.
- `random_state`: This is an optional input parameter for the random number generation.
- `n_iter`: This is an optional input parameter denoting the number of iterations for the model.
- `tol`: This is an optional input parameter denoting the convergence threshold for the model.
- `verbose`: This is an optional Boolean input parameter denoting whether the convergence report needs to be printed.
- `params, init_params`: These are optional parameters denoting the parameters to be initialized during or before the model training.
- `implementation`: This is an optional input parameter for the scaling logic.

Let us now proceed with the implementation of HMM on time series data.

Application of HMM on Time Series Data

In this example, we will be forecasting the `Units Sold` variable from `ProductSalesData`.

Let us start by importing the relevant libraries as follows:
- **Pandas** for data manipulation and analysis.
- **Hmmlearn.hmm** to use the Hidden Markov Model for time series analysis.
- **Sklearn.model_selection** for splitting the dataset into training and testing sets.
- **Sklearn.metrics** to compute the mean squared error and mean absolute for model evaluation.
- **Numpy** for numerical computations.
- **Matplotlib** to vitalize the output.

Code:

```
import pandas as pd
from hmmlearn import hmm
from sklearn.model_selection import train_test_split
from sklearn.metrics import mean_squared_error, mean_absolute_error
import numpy as np
import matplotlib.pyplot as plt
```

Let us then load the data from a CSV file named '**ProductSalesData.csv**' into a Pandas DataFrame and drop the column with no name.

Code:

```
data = pd.read_csv('ProductSalesData.csv')
data.drop(columns = ['Unnamed: 0'], inplace = True)
```

The next step is to perform data preparation by extracting the Units Sold column for further analysis.

Code:

```
units_sold = data['Units Sold'].values
```

Let us now split the data into training and testing sets using the **train_test_split** function, with 20% of the data as the test set. Ensure that the data is not shuffled so that the time series order can be maintained.

Code:

train, test = train_test_split(units_sold, test_size=0.2, shuffle=False)

Let us now create an instance of **GaussianHMM** with the following parameters:

n_components=4,

covariance_type='diag',

min_covar=0.001,

startprob_prior=1.0,

transmat_prior=1.0,

means_prior=0,

means_weight=0,

covars_prior=0.01,

covars_weight=1,

algorithm='viterbi',

random_state=None,

n_iter=10,

tol=0.01,

verbose=False,

params='stmc',

init_params='stmc',

implementation='log'

Code:

model = hmm.GaussianHMM(n_components=4, covariance_type="diag", n_iter=100)

The next step is to train the model using training data and reshape it to fit with the expected data format.

Code:

```
model.fit(train.reshape(-1, 1))
```

The output of the model is displayed as follows:

```
                    GaussianHMM
GaussianHMM(n_components=4, n_iter=100)
```

Figure 7.1: Gaussian HMM

Let us further make predictions for the test set. For each step, the model predicts the next value based on the last observed value or the last predicted value in subsequent iterations.

Code:

```
predicted = []

for i in range(len(test)):

    previous = np.array(train[-1]).reshape(1, -1) if i == 0 else np.array(predicted[-1]).reshape(1, -1)

    next_step = model.predict(previous)

    predicted.append(next_step[0])
```

We will then evaluate the model's performance using mean squared error (MSE), root mean squared error (RMSE), and mean absolute error (MAE).

Code:

```
mse = mean_squared_error(test, predicted)

rmse = np.sqrt(mse)

mae = mean_absolute_error(test, predicted)


print('Mean Squared Error:', mse)

print('Root Mean Squared Error:', rmse)

print('Mean Absolute Error:', mae)
```

Output:

```
Mean Squared Error: 81259.7353815659

Root Mean Squared Error: 285.06093275222037

Mean Absolute Error: 234.79187314172447
```

Let us further plot the actual and forecasted `Units Sold` for visual comparison:

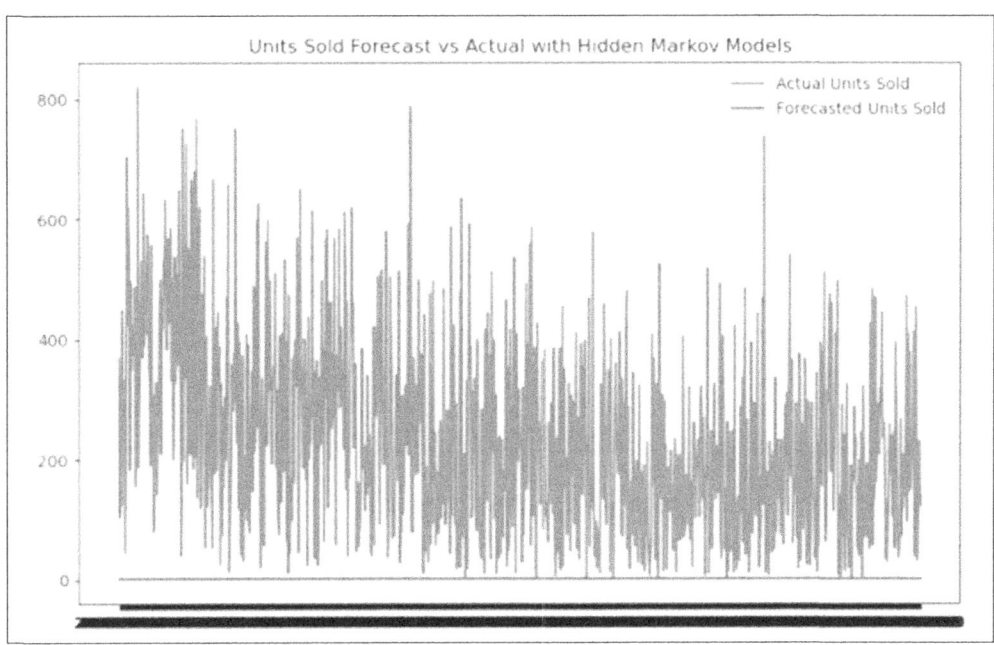

Figure 7.2: Actual vs. Forecast – HMM

In *Figure* 7.2, the forecasted value looks to be flat, while the actual values are different. Let us check the forecasted and actual values for the first 10 records in the test data.

Code:

```
predicted[0:10]
```

Output:

```
[1, 1, 1, 1, 1, 1, 1, 1, 1, 1]
```

Code:

```
test[0:10]
```

Output:

```
array([369., 104., 332., 124., 449., 314., 332., 138.,  45., 164.])
```

The forecasted values are a flat value of 1 for all entries, while the test data is completely different from the forecasted values. The relatively high error values of 81259.73 for MSE, 285.06 for RMSE, and 234.79 for MAE also indicate that HMM may not be a suitable model, or the data may require transformations before applying the model to it.

With this understanding, let us explore Gaussian Process Regressor in the next section.

Understanding Gaussian Process

A Gaussian Process Regressor (GPR) is a non-parametric Bayesian approach to regression. This concept in probability theory and statistics has a long history with multiple researches and literature in this area. The most prominent and seminal work that popularized this concept was the book titled *Gaussian Processes for Machine Learning* authored by Carl Edward Rasmussen and Christopher K. I. Williams, published in 2005.

A Gaussian Process, being a non-parametric Bayesian model, defines a prior over functions and uses observed data to update this prior to a posterior. It is a collection of random variables having a joint Gaussian distribution and is specified by its mean and covariance functions. The covariance function is also known as Kernel. Additionally, Gaussian Process applies a Bayesian framework to predict the distribution of possible functions that fit the data.

Library Documentation

The model documentation and its parameter information for the Gaussian Process Regressor are available in the documentation at:

https://scikit-learn.org/stable/modules/generated/sklearn.gaussian_process.GaussianProcessRegressor.html

The brief descriptions of the parameters of the model as described in the library are provided here. For more details on the parameters, refer to the sklearn documentation provided in the preceding link:

- `kernel`: This parameter is used to input the kernel instance that defines the covariance function for the Gaussian Process.

- **alpha:** This parameter is used to input the value for the diagonal of the kernel matrix during the model fitting process.
- **optimizer:** This parameter is used to input the optimizer for the model.
- **n_restarts_optimizer:** This parameter is used to input the number of restarts for the optimizer of the model.
- **normalize_y:** This parameter is used to determine whether the y value needs to be standardized.
- **copy_X_train:** This parameter is provided as a boolean value and determines if the train data needs to be a deep copy within the object or a reference instead.
- **n_targets:** This parameter is provided as the input to determine the dimensionality of the target values.
- **random_state:** This parameter is used to input the random state value, which determines the random number generation method employed for initializing the centers.

Let us now proceed with the implementation of the GP Regressor on time series data.

Application of Gaussian Process on Time Series Data

In this example, we will be forecasting the `Units Sold` variable from `ProductSalesData`.

Let us start by importing the relevant libraries as follows:
- **Pandas** for data manipulation and analysis.
- **Sklearn.gaussian_process** for the Gaussian Process Regressor and kernels.
- **Sklearn.model_selection** for splitting the dataset into training and testing sets.
- **Sklearn.metrics** to compute the mean squared error and mean absolute error for model evaluation.
- **Numpy** for numerical computations.
- **Matplotlib** to vitalize the output.

Code:

```
import pandas as pd
import numpy as np
from sklearn.gaussian_process import GaussianProcessRegressor
from sklearn.gaussian_process.kernels import RBF, ConstantKernel as C
from sklearn.model_selection import train_test_split
from sklearn.metrics import mean_squared_error, mean_absolute_error
import matplotlib.pyplot as plt
```

Let us then load the data from a CSV file named '**ProductSalesData.csv**' into a Pandas DataFrame.

Code:

```
data = pd.read_csv('ProductSalesData.csv')
```

The next step is to perform data preparation by extracting the Units Sold column for further analysis.

Code:

```
units_sold = data['Units Sold'].values
```

In the next step, let us create time indices as a simple range from 0 to the length of the data minus one. These indices represent the time component in the time series data.

Code:

```
time_indices = np.arange(len(units_sold)).reshape(-1, 1)
```

Let us now split the data into training and testing sets using the **train_test_split** function, with 20% of the data as the test set. Ensure that the data is not shuffled so that the time series order can be maintained.

Code:

```
X_train, X_test, y_train, y_test = train_test_split(time_indices, units_sold, test_size=0.2, shuffle = False)
```

Let us now instantiate a Gaussian Process model with a specific kernel. We will use the kernel as a combination of a Constant Kernel (C) and a Radial-basis function (RBF). These kernels define the covariance function of the GP.

Let us set the optimizer to run 10 times to find the kernel parameters that maximize the likelihood.

Code:

kernel = C(1.0, (1e-3, 1e3)) * RBF(10, (1e-2, 1e2))

gp = GaussianProcessRegressor(kernel=kernel, n_restarts_optimizer=10)

In the next step, we will train the GP model on the training data. This process involves adjusting the kernel's parameters to best explain the observed data.

Code:

gp.fit(X_train, y_train)

The output of the model is as follows:

```
                    GaussianProcessRegressor
GaussianProcessRegressor(kernel=1**2 * RBF(length_scale=10),
                         n_restarts_optimizer=10)
```

Figure 7.3: *Gaussian Process Regressor*

Let us now make predictions on the test set using **predict** method. The method also returns the standard deviation of the predictions, which provides an estimate of the prediction uncertainty.

Code:

y_pred, sigma = gp.predict(X_test, return_std=True)

Output of y_pred:

array([-6.21510914e+01, -4.09202778e+00, -3.46638549e-02, ...,

0.00000000e+00, 0.00000000e+00, 0.00000000e+00])

Output of sigma:

array([28.83326584, 31.61394076, 31.62277599, ..., 31.6227766 ,

31.6227766 , 31.6227766])

In the next step, we will evaluate the model's performance using mean squared error (MSE), root mean squared error (RMSE), and mean absolute error (MAE).

Code:

```
mse = mean_squared_error(y_test, y_pred)
rmse = np.sqrt(mse)
mae = mean_absolute_error(y_test, y_pred)

print('Mean Squared Error:', mse)
print('Root Mean Squared Error:', rmse)
print('Mean Absolute Error:', mae)
```

Output:

```
Mean Squared Error: 81780.4887795851
Root Mean Squared Error: 285.9728811960762
Mean Absolute Error: 235.85755978736452
```

Let us now create a plot to visualize the actual vs. forecasted **Units Sold**.

Code:

```
plt.figure(figsize=(10,6))
plt.plot(y_test, label='Actual Units Sold')
plt.plot(y_pred, label='Forecasted Units Sold', color='red')
plt.title('Units Sold Forecast vs Actual with Gaussian Process')
plt.legend()
plt.show()
```

The output of the plot is displayed as follows:

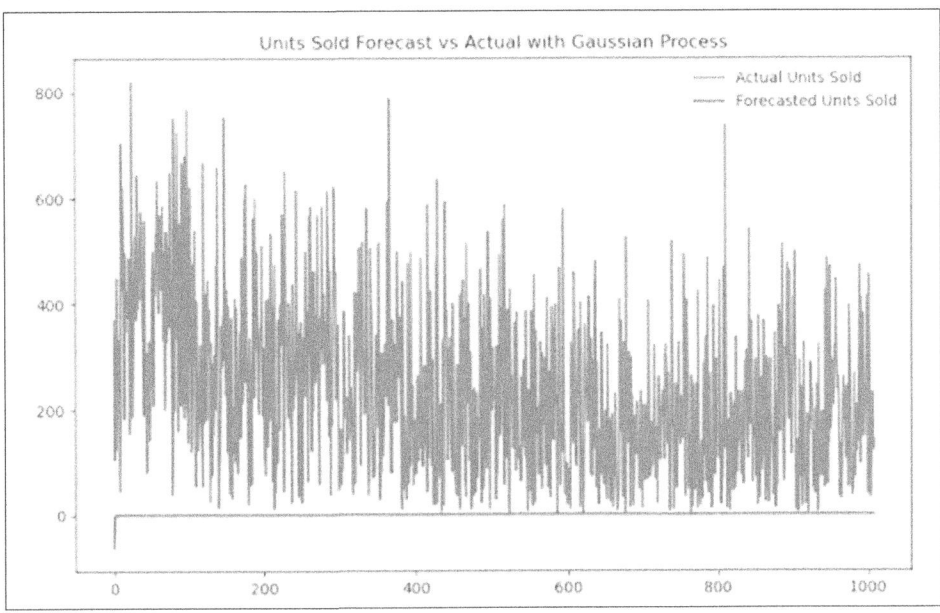

Figure 7.4: *Actual vs. Predicted - Gaussian Process Regressor*

The `Actual Units Sold` line in *Figure* 7.4 fluctuates significantly throughout the entire time series, indicating variability in the number of units sold over time. This variability could be due to seasonal trends, cyclic patterns, or other factors affecting sales. The `Forecasted Units Sold` is represented by a flat line near the x-axis, suggesting that the Gaussian Process Regressor predicted nearly the same value for the entire test set. This flat line indicates that the model did not capture the variability in the actual sales data, implying that the model has not performed well in forecasting the future values of the series. This suggests that either the model is not suitable for forecasting this data, or we might need to do more data preprocessing and transformation to make this model fit the data.

Let us now move to the next set of machine learning algorithms.

Developing an ML-Based Approach for Time Series Forecasting

In this section, we will create a common approach and a set of functions that can be applied to time series data to forecast future values using various machine learning algorithms.

The flow of various operations or functions in this approach is represented in *Figure 7.5*:

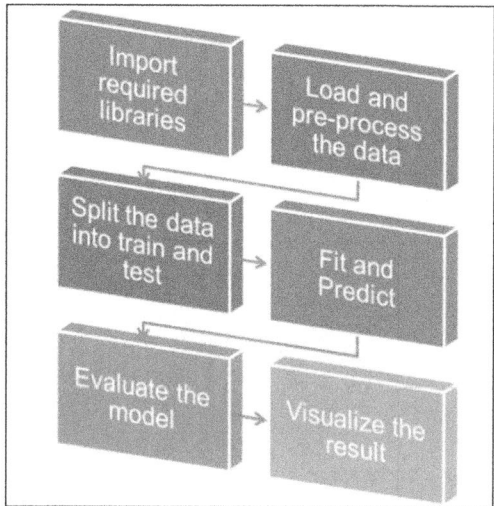

Figure 7.5: *Process flow for a machine learning-based approach*

To begin with, let us import the common libraries that will be needed to define the functions for this approach. The following libraries will be imported:

- **Pandas** will be used for data manipulation and analysis.
- **Numpy** will be used to add support for large, multi-dimensional arrays and matrices, along with a large collection of high-level mathematical functions to operate on these arrays.
- **Matplotlib** will be used to provide plotting capabilities for creating static, animated, and interactive visualizations in Python.
- **Sklearn.model_selection** will be used for splitting the dataset into training and testing sets.
- **Sklearn.metrics** will be used to compute the **mean squared error** and **mean absolute** for model evaluation.

Code:

```
import pandas as pd

import numpy as np

import matplotlib.pyplot as plt

from sklearn.metrics import mean_squared_error, mean_absolute_error

from sklearn.model_selection import train_test_split
```

In the next step, we will develop a function to load and pre-process the data. This function performs the following operations:
1. Loads the data from a CSV file.
2. Convert the `Date` column to a `datetime` object and sets it as the index, facilitating time series analysis.
3. Create a lag feature `Lag_1`, which is a common technique in time series forecasting where previous time steps are used as input variables.
4. Drops any rows with missing values.

Code:

```
def load_and_preprocess_data(file_name):
    df = pd.read_csv(file_name)
    df['Date'] = pd.to_datetime(df['Date'])
    df.set_index('Date', inplace=True)
    df['Lag_1'] = df['Units Sold'].shift(1)
    df.dropna(inplace=True)
    return df
```

We will now develop a function to split the data into train and test datasets. This function performs the following operations:
1. Split the data into features `X` and target variable `y`. Here, `Lag_1` is used as the feature and `Units Sold` is the target.
2. Split the dataset into training and testing sets, with 20% of the data reserved for testing. The `shuffle=False` parameter ensures that the splitting is done sequentially, preserving the time series order.

Code:

```
def split_data(df):
    X = df[['Lag_1']]
    y = df['Units Sold']
    return train_test_split(X, y, test_size=0.2, shuffle=False)
```

In the next step, let us define a function to fit the model and predict future values. This function performs the following operations:

1. Fit the specified model to the training data.
2. Make predictions on the test data.
3. Return the predicted values.

Code:

```
def fit_and_predict(model, X_train, y_train, X_test):
    model.fit(X_train, y_train)
    return model.predict(X_test)
```

In the next step, let us develop a function to evaluate the model results. This function performs the following operations:

1. Compute the common metrics used to evaluate the performance of regression models.
2. Return the results of the following metrics between the actual and predicted values: Mean Squared Error (MSE), Root Mean Squared Error (RMSE), and Mean Absolute Error (MAE).

Code:

```
def evaluate_model(y_test, y_pred):
    mse = mean_squared_error(y_test, y_pred)
    rmse = np.sqrt(mse)
    mae = mean_absolute_error(y_test, y_pred)
    return mse, rmse, mae
```

We will finally define a function to plot the results of the predictions. This function performs the following operation:

1. Plot the actual vs. predicted values of the **Units Sold**. This function is useful for visually comparing the model's predictions against the actual values.

Data Preparation

Let us now load the data and split it into train and test so that it can be easily used for various time series modeling activities.

Code:

```
df = load_and_preprocess_data('ProductSalesData.csv')
```

```
X_train, X_test, y_train, y_test = split_data(df)
```

The output displays a sample of the first five records of train data:

	Lag_1
Date	
2010-01-02	59.0
2010-01-03	203.0
2010-01-04	33.0
2010-01-05	117.0
2010-01-06	71.0

Figure 7.6: Sample train data with Lag feature

With these steps, we have defined all the functions needed to apply various machine learning models to the time series data.

In the next section, let us begin by applying Support Vector Machine (SVM) on the Product Sales data using this approach.

Applying Support Vector Machine

Support Vector Machines (SVMs) are supervised learning algorithms used for classification and regression problems. SVMs can also be used for time series forecasting after making relevant changes and data transformations to make it efficient for solving the problem. SVMs are capable of handling both linear and non-linear relationships in data. For non-linear relationships, SVMs use a technique called the kernel trick to transform data into a higher dimension where a linear separator can be found. The goal of the SVM algorithm is to find a decision boundary or hyperplane that maximizes the margin between different classes of data in the case of classification problems. In the context of regression or time series forecasting, this concept translates into fitting a line or hyperplane in multi-dimensional space that best captures the trends in the data.

The initial conceptualization of the SVMs algorithm was discussed in the Support-Vector Networks paper (Cortes and Vapnik, 1995), and later it was applied in multiple researches and problems.

Library Documentation

The SVM model documentation and its parameter information are available in the sklearn documentation at:

https://scikit-learn.org/stable/modules/generated/sklearn.svm.SVR.html

Support Vector Regression model in **sklearn** has the following class structure and parameters:

class sklearn.svm.SVR

(*,

kernel='rbf',

degree=3,

gamma='scale',

coef0=0.0,

tol=0.001,

C=1.0,

epsilon=0.1,

shrinking=True,

cache_size=200,

verbose=False,

max_iter=-1)

The parameters of the model as described in the library are as follows:
- **kernel:** This parameter is used to input the type of kernel to be utilized in the algorithm.
- **degree:** This parameter is used to input the degree of polynomial function value.
- **gamma:** This parameter is used to input the kernel coefficient.
- **coef:** This parameter is used to input the independent coefficient for the kernel function.
- **tol:** This parameter is used to input the tolerance value.
- **C:** This parameter is used to input the regularization parameter.
- **epsilon:** This parameter is used to input the epsilon value for the SVM model.
- **shrinking:** This is a boolean parameter provided as input to determine whether a shrinking heuristic needs to be used.

- **cache_size:** This parameter is used to input the size of the kernel cache.
- **verbose:** This parameter is a boolean value provided as input to determine if the verbose output needs to be enabled.
- **max_iter:** This parameter is used to input the maximum number of iterations for the model.

For more details and an understanding of the parameters, refer to the sklearn documentation.

Let us now proceed with the implementation of SVM on time series data.

Application of SVM on Time Series Data

In this example, we will be forecasting the Units Sold variable from **ProductSalesData**.

Let us start by importing the relevant libraries as follows:

In this step, let us import the SVR class from the SVM module of the scikit-learn library. SVR is the regression variant of the SVM algorithm, used for predicting continuous outcomes.

Code:

```
from sklearn.svm import SVR
```

In the next step, let us create an instance of the SVR class and assign it to the variable **svm_model**. This instance is created with default parameters, which can be adjusted, based on specific requirements or after hyperparameter tuning.

Code:

```
svm_model = SVR()
```

Let us now train the model and make predictions. The **fit_and_predict** function, which was defined in the machine learning approach in this chapter, is used here. It takes the **svm_model**, training data (**X_train**, **y_train**), and test data (**X_test**) as inputs. The function trains the **svm_model** using X_train and y_train, and then makes predictions on X_test. These predictions are stored in y_pred_svm.

Code:

```
y_pred_svm = fit_and_predict(svm_model, X_train, y_train, X_test)
```

In the next step, let us use another user-defined function, **evaluate_model**, which calculates various performance metrics. It takes the actual test outcomes (**y_test**) and the predicted values (**y_pred_svm**) as inputs and returns the Mean Squared Error (MSE), Root Mean Squared Error (RMSE), and Mean Absolute Error (MAE) of the model. These metrics are common for evaluating regression models, measuring the difference between actual and predicted values.

Code:

```
mse_svm, rmse_svm, mae_svm = evaluate_model(y_test, y_pred_svm)
print('Mean Squared Error:', mse_svm)
print('Root Mean Squared Error:', rmse_svm)
print('Mean Absolute Error:', mae_svm)
```

Output:

```
Mean Squared Error: 30717.93826290258
Root Mean Squared Error: 175.2653367409043
Mean Absolute Error: 146.8309981075176
```

An MSE of 30717.93 indicates that, on average, the square of the error of the forecasted units sold is quite high. Since MSE is sensitive to outliers due to squaring the errors, this high value could be influenced by large deviations in predictions for certain data points.

An RMSE of 175.26 means that the standard deviation of the prediction errors is about 175 units. This gives an idea of how much the predictions deviate from the actual values on average.

An MAE of 146.83 suggests that, on average, the absolute error of the forecast is 146.83 units.

The relatively high values of MSE and RMSE indicate that the model has a tendency to be off by a considerable number of units in its predictions. Given the scale of sales, an RMSE of 175.26 is significant, suggesting that the model's forecasts are often far from the actual sales figures. The MAE provides a clearer picture of the average magnitude of the errors. With an MAE of 146.83, it means that, on average, the model's forecasts are about 147 units away from the actual sales figures. This is also quite high, considering the range of sales numbers.

The metrics suggest that while the SVM model might be capturing the general level around which the sales oscillate, it is not accurately predicting the actual sales figures. This might be due to model under-fitting or inherent variability and noise in the sales data that the model cannot account for.

Finally, let us call the function **plot_results**, which creates a plot comparing the actual values (**y_test**) with the predicted values (**y_pred_svm**).

Code:

```
plot_results(y_test, y_pred_svm, 'Units Sold Forecast vs Actual with SVM')
```

The output of the plot is displayed as follows:

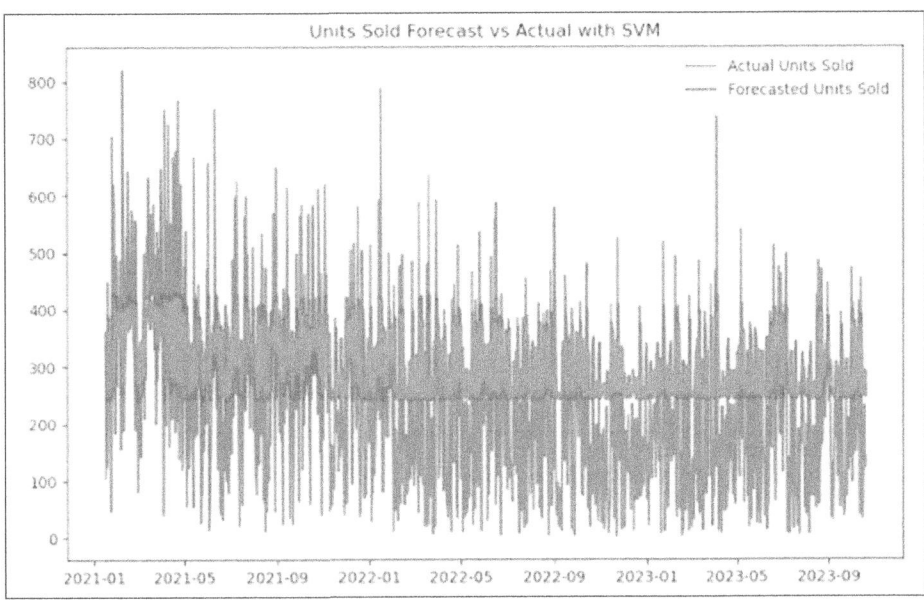

Figure 7.7: *Actual vs. Predicted – SVM*

The blue line in *Figure* 7.7 represents the actual number of units sold over the given time period. The line has many spikes and variations, which suggests significant variability in the actual sales data. This could be due to seasonal trends, irregular demand, promotions, or other factors affecting sales.

The red line in *Figure* 7.7 represents the number of units that were forecasted to be sold, as predicted by the Support Vector Machine (SVM) model. The red line looks smoother than the blue line, indicating that the SVM model has possibly captured the general trend but not the finer fluctuations in the actual Units Sold.

When comparing the two lines, it is evident that the forecast did not capture the peaks and troughs of the actual Units Sold. The forecasted values are consistently around a certain level without matching the actual sales' variability. This could imply that the SVM model used for forecasting may be under-fitting or not complex enough to capture the underlying patterns in the sales data.

Alternatively, it could also mean that there are external factors affecting the sales that the model has not considered.

With this understanding, let us proceed further to the next model in this chapter, which will be KNN.

Applying K-Nearest Neighbor (KNN)

K-Nearest Neighbors (KNN) is a simple and widely-used machine learning algorithm, which can also be applied to time series forecasting. KNN works on the principle of similarity. In the context of time series forecasting, *'similarity'* is usually based on how closely the patterns in the data match. In forecasting time series data, KNN examines the **k** most similar time points in the past in the dataset. These are the **nearest neighbors**. Similarity is often measured using distance metrics such as Euclidean distance. Once the algorithm identifies the nearest neighbors, the forecast is made by averaging the values of these neighbors.

The concept of the KNN algorithm was first introduced in a 1951 paper by Evelyn Fix and Joseph Hodges titled *"Discriminatory Analysis. Nonparametric Discrimination: Consistency Properties"*. This paper laid the groundwork for what would later be formalized as the KNN algorithm.

Library Documentation

The KNN model documentation and its parameter information are available in the sklearn documentation at:

https://scikit-learn.org/stable/modules/generated/sklearn.neighbors.KNeighborsRegressor.html

K-Nearest Neighbors model in `sklearn` has the following class structure and parameters:

class sklearn.neighbors.KNeighborsRegressor

(

n_neighbors=5,

*,

weights='uniform',

algorithm='auto',

leaf_size=30,

```
p=2,
metric='minkowski',
metric_params=None,
n_jobs=None
)
```

The parameters of the model as described in the library are as follows:
- **n_neighbors**: This parameter is used to provide the input for the number of neighbors for the KNN model.
- **weights**: This parameter is used to input the weight function that needs to be used in the model.
- **algorithm**: This parameter is used to input the name of the algorithm that needs to be used to calculate the nearest neighbors from the data.
- **leaf_size**: This parameter is used to input the leaf size for the nearest neighbors algorithm.
- **p**: This parameter is used to input the power value for the distance metric chosen to calculate the nearest neighbors.
- **metric**: This parameter is used to input the distance metric.
- **metric_params**: This parameter is used to input the additional arguments needed for the distance metric.
- **n_jobs**: This parameter is used to input the number of jobs that need to run in parallel to calculate the nearest neighbors.

For more details and an understanding of the parameters, refer to the sklearn documentation.

Let us now proceed with the implementation of KNN on time series data.

Application of KNN on Time Series Data

In this example, we will be forecasting the Units Sold variable from **ProductSalesData**.

Let us start by importing the relevant libraries as follows:

In this step, let us import the KNN class from the neighbors module of the scikit-learn library. **KNeighborsRegressor** is the regression variant of the KNN algorithm, used for predicting continuous outcomes.

Code:

```
from sklearn.neighbors import KNeighborsRegressor
```

In the next step, let us create an instance of the **KNeighborsRegressor** class and assign it to the variable **knn_model**. This instance is created with the number of neighbors as 5 and other default parameters, which can be adjusted, based on specific requirements or after hyperparameter tuning.

Code:

```
knn_model = KNeighborsRegressor(n_neighbors=5)
```

Let us now train the model and make the prediction. The **fit_and_predict** function, which was defined in the machine learning approach in this chapter, is used here. It takes the knn_model, training data (**X_train, y_train**), and test data (**X_test**) as inputs. The function trains the **knn_model** using **X_train** and **y_train**, and then makes predictions on **X_test**. These predictions are stored in **y_pred_knn**.

Code:

```
y_pred_knn = fit_and_predict(knn_model, X_train, y_train, X_test)
```

In the next step, let us use another user-defined function, **evaluate_model**, which calculates various performance metrics. It takes the actual test outcomes (**y_test**) and the predicted values (**y_pred_knn**) as inputs and returns the Mean Squared Error (MSE), Root Mean Squared Error (RMSE), and Mean Absolute Error (MAE) of the model. These metrics are common for evaluating regression models, measuring the difference between actual and predicted values.

Code:

```
mse_knn, rmse_knn, mae_knn = evaluate_model(y_test, y_pred_knn)
print('Mean Squared Error:', mse_knn)
print('Root Mean Squared Error:', rmse_knn)
print('Mean Absolute Error:', mae_knn)
```

Output:

```
Mean Squared Error: 36146.26813492064
Root Mean Squared Error: 190.12171926142642
Mean Absolute Error: 156.84345238095239
```

An MSE of 36146.26 indicates that, on average, the square of the error of the forecasted units sold is quite high. Since MSE is sensitive to outliers due to squaring the errors, this high value could be influenced by large deviations in predictions for certain data points.

An RMSE of 190.12 means that the standard deviation of the prediction errors is about 190 units. This gives an idea of how much the predictions deviate from the actual values on average.

An MAE of 156.84 suggests that, on average, the absolute error of the forecast is 156.84 units.

These metrics suggest that while the KNN model might be capturing the general level around which the sales oscillate, it is not accurately predicting the actual sales figures. This might be due to model under-fitting or inherent variability and noise in the sales data that the model cannot account for.

Finally, let us call the function **plot_results**, which creates a plot comparing the actual values (**y_test**) with the predicted values (**y_pred_knn**).

Code:

```
plot_results(y_test, y_pred_knn, 'Units Sold Forecast vs Actual with KNN')
```

The output of the plot is displayed as follows:

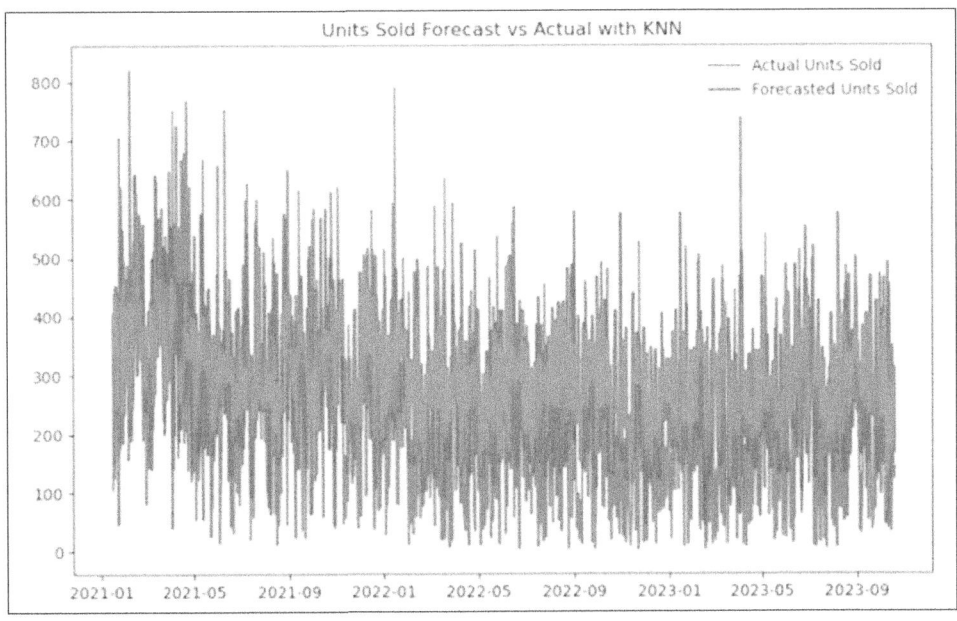

Figure 7.8: *Actual vs. Predicted – KNN*

The blue line in *Figure* 7.8 represents the actual number of units sold over the given time period. The line has many spikes and variations, which suggests significant variability in the actual sales data. This could be due to seasonal trends, irregular demand, promotions, or other factors affecting sales.

The red line in *Figure* 7.8 represents the number of units that were forecasted to be sold, as predicted by the K-Nearest Neighbors (KNN) model. The red line also shows fluctuations and seems to follow the pattern of the actual Units Sold to some extent.

When comparing the two lines, it is evident that the forecast does capture some of the peaks and troughs of the actual Units Sold. This could imply that the KNN model used for forecasting may be getting closer to capturing the underlying patterns in the sales data.

Let us now move forward to the next model in this chapter, which will be Random Forest.

Implementing with Random Forest

Random Forest is a popular machine learning technique that can be adapted for time series forecasting. It is an ensemble learning method that combines multiple decision trees to produce a more accurate and stable prediction. Each tree in the forest makes a prediction, and the final output is determined by averaging these predictions for regression tasks. Random Forest can be a powerful tool for time series forecasting, especially when the data exhibits complex patterns and non-linear relationships.

The original concept of the Random Forest algorithm was introduced by Leo Breiman. The foundational paper is titled "*Random Forests*", published in 2001 in the journal "Machine Learning". In this paper, Breiman laid out the fundamental principles of the Random Forest algorithm, explaining how it builds multiple decision trees and merges them together to get a more accurate and stable prediction.

Library Documentation

The Random Forest model documentation and its parameter information are available in the sklearn documentation at:

https://scikit-learn.org/stable/modules/generated/sklearn.ensemble.RandomForestRegressor.html

Random Forest model in sklearn has the following class structure and parameters:

```
class sklearn.ensemble.RandomForestRegressor
(n_estimators=100,
 *,
 criterion='squared_error',
 max_depth=None,
 min_samples_split=2,
 min_samples_leaf=1,
 min_weight_fraction_leaf=0.0,
 max_features=1.0,
 max_leaf_nodes=None,
 min_impurity_decrease=0.0,
 bootstrap=True,
 oob_score=False,
 n_jobs=None,
 random_state=None,
 verbose=0,
 warm_start=False,
 ccp_alpha=0.0,
 max_samples=None)
```

The parameters of the model as described in the library are as follows:
- **n_estimators:** This parameter is used to input the number of trees to be considered in the random forest model.
- **criterion:** This parameter is used to input the function that needs to be used to calculate the quality of the splits that are performed by the model.
- **max_depth:** This parameter is used to provide a value that is used for deciding the maximum depth of the tree in the model.

- **min_samples_split**: This parameter is used to provide the minimum number of samples that need to be considered to split the nodes within the model.
- **min_samples_leaf**: This parameter is used to input the minimum number of samples that need to be considered at a lead node by the model.
- **min_weight_fraction_leaf**: This parameter is used to input the minimum weight fraction that needs to be available at a leaf node out of the total weights of all the samples in the data.
- **max_features**: This parameter is to input the number of features to be considered by the model while creating the splits.
- **max_leaf_nodes**: This parameter is used to input the maximum number of leaf nodes for the trees in the model.
- **min_impurity_decrease**: This parameter is used to input the impurity check value that can be used to determine the value at which a node should be split within the model.
- **bootstrap**: This is a boolean parameter used to determine if bootstrap samples need to be used by the model.
- **oob_score**: This is a boolean parameter used to determine if out-of-bag samples need to be used for scores in the model.
- **n_jobs**: This parameter is used to input the number of parallel jobs to be run for the model.
- **random_state**: This parameter is used to provide a value that handles the randomness in the model development process at various stages of sampling.
- **verbose**: This parameter is used to provide a value that determines the verbosity of the model.
- **warm_start**: This boolean parameter is used to determine whether an existing model estimator and fitted model can be used for the current process or a new model needs to be fit.
- **ccp_alpha**: This parameter is used to provide an input value for cost-complexity pruning of the model.
- **max_samples**: This parameter is used to input the number of samples to be used for each model estimator.

For more details and an understanding of the parameters, refer to the sklearn documentation.

Let us now proceed with the implementation of Random Forest on time series data.

Application of Random Forest on Time Series Data

In this example, we will be forecasting the Units Sold variable from ProductSalesData.

Let us start by importing the relevant libraries as follows:

In this step, let us import the **RandomForestRegressor** class from the ensemble module of the scikit-learn library. **RandomForestRegressor** is the regression variant of the Random Forest algorithm, used for predicting continuous outcomes.

Code:

```
from sklearn.ensemble import RandomForestRegressor
```

In the next step, let us create an instance of the **RandomForestRegressor** class and assign it to the variable **rf_model**. This instance is created with the number of **n_estimators** as 100 and other default parameters, which can be adjusted, based on specific requirements or after hyperparameter tuning.

Code:

```
rf_model = RandomForestRegressor(n_estimators=100)
```

Let us now train the model and make the prediction. The **fit_and_predict** function, defined earlier in the machine learning approach in this chapter, is used here. It takes the **rf_model**, training data (**X_train, y_train**), and test data (**X_test**) as inputs. The function trains the **rf_model** using **X_train** and **y_train**, and then makes predictions on **X_test**. These predictions are stored in **y_pred_rf**.

Code:

```
y_pred_rf = fit_and_predict(rf_model, X_train, y_train, X_test)
```

In the next step, let us use another user-defined function, **evaluate_model**, which calculates various performance metrics. It takes the actual test outcomes (**y_test**) and the predicted values (**y_pred_rf**) as inputs and returns the Mean Squared Error (MSE), Root Mean Squared Error (RMSE), and Mean Absolute

Error (MAE) of the model. These metrics are common for evaluating regression models, measuring the difference between actual and predicted values.

Code:

```
mse_rf, rmse_rf, mae_rf = evaluate_model(y_test, y_pred_rf)
print('Mean Squared Error:', mse_rf)
print('Root Mean Squared Error:', rmse_rf)
print('Mean Absolute Error:', mae_rf)
```

Output:

```
Mean Squared Error: 37481.6298468256
Root Mean Squared Error: 193.60172996857648
Mean Absolute Error: 158.8789766787894
```

An MSE of 37481.62 indicates that, on average, the square of the error of the forecasted **Units Sold** is quite high. Since MSE is sensitive to outliers due to squaring the errors, this high value could be influenced by large deviations in predictions for certain data points.

An RMSE of 193.60 means that the standard deviation of the prediction errors is about 193 units. This gives an idea of how much the predictions deviate from the actual values on average.

An MAE of 158.87 suggests that, on average, the absolute error of the forecast is 158.87 units.

These metrics suggest that while the Random Forest model might be capturing the general level around which the sales oscillate, it is not accurately predicting the actual sales figures. This might be due to model under-fitting or inherent variability and noise in the sales data that the model cannot account for.

Finally, let us call the function plot_results, which creates a plot comparing the actual values (**y_test**) with the predicted values (**y_pred_rf**).

Code:

```
plot_results(y_test, y_pred_rf, 'Units Sold Forecast vs Actual with Random Forest')
```

The output of the plot is displayed as follows:

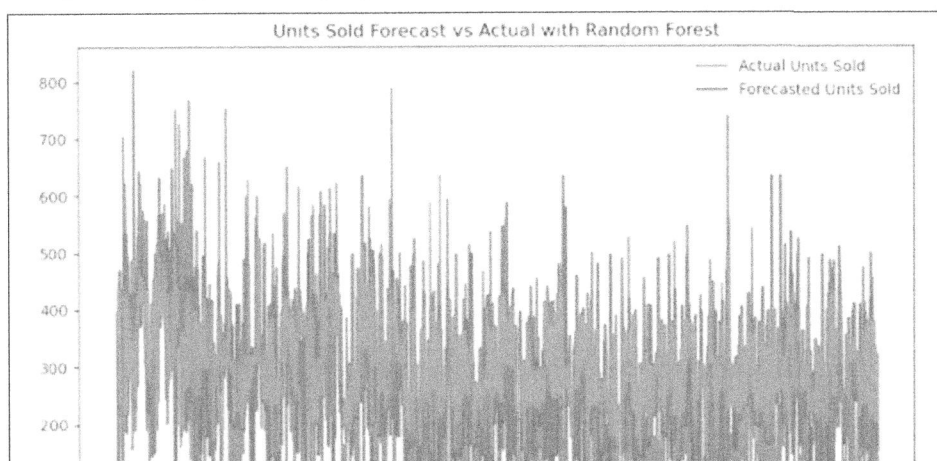

Figure 7.9: *Actual vs. Predicted – Random Forest*

The blue line in *Figure* 7.9 represents the actual number of units sold over the given time period. The line has many spikes and variations, which suggests significant variability in the actual sales data. This could be due to seasonal trends, irregular demand, promotions, or other factors affecting sales.

The red line in *Figure* 7.9 represents the number of units that were forecasted to be sold, as predicted by the Random Forest model. The red line also shows fluctuations and seems to follow the pattern of the actual `Units Sold` to some extent.

When comparing the two lines, it is evident that the forecast does capture some of the peaks and troughs of the actual `Units Sold`. This could imply that the Random Forest model used for forecasting may also be getting closer to capturing the underlying patterns in the sales data.

Implementing with Gradient Boosting

Gradient boosting is a powerful machine-learning technique that can be applied to various types of data, including time series forecasting. Gradient boosting combines multiple weak predictive models (decision trees) to create a strong model. Each new model focuses on and corrects the errors made by the previous ones. This optimization technique is used to minimize the loss by adjusting the model in the direction that reduces the loss the most. Gradient boosting, with its ability to iteratively learn from past errors and adapt to complex data patterns, can be a potential tool for time series forecasting.

The original concept of gradient boosting was introduced by Jerome H. Friedman in his paper *"Greedy Function Approximation: A Gradient Boosting Machine"*. This seminal work laid the foundation for gradient boosting algorithms, which have since evolved and been adapted in various forms, including popular implementations like XGBoost, LightGBM, and CatBoost.

Library Documentation

The Gradient Boosting model documentation and its parameter information are available in the sklearn documentation at:

https://scikit-learn.org/stable/modules/generated/sklearn.ensemble.GradientBoostingRegressor.html

Gradient Boosting model in sklearn has the following class structure and parameters:

```
class sklearn.ensemble.GradientBoostingRegressor
(*,
 loss='squared_error',
 learning_rate=0.1,
 n_estimators=100,
 subsample=1.0,
 criterion='friedman_mse',
 min_samples_split=2,
 min_samples_leaf=1,
 min_weight_fraction_leaf=0.0,
 max_depth=3,
 min_impurity_decrease=0.0,
 init=None,
 random_state=None,
 max_features=None,
```

```
    alpha=0.9,
    verbose=0,
    max_leaf_nodes=None,
    warm_start=False,
    validation_fraction=0.1,
    n_iter_no_change=None,
    tol=0.0001,
    ccp_alpha=0.0)
```

The parameters of the model as described in the library are as follows:

- **loss:** This parameter is used to input the loss function for the model.
- **learning_rate:** This parameter is used to input the learning rate for the model.
- **n_estimators:** This parameter is used to determine the number of estimators for the model.
- **subsample:** This parameter is used to input the sub-sample fraction to be used to fit on each base estimator for the model.
- **criterion:** This parameter is used to input the function that needs to be used to calculate the quality of the splits that are performed by the model.
- **min_samples_split:** This parameter is used to provide the minimum number of samples that need to be considered to split the nodes within the model.
- **min_samples_leaf:** This parameter is used to input the minimum number of samples that need to be considered at a lead node by the model.
- **min_weight_fraction_leaf:** This parameter is used to input the minimum weight fraction that needs to be available at a leaf node out of the total weights of all the samples in the data.
- **max_depth:** This parameter is used to provide a value that is used for deciding the maximum depth of the estimator in the model.
- **min_impurity_decrease:** This parameter is used to input the impurity check value that can be used to determine the value at which a node should be split within the model.

- **init:** This parameter is used to input the initial prediction estimator object for the model.
- **random_state:** This parameter is used to provide a value that handles the randomness in the model development process at various stages of sampling.
- **max_features:** This parameter is used to input the number of features to be considered by the model while creating the splits.
- **alpha:** This parameter is used to input the alpha-quantile of the loss function.
- **verbose:** This parameter is used to input a value that decides the frequency at which the model progress and performance need to be printed.
- **max_leaf_nodes:** This parameter is used to input the maximum number of leaf nodes for the trees in the model.
- **warm_start:** This boolean parameter is used to determine whether an existing model estimator and fitted model can be used for the current process or a new model needs to be fit.
- **validation_fraction:** The proportion of training data to set aside as validation set for early stopping.
- **n_iter_no_change:** This parameter is used to input a value that decides if early stopping of the iterations is needed during the model training process.
- **tol:** This is an optional input parameter denoting the early stopping threshold for the model.
- **ccp_alpha:** This parameter is used to provide an input value for cost-complexity pruning of the model.

For more details and an understanding of the parameters, refer to the sklearn documentation.

Let us now proceed with the implementation of Gradient Boosting on time series data.

Application of Gradient Boosting on Time Series Data

In this example, we will be forecasting the **Units Sold** variable from **ProductSalesData**.

Let us start by importing the relevant libraries as follows:

In this step, let us import the **GradientBoostingRegressor** class from the ensemble module of the scikit-learn library. **GradientBoostingRegressor** is the regression variant of the Gradient Boosting algorithm, used for predicting continuous outcomes.

Code:

```
from sklearn.ensemble import GradientBoostingRegressor
```

In the next step, let us create an instance of the **GradientBoostingRegressor** or class and assign it to the variable **gb_model**. This instance is created with the number of **n_estimators** as 100 and other default parameters, which can be adjusted, based on specific requirements or after hyperparameter tuning.

Code:

```
gb_model = GradientBoostingRegressor(n_estimators=100)
```

Let us now train the model and make the prediction. The **fit_and_predict** function, which was defined in the machine learning approach in this chapter, is used here. It takes the **gb_model**, training data (**X_train, y_train**), and test data (**X_test**) as inputs. The function trains the **gb_model** using **X_train** and **y_train**, and then makes predictions on **X_test**. These predictions are stored in **y_pred_gb**.

Code:

```
y_pred_gb = fit_and_predict(gb_model, X_train, y_train, X_test)
```

In the next step, let us use another user-defined function, evaluate_model, which calculates various performance metrics. It takes the actual test outcomes (**y_test**) and the predicted values (**y_pred_gb**) as inputs and returns the Mean Squared Error (MSE), Root Mean Squared Error (RMSE), and Mean Absolute Error (MAE) of the model. These metrics are common for evaluating regression models, measuring the difference between actual and predicted values.

Code:

mse_gb, rmse_gb, mae_gb = evaluate_model(y_test, y_pred_gb)

print('Mean Squared Error:', mse_gb)

print('Root Mean Squared Error:', rmse_gb)

print('Mean Absolute Error:', mae_gb)

Output:

Mean Squared Error: 31976.61504444344

Root Mean Squared Error: 178.82006331629412

Mean Absolute Error: 149.4313760353675

An MSE of 31976.61 indicates that, on average, the square of the error of the forecasted units sold is quite high. Since MSE is sensitive to outliers due to squaring the errors, this high value could be influenced by large deviations in predictions for certain data points.

An RMSE of 178.82 means that the standard deviation of the prediction errors is about 178 units. This gives an idea of how much the predictions deviate from the actual values on average.

An MAE of 149.43 suggests that, on average, the absolute error of the forecast is 149.43 units.

The relatively high values of MSE and RMSE indicate that the model has a tendency to be off by a considerable number of units in its predictions. Given the scale of sales, an RMSE of 178.82 is significant, suggesting that the model's forecasts are often far from the actual sales figures. The MAE provides a clearer picture of the average magnitude of the errors. With an MAE of 149.43, it means that, on average, the model's forecasts are about 149 units away from the actual sales figures. This is also quite high, considering the range of sales numbers.

The metrics suggest that while the Gradient Boosting model similar to SVM might be capturing the general level around which the sales oscillate, it is not accurately predicting the actual sales figures. This might be due to model underfitting or inherent variability and noise in the sales data that the model cannot account for.

Finally, let us call the function **plot_results**, which creates a plot comparing the actual values (**y_test**) with the predicted values (**y_pred_gb**).

Code:

```
plot_results(y_test, y_pred_gb, 'Units Sold Forecast vs Actual with Gradient Boosting')
```

The output of the plot is displayed as follows:

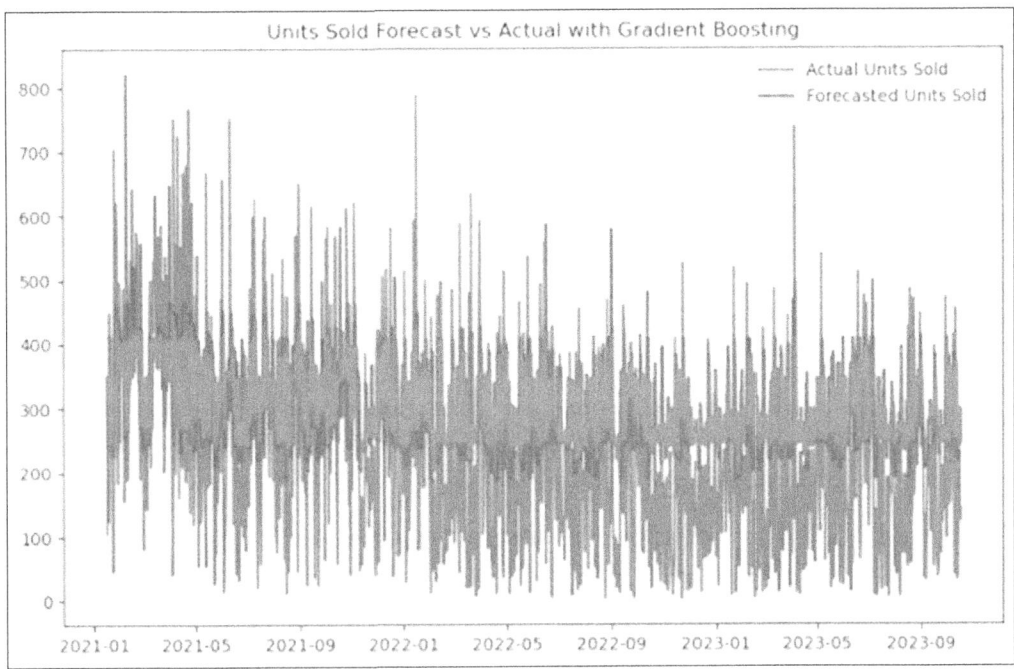

Figure 7.10: *Actual vs. Predicted – Gradient Boosting*

The blue line in *Figure 7.10* represents the actual number of units sold over the given time period. The line has many spikes and variations, which suggests significant variability in the actual sales data. This could be due to seasonal trends, irregular demand, promotions, or other factors affecting sales.

The red line in *Figure 7.10* represents the number of units that were forecasted to be sold, as predicted by the Gradient Boosting model. The red line looks smoother than the blue line, indicating that the Gradient Boosting model similar to SVM has possibly captured the general trend but not the finer fluctuations in the actual **Units Sold**.

When comparing the two lines, it is evident that the forecast did not capture the peaks and troughs of the actual **Units Sold**. The forecasted values are consistently around a certain level without matching the actual sales' variability. This could imply that the Gradient Boosting model used for forecasting may be under-fitting or not complex enough to capture the underlying patterns in the sales data. Alternatively, it could also mean that there are external factors affecting the sales that the model has not considered.

These are various examples of machine learning models that can be used to forecast time series data.

Conclusion

In this chapter, we have learned about the various machine learning algorithms that can be used in forecasting time series data by modifying the input features.

We also explored the parameters, documentation, and examples of understanding the Hidden Markov Model and the Gaussian Process model.

Additionally, we developed a common set of functions that can be reused to apply multiple machine-learning algorithms.

Furthermore, we learned to reuse the functions and apply Support Vector Machine (SVM), K-Nearest Neighbor (KNN), Random Forest, and Gradient Boosting on the time series data.

In the next chapter, we will delve into applying deep learning algorithms to forecast future values.

References

- Baum, L.E., 1972. An inequality and associated maximization technique in statistical estimation for probabilistic functions of Markov processes. Inequalities, 3(1), pp.1-8.
- API reference (no date) API Reference - hmmlearn 0.3.0.post3+g23c0f13 documentation. Available at: https://hmmlearn.readthedocs.io/en/latest/api.html (Accessed: 04 December 2023).
- Rasmussen, C. and Williams, C. (2005) Gaussian processes for machine learning [Preprint]. doi:10.7551/mitpress/3206.001.0001.
- Sklearn.gaussian_process.Gaussianprocessregressor (no date) scikit. Available at: https://scikit-learn.org/stable/modules/generated/sklearn.gaussian_process.GaussianProcessRegressor.html (Accessed: 04 December 2023).

- Cortes, C. and Vapnik, V. (1995) 'Support-Vector Networks', Machine Learning, 20(3), pp. 273–297. doi:10.1007/bf00994018.
- Sklearn.svm.SVR (no date) scikit. Available at: https://scikit-learn.org/stable/modules/generated/sklearn.svm.SVR.html (Accessed: 04 December 2023).
- Fix, E. and Hodges, J.L. (1951) 'Discriminatory analysis: Nonparametric discrimination: Consistency properties', PsycEXTRA Dataset [Preprint]. doi:10.1037/e471672008-001.
- Sklearn.neighbors.kneighborsregressor (no date) scikit. Available at: https://scikit-learn.org/stable/modules/generated/sklearn.neighbors.KNeighborsRegressor.html (Accessed: 04 December 2023).
- Breiman, L. (2001) Random Forests, 45(1), pp. 5–32. doi:10.1023/a:1010933404324.
- Sklearn.ensemble.randomforestregressor (no date) scikit. Available at: https://scikit-learn.org/stable/modules/generated/sklearn.ensemble.RandomForestRegressor.html (Accessed: 04 December 2023).
- Friedman, J.H. (2001) 'Greedy function approximation: A gradient boosting machine.', The Annals of Statistics, 29(5). doi:10.1214/aos/1013203451.
- Sklearn.ensemble.gradientboostingregressor (no date) scikit. Available at: https://scikit-learn.org/stable/modules/generated/sklearn.ensemble.GradientBoostingRegressor.html (Accessed: 04 December 2023).

CHAPTER 8
Time Series Forecasting - DL Approach

In this chapter, we will explore the applications of deep learning to forecast time series data. Deep learning is a branch of machine learning where multiple layers of neural networks are used to develop models that can perform various prediction tasks on the data. There are multiple variations of these deep learning algorithms. We will examine the relevant algorithms that can be customized and applied to time series data for forecasting tasks. Some of the popular deep learning algorithms include Recurrent Neural Networks (RNNs), Long Short-Term Memory (LSTM) networks, and Convolutional Neural Networks (CNNs). We will cover these algorithms and a few more variations of them in this chapter.

Structure

In this chapter, the following topics will be covered:
- Understanding Long Short-Term Memory Networks
- Developing a Deep Learning-Based Approach for Time Series Forecasting
- Applying Gated Recurrent Units
- Applying Convolutional Neural Networks

Data Introduction

Throughout this chapter, we will continue to make use of one dataset, and a single variable from the dataset will be focused on forecasting future values based on various machine learning algorithms that support time series data. The dataset used for this section is synthetically generated data developed to illustrate the examples in this chapter, and the data is available in the GitHub repository: https://github.com/OrangeAVA/Mastering Time Series Analysis and Forecasting with Python.

The variables of interest from this dataset for this chapter are as follows:
- **Date:** Date of Sales
- **Units Sold:** Number of units of a product sold in a day. Values ranging between 1 and 1000

Understanding Long Short-Term Memory Networks

Long Short-Term Memory (LSTM) networks are a type of recurrent neural network (RNN) used for solving data problems such as time series forecasting. RNNs are suitable for handling and predicting sequential data since they can use their internal memory state to process sequences of data. LSTM is an extension or modification of RNNs, and the internal memory state of LSTM is more complex than RNNs. It is designed in such a way to handle long-term dependencies in the data.

The core components of LSTM include the following:
- **Memory Cell**: This is the most important component of the LSTM unit, which can remember past data in a sequential input and can maintain its state over a period of time as well.
- **Input Gate**: This is the component where the input is provided to the memory cell to keep it updated with new information.
- **Output Gate**: This is the component where a decision is made on the next hidden state of the information that is used in the prediction of the current time step.
- **Forget Gate**: This is the component where the decision is made on the information that needs to be discarded from the state of the cell.

The fundamental concept of Long Short-Term Memory (LSTM) networks was introduced by Sepp Hochreiter and Jürgen Schmidhuber in 1997 in their research paper titled *Long Short-Term Memory*. In this paper, the architecture of LSTM was introduced as an improvement to handle the challenges involved in the recurrent neural networks (RNNs). LSTM was designed to address the vanishing gradient problem of RNNs.

Library Documentation

The model documentation and parameters for LSTM are available in the TensorFlow documentation at:

https://www.tensorflow.org/api_docs/python/tf/keras/layers/LSTM

LSTM in the TensorFlow library has the following class structure and parameters:

```
tf.keras.layers.LSTM(
    units,
    activation='tanh',
    recurrent_activation='sigmoid',
    use_bias=True,
    kernel_initializer='glorot_uniform',
    recurrent_initializer='orthogonal',
    bias_initializer='zeros',
    unit_forget_bias=True,
    kernel_regularizer=None,
    recurrent_regularizer=None,
    bias_regularizer=None,
    activity_regularizer=None,
    kernel_constraint=None,
    recurrent_constraint=None,
    bias_constraint=None,
    dropout=0.0,
    recurrent_dropout=0.0,
```

```
        return_sequences=False,

        return_state=False,

        go_backwards=False,

        stateful=False,

        time_major=False,

        unroll=False,

        **kwargs
)
```

The parameters of the model as described in the library are as follows:
- **units**: This parameter is used to input a positive integer denoting the dimensionality of the output space.
- **activation**: This parameter is used to input a function name that denotes the Activation function to use.
- **use_bias**: This parameter is used to determine if a bias vector needs to be used in a model layer.
- **kernel_initializer**: This parameter is used to provide a kernel initializer for the model inputs.
- **recurrent_initializer**: This parameter is used to provide a kernel initializer for the recurrent states of the model.
- **bias_initializer**: This parameter is used to provide an initializer for the bias vector of the model.
- **unit_forget_bias**: This parameter is used to provide a boolean input for the unit forget bias.
- **kernel_regularizer**: This parameter is used to input the kernel regularizer function for the model.
- **recurrent_regularizer**: This parameter is used to input the recurrent regularizer function for the model.
- **bias_regularizer**: This parameter is used to input the bias **regularizer** function for the model.
- **activity_regularizer**: This parameter is used to input the activity regularizer function for the model.
- **kernel_constraint**: This parameter is used to input the kernel constraint function for the model.

- **recurrent_constraint**: This parameter is used to input the recurrent constraint function for the model.
- **bias_constraint**: This parameter is used to input the bias constraint function for the model.
- **dropout**: This parameter is used to input a value that determines the number of units that need to be dropped at the input state.
- **recurrent_dropout**: This parameter is used to input a value that determines the number of units that need to be dropped at the recurrent state.
- **return_sequences**: This parameter is used to determine the sequences that need to be provided in the output.
- **return_state**: This parameter is used to determine the states that need to be provided in the output.
- **go_backwards**: This parameter is used to determine the direction in which the input sequence needs to be processed by the model.
- **stateful**: This parameter is used to determine if the previous state needs to be used in the next state in the model.
- **time_major**: This parameter is used to determine the shape format of the inputs and outputs tensors.
- **unroll:** This parameter is used to input a boolean value that determines if the network needs to be unrolled.

For more details and understanding of the parameters, refer to the TensorFlow documentation.

Let us now proceed with the implementation of LSTM on time series data.

Application of LSTM on Time Series Data

In this example, we will be forecasting the `Units Sold` variable from `ProductSalesData`.

Let us start by importing the relevant libraries as follows:
- **Pandas**: imported for data manipulation and analysis.
- **Numpy**: imported for numerical computation.
- **Matplotlib**: imported for visualizing the output.
- **Math**: imported for mathematical computation.
- **Sklearn**: imported for data preprocessing and metrics.
- **Tensorflow**: imported for neural networks model development.

Code:

```
import pandas as pd
import numpy as np
from sklearn.preprocessing import MinMaxScaler
from sklearn.model_selection import train_test_split
from tensorflow.keras.models import Sequential
from tensorflow.keras.layers import LSTM, Dense
from tensorflow.keras.optimizers import Adam
import matplotlib.pyplot as plt
import math
from sklearn.metrics import mean_squared_error
```

Let us then load the data from a CSV file named '**ProductSalesData.csv**' into a Pandas DataFrame and drop the column with no name.

Code:

```
data = pd.read_csv('ProductSalesData.csv')
```

In the next step, let us convert the **Date** column into **DateTime** format and sort the data by date.

Code:

```
data['Date'] = pd.to_datetime(data['Date'])
data.sort_values('Date', inplace=True)
```

Let us further get the target variable **Units Sold** ready for prediction.

Code:

```
df = data[['Units Sold']]
```

In the next step, let us normalize the target variable using **MinMaxScaler** to scale the values between 0 and 1.

Code:

```
scaler = MinMaxScaler(feature_range=(0, 1))
df_scaled = scaler.fit_transform(df)
```

Time Series Forecasting - DL Approach

In the next step, let us define a function named **create_dataset** to prepare the data for the model development process. This function creates sequences of Product Sales data X and the corresponding next value to predict Y.

Code:

```
def create_dataset(data, ts=1):
    X, Y = [], []
    for i in range(len(data) - ts - 1):
        a = data[i:(i + ts), 0]
        X.append(a)
        Y.append(data[i + ts, 0])
    return np.array(X), np.array(Y)
ts = 3
X, Y = create_dataset(df_scaled, ts)
```

The input parameter **ts** in **create_dataset** denotes the time step.

In the next step, let us split the data into a train set as **80%** and a test set as **20%**.

Code:

```
X_train, X_test, y_train, y_test = train_test_split(X, Y, test_size=0.2, random_state=42)
```

In the next step, let us reshape the data into **samples**, **time**, **steps**, and **features** so that it can be provided as input to the LSTM model.

Code:

```
X_train = X_train.reshape(X_train.shape[0], X_train.shape[1], 1)
X_test = X_test.reshape(X_test.shape[0], X_test.shape[1], 1)
```

The most interesting part of this application lies in the development of the LSTM model with multiple sequential layers. Let us develop the model with four layers: two layers of the model will be LSTM and two layers will be Dense.

Code:

```
model = Sequential()
model.add(LSTM(50, return_sequences=True, input_shape=(ts, 1)))
```

```
model.add(LSTM(50, return_sequences=False))
model.add(Dense(25))
model.add(Dense(1))
```

These layers can be increased or decreased based on the accuracy of the model results and the availability of computation power and resources needed to develop these models.

In the next step, let us compile the model with optimizer as **Adam**, learning rate as **0.001**, and loss function as **mean_squared_error**.

Code:

```
model.compile(optimizer=Adam(learning_rate=0.001), loss='mean_squared_error')
```

Let us train this model on the training data with **100** epochs and a batch size of **64**.

Code:

```
model.fit(X_train, y_train, validation_data=(X_test, y_test), epochs=100, batch_size=64, verbose=1)
```

Output:

```
Epoch 1/100
63/63 [==============================] - 4s 18ms/step - loss: 0.0466 - val_loss: 0.0308
Epoch 2/100
63/63 [==============================] - 0s 6ms/step - loss: 0.0302 - val_loss: 0.0289
Epoch 3/100
63/63 [==============================] - 0s 6ms/step - loss: 0.0300 - val_loss: 0.0289
...
Epoch 98/100
63/63 [==============================] - 0s 6ms/step - loss: 0.0294 - val_loss: 0.0284
```

```
Epoch 99/100
63/63 [==============================] - 0s 6ms/step - loss: 0.0295 - val_loss: 0.0284
Epoch 100/100
63/63 [==============================] - 0s 6ms/step - loss: 0.0294 - val_loss: 0.0286
```

Let us now review the summary of the model.

Code:

```
model.summary()
```

Output:

```
Model: "sequential"
```

Layer (type)	Output Shape	Param #
lstm (LSTM)	(None, 3, 50)	10400
lstm_1 (LSTM)	(None, 50)	20200
dense (Dense)	(None, 25)	1275
dense_1 (Dense)	(None, 1)	26

```
Total params: 31,901
Trainable params: 31,901
Non-trainable params: 0
```

Each layer, its dimensions, and the number of parameters are described in the preceding model summary.

Let us now **predict** the **train** and **test** data using this model.

Code:

train_predict = model.predict(X_train)

test_predict = model.predict(X_test)

Output:

126/126 [==============================] - 1s 1ms/step

32/32 [==============================] - 0s 2ms/step

Let us inverse the data that was normalized before applying the model.

Code:

train_predict = scaler.inverse_transform(train_predict)

test_predict = scaler.inverse_transform(test_predict)

test_predict

Output:

array([[194.84602],

[501.15582],

[289.13095],

...,

[420.15256],

[502.0417],

[303.7021]], dtype=float32)

Let us calculate the Root Mean Squared Error (RMSE) for both training and testing predictions to evaluate the model's performance.

Code:

train_rmse = math.sqrt(mean_squared_error(y_train, train_predict))

test_rmse = math.sqrt(mean_squared_error(y_test, test_predict))

Time Series Forecasting - DL Approach

```
print(f"Train RMSE: {train_rmse}, Test RMSE: {test_rmse}")
```

Output:

Train RMSE: 346.6493006673652, Test RMSE: 341.3032681988748

A train RMSE of 326.43 and a test RMSE of 341.30 explain how much the model deviates from the actual values on average. This is also an indicator of how well the model is likely to perform on unseen data in practice. The magnitude of the RMSE values should be considered relative to the scale of the `Units Sold`. If the average number of units sold is in the thousands, an RMSE of around 341 to 346 may be relatively small. However, if the average units sold are lower, this could be a significant error. Since the train and test RMSE values are close, it suggests that the model is generalizing well.

Let us finally plot the results of the model using the following code:

Code:

```
train_predict_plot = np.empty_like(df_scaled)

train_predict_plot[:, :] = np.nan

train_predict_plot[ts:len(train_predict)+ts, :] = train_predict

test_predict_plot = np.empty_like(df_scaled)

test_predict_plot[:, :] = np.nan

test_predict_plot[len(train_predict)+(ts):len(df_scaled)-1, :] = test_predict
```

In the preceding code, we have prepared the train and test data in the format required for visual representation. Following this, let us proceed to create the code for plotting the data to show the comparison between predicted versus actual datasets.

Code:

```
plt.figure(figsize=(12,6))

plt.plot(scaler.inverse_transform(df_scaled), label='Actual Units Sold')

plt.plot(train_predict_plot, label='Train Predict')

plt.plot(test_predict_plot, label='Test Predict')

plt.title('Units Sold Prediction')
```

```
plt.xlabel('Time')

plt.ylabel('Units Sold')

plt.legend()

plt.show()
```

The output of the plot is displayed as follows:

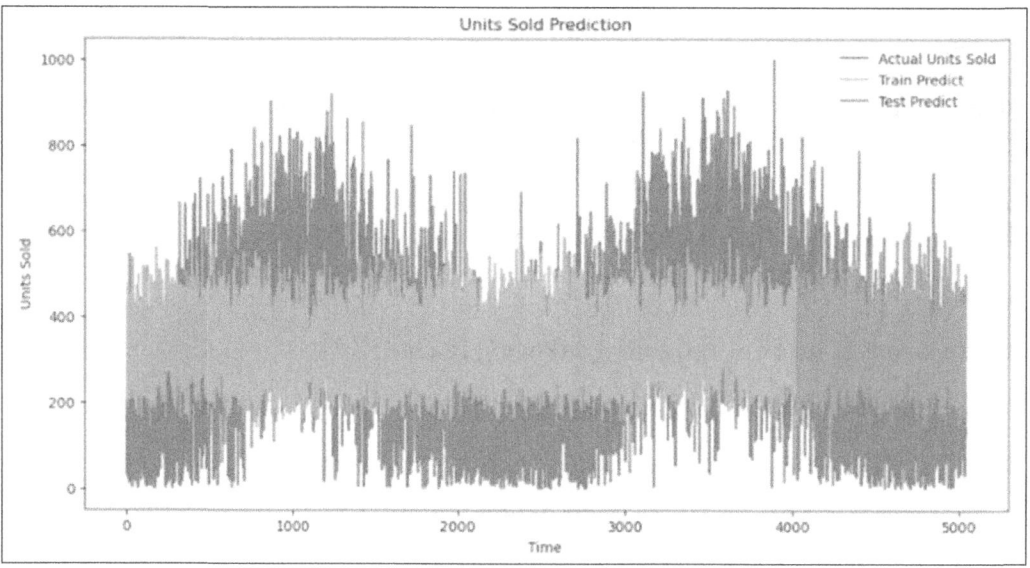

Figure 8.1: Actual vs. Predicted – LSTM

The preceding plot represents the predicted vs. actual values of the model. Orange lines indicate the train prediction, while green lines indicate the test prediction. Blue lines indicate the actual values of the data. The gap between the blue and orange lines is more pronounced in certain areas compared to others. Wherever the gap is smaller, the predictions are better.

With this understanding, let us proceed to create a library capable of performing common tasks across multiple deep learning models.

Developing a Deep Learning-Based Approach for Time Series Forecasting

In this section, we will create a common approach and a set of functions that can be applied to time series data to forecast future values using various deep learning algorithms.

The flow of various operations or functions in this approach is represented in *Figure 8.2*:

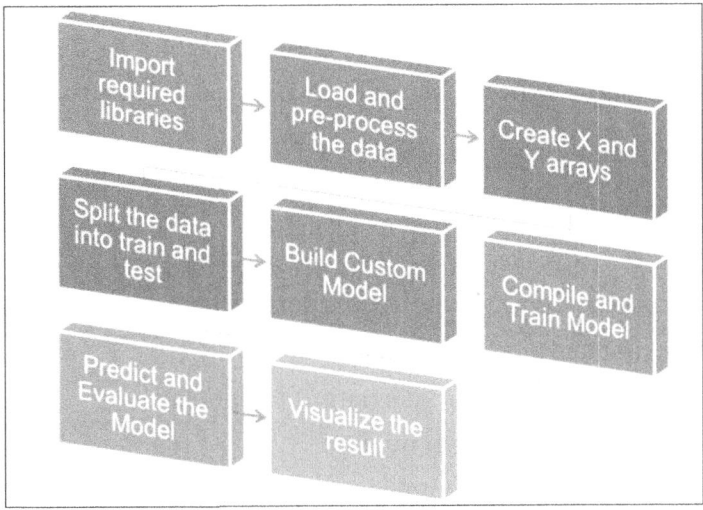

Figure 8.2: *Process flow for a deep learning-based approach*

To begin with, let us import the common libraries that will be needed to define the functions for this approach. The following libraries will be imported:

- `Pandas` will be used for data manipulation and analysis.
- `Numpy` will be used to add support for large, multi-dimensional arrays and matrices, along with a large collection of high-level mathematical functions to operate on these arrays.
- `Math` will be used for mathematical computations.
- `Matplotlib` will be used to provide plotting capabilities for creating static, animated, and interactive visualizations in Python.
- `Sklearn.preprocessing` will be used for data normalization.
- `Sklearn.model_selection` will be used for splitting the dataset into training and testing sets.
- `Sklearn.metrics` will be used to compute the mean squared error.
- `Tensorflow.keras.optimizers` will be used to include Adam optimizer for the Tensorflow models.

Code:

```
import pandas as pd
import numpy as np
```

```
import math
from sklearn.preprocessing import MinMaxScaler
from sklearn.model_selection import train_test_split
from tensorflow.keras.optimizers import Adam
from sklearn.metrics import mean_squared_error
import matplotlib.pyplot as plt
```

In the next step, we will develop a function to load and preprocess the data, named **load_and_preprocess_data**. This function performs the following operations:

1. Load the data as a CSV file.
2. Convert the date into Pandas datetime data type.
3. Sort the values in the data by date.
4. Create a new DataFrame named **df** with the target column.
5. Normalize the data using **MinMaxScaler**.
6. Return the scaled data and the scaler.

The parameters of **load_and_preprocess_data** are:

- **file_path**: This parameter is used to provide the input data file.
- **date_col**: This parameter is used to provide the date column as input.
- **target_col**: This parameter is used to provide the target column as input.

Code:

```
def load_and_preprocess_data(file_path, date_col, target_col):
    data = pd.read_csv(file_path)
    data[date_col] = pd.to_datetime(data[date_col])
    data.sort_values(date_col, inplace=True)
    df = data[[target_col]]
    scaler = MinMaxScaler(feature_range=(0, 1))
    df_scaled = scaler.fit_transform(df)
    return df_scaled, scaler
```

In the next step, let us create a function named **create_XY**. This function performs the following operations:

Time Series Forecasting - DL Approach

1. Create two arrays – X and Y.
2. Create sequences of Product Sales data X and the corresponding next value to predict Y using a time step.

The parameters of **create_XY** are:
- **data**: This parameter is used to provide the input data that is scaled and output from `load_and_preprocess_data`.
- **ts**: This parameter is used to provide the number of time steps for feature creation.

Code:

```
def create_XY(data, ts=1):
    X, Y = [], []
    for i in range(len(data) - ts - 1):
        a = data[i:(i + ts), 0]
        X.append(a)
        Y.append(data[i + ts, 0])
    return np.array(X), np.array(Y)
```

In the next step, let us define another function, **split_data**, that performs the following operations:

1. Split the data into train 80% and test 20%.
2. Reshape the data into samples, time steps, and features so that it can be provided as input to the model.

The parameters of **split_data** are:
- **X**: Independent variable
- **Y**: Target variable

Code:

```
def split_data(X, Y):
    X_train, X_test, y_train, y_test = train_test_split(X, Y, test_size=0.2, random_state=42)
    X_train = X_train.reshape(X_train.shape[0], X_train.shape[1], 1)
    X_test = X_test.reshape(X_test.shape[0], X_test.shape[1], 1)
```

```
    return X_train, X_test, y_train, y_test
```

In the next step, let us create a function named **compile_and_train** that performs the following operations:

1. Compile the model with Adam as the optimizer with a learning rate of 0.001 and the loss function as **mean_squared_error**.
2. Fit the model on the data and return the model.

The parameters of **compile_and_train** are:

- **model**: The deep learning model will be provided as input.
- **X_train**: The X variable from the training set.
- **y_train**: The y variable from the training set.
- **X_test**: The X variable from the test set.
- **y_test**: The y variable from the test set.
- **epochs**: The number of epochs for training.
- **batch_size**: The input batch size for training.

Code:

```
def compile_and_train(model, X_train, y_train, X_test, y_test, epochs=100, batch_size=64):
    model.compile(optimizer=Adam(learning_rate=0.001), loss='mean_squared_error')
    model.fit(X_train, y_train, validation_data=(X_test, y_test), epochs=epochs, batch_size=batch_size, verbose=1)
    return model
```

In the next step, let us define another function, **predict_evaluate_model**, that performs the following operations:

1. Predict the target variable.
2. Inverse transform the predicted data.
3. Calculate root mean squared error.
4. Return the prediction and RMSE.

The parameters of **predict_evaluate_model** are:

- **model**: The compiled and trained deep learning model will be provided as input.
- **X**: The independent variable from data.

Time Series Forecasting - DL Approach

- **Y**: The target variable from data.
- **scaler**: The `scaler` function from `load_and_preprocess_data`.

Code:

```
def predict_evaluate_model(model, X, y, scaler):
    predict = model.predict(X)
    predict = scaler.inverse_transform(predict)
    rmse = math.sqrt(mean_squared_error(y, predict))
    return predict, rmse
```

Let us now define the function `plot_predictions`, which performs the following operations:

1. Get the train and test predictions data in the required format.
2. Create a plot that compares Actual data with Train and Test predictions.

The parameters of `plot_predictions` are:

- **df_scaled**: The actual values of the target variable.
- **train_predict**: The predictions from the train dataset.
- **test_predict**: The predictions from the test dataset.
- **title**: The title of the plot.

Code:

```
def  plot_predictions(df_scaled,   train_predict,   test_predict,
title='Prediction'):
    train_predict_plot = np.empty_like(df_scaled)
    train_predict_plot[:, :] = np.nan
    train_predict_plot[ts:len(train_predict)+ts, :] = train_predict

    test_predict_plot = np.empty_like(df_scaled)
    test_predict_plot[:, :] = np.nan
    test_predict_plot[len(train_predict)+(ts):len(df_scaled)-1, :] = test_predict
```

```
plt.figure(figsize=(12,6))
plt.plot(scaler.inverse_transform(df_scaled), label='Actual')
plt.plot(train_predict_plot, label='Train Predict')
plt.plot(test_predict_plot, label='Test Predict')
plt.title(title)
plt.xlabel('Time')
plt.ylabel('Value')
plt.legend()
plt.show()
```

With these steps, we have defined all the functions needed to apply various deep learning models to the time series data.

In the next section, let us start by applying the GRU algorithm to the Product Sales data using this approach.

Applying Gated Recurrent Units

Gated Recurrent Units (GRUs) is another deep learning algorithm that is also suitable for handling sequential data. It is a variation of recurrent neural networks (RNN).

The core components of GRUs include the following:

- **Update Gate**: This is the component that determines how much of the past information needs to be passed along to the future and also helps the model to decide whether to keep or discard information from the past.
- **Reset Gate**: This component helps the model to decide how much of the past information to forget based on scenarios where the relevance of past information diminishes over time.

The fundamental concepts of Gated Recurrent Units (GRUs) were introduced by Kyunghyun Cho, Bart van Merrienboer, Caglar Gulcehre, Dzmitry Bahdanau, Fethi Bougares, Holger Schwenk, and Yoshua Bengio in the paper titled *Learning Phrase Representations using RNN Encoder-Decoder for Statistical Machine Translation*. The authors in this paper extended the concept of RNN by handling the vanishing gradient problem and at the same time simplifying the network so that it is simpler than LSTM.

Library Documentation

The model documentation and parameters for GRUs are available in the TensorFlow documentation at:

https://www.tensorflow.org/api_docs/python/tf/keras/layers/GRU

GRU in the TensorFlow library has the following structure and parameters:

```
tf.keras.layers.GRU(
    units,
    activation='tanh',
    recurrent_activation='sigmoid',
    use_bias=True,
    kernel_initializer='glorot_uniform',
    recurrent_initializer='orthogonal',
    bias_initializer='zeros',
    kernel_regularizer=None,
    recurrent_regularizer=None,
    bias_regularizer=None,
    activity_regularizer=None,
    kernel_constraint=None,
    recurrent_constraint=None,
    bias_constraint=None,
    dropout=0.0,
    recurrent_dropout=0.0,
    return_sequences=False,
    return_state=False,
    go_backwards=False,
```

```
        stateful=False,
        unroll=False,
        time_major=False,
        reset_after=True,
        **kwargs
)
```

The parameters of the model as described in the library are as follows:

- **units**: This parameter is used to input a positive integer denoting the dimensionality of the output space.
- **activation**: This parameter is used to input a function name that denotes the Activation function to use.
- **use_bias**: This parameter is used to determine if a bias vector needs to be used in a model layer.
- **kernel_initializer**: This parameter is used to provide a kernel initializer for the model inputs.
- **recurrent_initializer**: This parameter is used to provide a kernel initializer for the recurrent states of the model.
- **bias_initializer**: This parameter is used to provide an initializer for the bias vector of the model.
- **kernel_regularizer**: This parameter is used to input the kernel regularizer function for the model.
- **recurrent_regularizer**: This parameter is used to input the recurrent regularizer function for the model.
- **bias_regularizer**: This parameter is used to input the bias regularizer function for the model.
- **activity_regularizer**: This parameter is used to input the activity regularizer function for the model.
- **kernel_constraint**: This parameter is used to input the kernel constraint function for the model.
- **recurrent_constraint**: This parameter is used to input the recurrent constraint function for the model.
- **bias_constraint**: This parameter is used to input the bias constraint function for the model.

- **dropout**: This parameter is used to input a value that determines the number of units that need to be dropped at the input state.
- **recurrent_dropout**: This parameter is used to input a value that determines the number of units that need to be dropped at the recurrent state.
- **return_sequences**: This parameter is used to determine the sequences that need to be provided in the output.
- **return_state**: This parameter is used to determine the states that need to be provided in the output.
- **go_backwards**: This parameter is used to determine the direction in which the input sequence needs to be processed by the model.
- **stateful**: This parameter is used to determine if the previous state needs to be used in the next state in the model.
- **unroll**: This parameter is used to input a boolean value that determines if the network needs to be unrolled.
- **time_major**: This parameter is used to determine the shape format of the inputs and outputs tensors.
- **reset_after**: This parameter is used to input the GRU convention.

For more details and understanding of the parameters, refer to the TensorFlow documentation.

Let us now proceed with the implementation of GRUs on the time series data.

Application of GRU on the Time Series Data

In this example, we will be forecasting the **Units Sold** variable from **ProductSalesData**.

Let us start by importing the GRU and Dense classes from the TensorFlow library along with the Sequential class.

Code:

```
from tensorflow.keras.models import Sequential

from tensorflow.keras.layers import GRU, Dense
```

In this example, we will create the sequential layers needed for the GRU model as a reusable function that performs the following operations:

1. Create a model variable to add **sequential** layers to it.
2. Add the first layer as **GRU** with the required parameters and input shape.

3. Add the second layer as GRU again.
4. Add the third layer as Dense with the required parameters.
5. Add the fourth layer as Dense with an output shape of 1.
6. Return the model.

Code:

```
def build_gru_model(input_shape, units=50, dense_units=25):
    model = Sequential()
    model.add(GRU(units, return_sequences=True, input_shape=input_shape))
    model.add(GRU(units))
    model.add(Dense(dense_units))
    model.add(Dense(1))
    return model
```

These layers can be increased or decreased based on the accuracy of the model results and the availability of computation power and resources needed to develop these models.

From the next step onwards, let us start using the functions that we developed in this chapter to implement the deep learning approach as a library.

In this step, let us load and process the data by calling the function **load_and_preprocess_data**.

Code:

```
df_scaled, scaler = load_and_preprocess_data('ProductSalesData.csv', 'Date', 'Units Sold')
```

In the next step, let us set the time step and create X and Y input by calling the function **create_XY**.

Code:

```
ts = 3
X, Y = create_XY(df_scaled, ts=ts)
```

In the next step, let us split the data into train and test by calling the function **split_data**.

Time Series Forecasting - DL Approach

Code:

X_train, X_test, y_train, y_test = split_data(X, Y)

Let us further call the GRU model, compile and train it on the data.

Code:

```
model = build_gru_model(input_shape=(3, 1))
model = compile_and_train(model, X_train, y_train, X_test, y_test)
```

Output:

```
Epoch 1/100
63/63 [==============================] - 4s 15ms/step - loss: 0.0384 - val_loss: 0.0285
Epoch 2/100
63/63 [==============================] - 0s 7ms/step - loss: 0.0295 - val_loss: 0.0284
Epoch 3/100
63/63 [==============================] - 0s 7ms/step - loss: 0.0295 - val_loss: 0.0284
...
Epoch 98/100
63/63 [==============================] - 0s 7ms/step - loss: 0.0293 - val_loss: 0.0285
Epoch 99/100
63/63 [==============================] - 0s 7ms/step - loss: 0.0294 - val_loss: 0.0284
Epoch 100/100
63/63 [==============================] - 0s 6ms/step - loss: 0.0293 - val_loss: 0.0283
```

Let us further review the layers in the model summary.

Code:

```
model.summary()
```

Output:

Model: "sequential_2"

Layer (type)	Output Shape	Param #
gru_2 (GRU)	(None, 3, 50)	7950
gru_3 (GRU)	(None, 50)	15300
dense_4 (Dense)	(None, 25)	1275
dense_5 (Dense)	(None, 1)	26

Total params: 24,551

Trainable params: 24,551

Non-trainable params: 0

Each layer, its dimensions, and the number of parameters are described in the preceding model summary.

In the next steps, let us predict and evaluate the model by calling the function **predict_evaluate_model**.

Code:

```
train_predict, train_rmse = predict_evaluate_model(model, X_train, y_train, scaler)

test_predict, test_rmse = predict_evaluate_model(model, X_test, y_test, scaler)
```

Output:

126/126 [==============================] - 1s 1ms/step 32/32 [==============================] - 0s 2ms/step

The RMSE values of train and test are as follows:

Code:

print(f"Train RMSE: {train_rmse}, Test RMSE: {test_rmse}")

Output:

Train RMSE: 353.5960839158617, Test RMSE: 346.95032073793726

A train RMSE of 353.59 and a test RMSE of 346.95 explain how much of the model deviates from the actual values on average. This is also an indicator of how well the model is likely to perform on unseen data in practice. The magnitude of the RMSE values should be considered relative to the scale of the Units Sold. If the average number of units sold is in the thousands, an RMSE of around 346 to 353 may be relatively small. However, if the average units sold are lower, this could be a significant error. Since the train and test RMSE values are close, it suggests that the model is generalizing well.

In the final step, let us visualize the predictions vs. actual values by calling the function **plot_predictions**.

Code:

plot_predictions(df_scaled, train_predict, test_predict, 'Units Sold Prediction')

The output of the plot is displayed as follows:

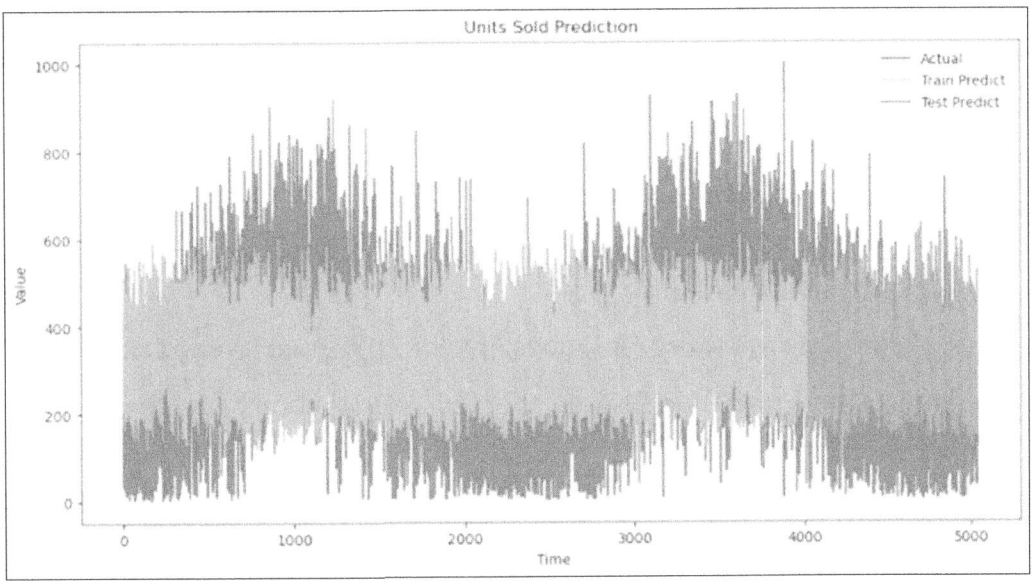

Figure 8.3: Actual vs. Predicted - GRU

The preceding plot represents the predicted vs. actual values of the model. Orange lines indicate the train prediction, while green lines indicate the test prediction. Blue lines indicate the actual values of the data. The gap between the blue and orange lines is more pronounced in certain areas compared to others. Wherever the gap is smaller, the predictions are better, similar to LSTM.

With this understanding, let us further explore an application of Convolutional Neural Networks.

Applying Convolutional Neural Networks

Convolutional Neural Networks (CNN) algorithm is widely used for applications involving image classification problems. However, CNN can also be extended to time series forecasting by creating the features in a suitable spatial pattern that can be processed by this algorithm.

CNNs use convolutional layers to automatically and adaptively learn spatial hierarchies of features from time series data and its corresponding time steps. This can be used to detect patterns in the data such as trends, seasonality, and cycles, which are crucial for accurate forecasting. CNNs use pooling layers to reduce time steps in the time series data. This in turn helps in reducing the computational load and also in extracting higher-level, more abstract features.

The fundamental concept of CNNs originated from a series of works, but the foundational idea is most commonly attributed to a paper by Yann LeCun et al. from 1998, titled *Gradient-Based Learning Applied to Document Recognition*. This paper is widely recognized for popularizing the use of CNNs in the field of machine learning, especially for image recognition tasks.

Library Documentation

The model documentation and parameters for CNNs are available in the TensorFlow documentation at:

https://www.tensorflow.org/api_docs/python/tf/keras/layers/Conv1D

The base class Conv1D for CNN in the TensorFlow library has the following structure and parameters:

```
tf.keras.layers.Conv1D(
    filters,
    kernel_size,
```

Time Series Forecasting - DL Approach

```
    strides=1,
    padding='valid',
    data_format='channels_last',
    dilation_rate=1,
    groups=1,
    activation=None,
    use_bias=True,
    kernel_initializer='glorot_uniform',
    bias_initializer='zeros',
    kernel_regularizer=None,
    bias_regularizer=None,
    activity_regularizer=None,
    kernel_constraint=None,
    bias_constraint=None,
    **kwargs
)
```

The parameters of the model as described in the library are as follows:
- **filters**: This parameter is used to input the dimensionality of the output space.
- **kernel_size**: This parameter is used to input kernel size for the model.
- **strides**: This parameter is used to input the stride length of the convolution.
- **padding**: This parameter is used to input the padding for the input data.
- **data_format**: This parameter is used to input the ordering of the dimensions in the inputs.
- **dilation_rate**: This parameter is used to input the dilation rate for the model.
- **groups**: This parameter is used to determine the number of groups required to split the inputs in the model development process.

- **activation**: This parameter is used to input a function name that denotes the Activation function to use.
- **use_bias**: This parameter is used to determine if a bias vector needs to be used in a model layer.
- **kernel_initializer**: This parameter is used to provide a kernel initializer for the model inputs.
- **bias_initializer**: This parameter is used to provide an initializer for the bias vector of the model.
- **kernel_regularizer**: This parameter is used to input the kernel **regularizer** function for the model.
- **bias_regularizer**: This parameter is used to input the bias **regularizer** function for the model.
- **activity_regularizer**: This parameter is used to input the activity **regularizer** function for the model.
- **kernel_constraint**: This parameter is used to input the kernel constraint function for the model.
- **bias_constraint**: This parameter is used to input the bias constraint function for the model.

For more details and understanding of the parameters, refer to the TensorFlow documentation.

Let us now proceed with the implementation of CNNs on the time series data.

Application of CNN on the time series data

In this example, we will be forecasting the **Units Sold** variable from **ProductSalesData**.

Let us start by importing the **Conv1D**, **MaxPooling1D**, **Flatten**, and **Dense** classes from the TensorFlow library along with the Sequential class.

Code:

from tensorflow.keras.models import import Sequential

from tensorflow.keras.layers import Conv1D, MaxPooling1D, Flatten, Dense

In this example, we will create the sequential layers needed for the CNN model as a reusable function that performs the following operations:

1. Create a model variable to add sequential layers to it.

2. Add the first layer as `Conv1D` with the required parameters and input shape.
3. Add the second layer as `MaxPooling1D` with the required parameters.
4. Add the third layer as `Flatten` with the required parameters.
5. Add the fourth layer as `Dense` with the required parameters.
6. Add the fifth layer as `Dense` with an output shape of 1.
7. Return the model.

Code:

```
def build_cnn_model(filters=64, kernel_size=2, activation='relu', dense_units = 50, time_step = 3, pool_size=2):
    model = Sequential()
    model.add(Conv1D(filters=filters, kernel_size=kernel_size, activation=activation, input_shape=(time_step, 1)))
    model.add(MaxPooling1D(pool_size=pool_size))
    model.add(Flatten())
    model.add(Dense(dense_units, activation=activation))
    model.add(Dense(1))
    return model
```

These layers can be increased or decreased based on the accuracy of the model results and the availability of computation power and resources needed to develop these models.

From the next step onwards, let us start using the functions that we developed in this chapter to implement the deep learning approach as a library.

In this step, let us load and process the data by calling the function `load_and_preprocess_data`.

Code:

```
df_scaled, scaler = load_and_preprocess_data('ProductSalesData.csv', 'Date', 'Units Sold')
```

In the next step, let us set the time step and create X and Y input by calling the function `create_XY`.

Code:

```
ts = 3
X, Y = create_XY(df_scaled, ts=ts)
```

In the next step, let us split the data into train and test by calling the function **split_data**.

Code:

```
X_train, X_test, y_train, y_test = split_data(X, Y)
```

Let us further call the CNN model, compile and train it on the data:

Code:

```
model = build_cnn_model(filters=64, kernel_size=2, activation='relu', dense_units = 50, time_step = 3, pool_size=2)
model = compile_and_train(model, X_train, y_train, X_test, y_test)
```

Output:

```
Epoch 1/100
63/63 [==============================] - 1s 3ms/step - loss: 0.0455 - val_loss: 0.0293
Epoch 2/100
63/63 [==============================] - 0s 2ms/step - loss: 0.0299 - val_loss: 0.0286
Epoch 3/100
63/63 [==============================] - 0s 3ms/step - loss: 0.0298 - val_loss: 0.0287
...
Epoch 98/100
63/63 [==============================] - 0s 2ms/step - loss: 0.0292 - val_loss: 0.0293
Epoch 99/100
63/63 [==============================] - 0s 2ms/step - loss: 0.0291 - val_loss: 0.0286
```

```
Epoch 100/100

63/63 [==============================] - 0s 2ms/step - loss: 0.0290 - val_loss: 0.0291
```

Let us further review the layers in the model summary.

Code:

```
model.summary()
```

Output:

Model: "sequential_2"

Layer (type)	Output Shape	Param #
conv1d (Conv1D)	(None, 2, 64)	192
max_pooling1d (MaxPooling1D)	(None, 1, 64)	0
flatten (Flatten)	(None, 64)	0
dense_4 (Dense)	(None, 50)	3250
dense_5 (Dense)	(None, 1)	51

Total params: 3,493

Trainable params: 3,493

Non-trainable params: 0

Each layer, its dimensions, and the number of parameters are described in the preceding model summary.

In the next steps, let us predict and evaluate the model by calling the function **predict_evaluate_model**.

Code:

```
train_predict, train_rmse = predict_evaluate_model(model, X_train, y_train, scaler)

test_predict, test_rmse = predict_evaluate_model(model, X_test, y_test, scaler)
```

Output:

```
126/126 [==============================] - 0s 859us/step
32/32 [==============================] - 0s 971us/step
```

The RMSE values of train and test are as follows:

Code:

```
print(f"Train RMSE: {train_rmse}, Test RMSE: {test_rmse}")
```

Output:

```
Train RMSE: 358.1935285787368, Test RMSE: 352.81608347385327
```

A train RMSE of 358.19 and a test RMSE of 352.81 explain how much of the model deviates from the actual values on average. This is also an indicator of how well the model is likely to perform on unseen data in practice. The magnitude of the RMSE values should be considered relative to the scale of the Units Sold. If the average number of units sold is in the thousands, an RMSE of around 352 to 358 may be relatively small. However, if the average units sold are lower, this could be a significant error. Since the train and test RMSE values are close, it suggests that the model is generalizing well.

In the final step, let us visualize the predictions vs. actual values by calling the function **plot_predictions**.

Code:

```
plot_predictions(df_scaled, train_predict, test_predict, 'Units Sold Prediction')
```

The output of the plot is displayed as follows:

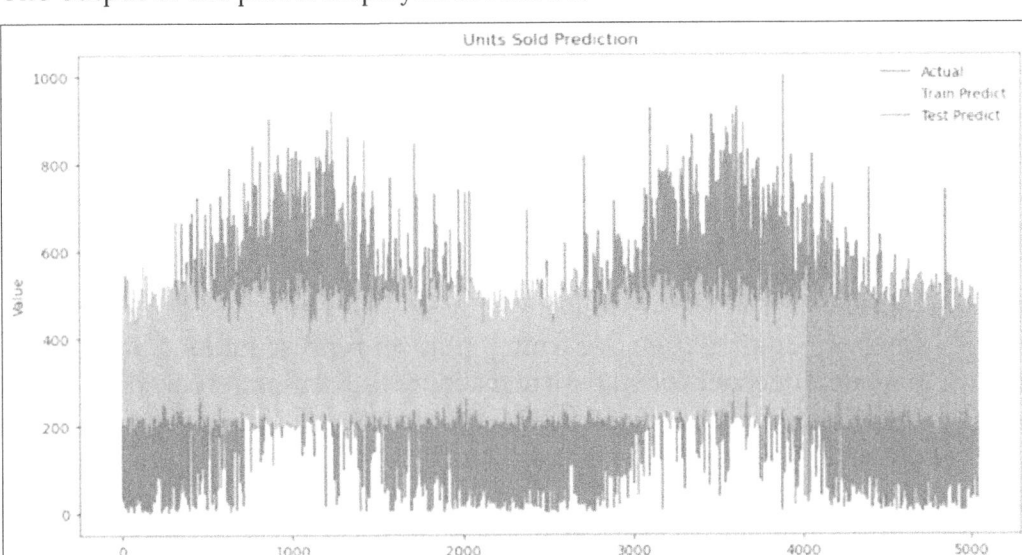

Figure 8.4: Actual vs. Predicted – CNN

The preceding plot represents the predicted vs. actual values of the model. Orange lines indicate the train prediction, while green lines indicate the test prediction. Blue lines indicate the actual values of the data. The gap between the blue and orange lines is more pronounced in certain areas compared to others. Wherever the gap is smaller, the predictions are better, similar to GRU.

These are some of the deep learning algorithms that can be used to predict future values of univariate time series data.

Conclusion

In this chapter, we have learned about various deep learning algorithms that can be used in forecasting future data for a time series.

We also explored the parameters, documentation, and examples of understanding Long Short-Term Memory (LSTM) networks.

Additionally, we developed a generic library with functions that can be reused for the application of various deep learning algorithms on the time series data. We also explored the Gated Recurrent Units (GRUs) for predicting time series data.

We also explored the Convolutional Neural Networks (CNN) for predicting time series data.

In the next chapter, we will delve into applying a few more machine learning algorithms to forecast future values on multiple time series data.

References

- Hochreiter, S. and Schmidhuber, J. (1997) 'Long short-term memory', Neural Computation, 9(8), pp. 1735–1780. doi:10.1162/neco.1997.9.8.1735.
- Cho, K. et al. (2014) 'Learning phrase representations using RNN encoder–decoder for statistical machine translation', Proceedings of the 2014 Conference on Empirical Methods in Natural Language Processing (EMNLP) [Preprint]. doi:10.3115/v1/d14-1179.
- Tf.keras.layers.LSTM: tensorflow V2.14.0 (no date) TensorFlow. Available at: https://www.tensorflow.org/api_docs/python/tf/keras/layers/LSTM (Accessed: 10 December 2023).
- Tf.keras.layers.GRU: tensorflow V2.14.0 (no date) TensorFlow. Available at: https://www.tensorflow.org/api_docs/python/tf/keras/layers/GRU (Accessed: 10 December 2023).
- TF.KERAS.LAYERS.CONV1D: tensorflow V2.14.0 (no date) TensorFlow. Available at: https://www.tensorflow.org/api_docs/python/tf/keras/layers/Conv1D (Accessed: 10 December 2023).

CHAPTER 9
Multivariate Time Series, Metrics, and Validation

We have entered the last chapter of this book, which will cover a few more important topics related to time series analysis and forecasting. The various examples and applications covered throughout this book involved univariate time series data and algorithms that can be applied to forecast future time series values on such data.

In this chapter, we will explore various algorithms that can be applied to multivariate time series data and their corresponding examples on a simulated multivariate dataset. We will further explore some of the common validation metrics that can be applied to both univariate and multivariate forecasting problems.

Structure

In this chapter, the following topics will be covered:
- Understanding Vector AutoRegression
- Applying Vector Error Correction Model
- Understanding VARMAX
- Metrics for Time Series

Data Introduction

Throughout this chapter, we will be using one dataset, and a single variable from the dataset will be focused on forecasting future values based on various multivariate forecasting algorithms that support time series data. The dataset used for this section is synthetically generated data developed to illustrate the examples in this chapter, and the data is available in the GitHub repository:

https://raw.githubusercontent.com/OrangeAVA/Time-Series-Analysis-and-Forecasting-with-Python/main/WeatherData.csv

The dataset has the following variables:

- **Unnamed: 0**: This is an index column. It doesn't contain meaningful data but is a unique identifier for each row. This field can be deleted during data preprocessing.
- **Date**: This represents the date for each observation. The data starts from January 1, 1970.
- **Temperature (Min)** and **Temperature (Max)**: These columns show the minimum and maximum temperatures recorded on each day. Values for Temperature (Min) are from 16 to 20 Celsius. Values for Temperature (Max) are from 28 to 38 Celsius.
- **Pressure**: This is the atmospheric pressure. Values are from 700 to 1000 hPa.
- **Direction of Wind**: This column indicates the direction from which the wind is coming. Values are **NorthEast**, **NorthWest**, **SouthEast**, and **SouthWest**.
- **Velocity of Wind**: This column indicates the speed of the wind. Values are from 0.5 to 65 Knots.
- **Humidity**: This column represents the relative humidity. Values are from 0% to 100%.
- **Carbon Monoxide**: This column is the concentration of carbon monoxide in the air. Values are from 0 to 1 ppm.
- **UV Rays**: This column indicates the intensity of ultraviolet radiation. The values are from 0 to 2.
- **Intensity of Light**: This column measures the light intensity. The values are from 10000 to 25000 lux.
- **Clouds**: This column describes the type of clouds observed. Values are ['Cirrus', 'Cirrostratus', 'Cirrocumulus', 'Altostratus', 'Altocumulus',

'Stratus', 'Stratocumulus', 'Nimbostratus', 'Cumulus: Fluffy', 'Cumulonimbus', 'Lenticular Clouds', 'Mammatus Clouds', 'Contrails']

- **Rainfall**: This column defines the amount of rainfall measured. Values are from 0 to 100 mm/h.

These are the various attributes of the dataset that will be used for the examples in this chapter.

Understanding Vector AutoRegression

Vector AutoRegression (VAR) is a statistical model used for time series forecasting, especially when multivariate time series data is available. VAR is a generalization of the AutoRegressive (AR) model and extends to multivariate data.

Lags are important features of VAR. Lags are the previous time points of the variables in the dataset. A VAR model predicts the future values of multiple time series using the past values of all the series in the system. In a VAR model, each variable will have an equation that describes its evolution based on its own lags and the lags of all the other variables in the model. The number of lags used is called the order of the VAR model. The effectiveness of the VAR model depends on careful selection of variables, correct specification of lag order, and appropriate handling of stationarity issues.

The fundamental concept of VAR was possibly introduced by economist Christopher A. Sims in his seminal paper titled "*Macroeconomics and Reality*," published in 1980. This paper marked a significant shift in macroeconomic analysis and time series econometrics. The VAR model allows each variable in a multivariate time series to be a linear function of past values of itself and past values of all other variables in the model, without requiring strict theoretical restrictions.

Library Documentation

The model documentation and parameters for the VAR model are available in the `statsmodels` documentation at:

https://www.statsmodels.org/dev/generated/statsmodels.tsa.vector_ar.var_model.VAR.html#statsmodels.tsa.vector_ar.var_model.VAR

VAR in the statsmodels library has the following class structure and parameters:

```
class statsmodels.tsa.vector_ar.var_model.VAR
(
```

```
    endog,

    exog=None,

    dates=None,

    freq=None,

    missing='none'
)
```

The parameters of the model as described in the library are as follows:

- **endogarray_like**: This parameter is used to input the 2-d endogenous response variable, which is an independent variable.
- **exogarray_like**: This parameter is used to input the 2-d exogenous variable.
- **datesarray_like**: This parameter is used to input the must match number of rows of endog.

For more details and understanding of the parameters, refer to the statsmodels documentation.

Let us now proceed with the implementation of VAR on multivariate time series data.

Application of VAR on Time Series Data

In this example, we will be demonstrating how to use a Vector AutoRegression (VAR) model for time series forecasting of WeatherData.csv.

Let us start by importing the following libraries needed for this example:

Code:

```
import pandas as pd

import numpy as np

from statsmodels.tsa.api import VAR

from statsmodels.tsa.stattools import adfuller

from statsmodels.tools.eval_measures import rmse
```

In the next step, let us load the dataset and set the **Date** column as the index, parsing it as date objects. Take the first 1000 records from the data.

Code:

```
df = pd.read_csv('WeatherData.csv', index_col='Date', parse_dates=['Date'])
df = df.head(1000)
```

Let us further process the data by dropping the unnecessary column **Unnamed: 0** and converting the categorical variables, **Direction of Wind**, **Clouds**, into dummy or indicator variables. This step is necessary because VAR models require numerical input.

Code:

```
df.drop(columns = 'Unnamed: 0', inplace = True)
df = pd.get_dummies(df, columns=['Direction of Wind', 'Clouds'], drop_first=True)
```

In the next step, let us define a function called **check_stationarity** to test each time series in the dataset for stationarity using the Augmented Dickey-Fuller test. If the p-value is greater than 0.05, the series is considered non-stationary.

Code:

```
def check_stationarity(series):
    result = adfuller(series)
    if result[1] > 0.05:
        print(f"{series.name} is not stationary")
    else:
        print(f"{series.name} is stationary")


for column in df.columns:
    check_stationarity(df[column])
```

Output:

```
Temperature (Min) is not stationary
Temperature (Max) is not stationary
Pressure is stationary
```

```
Velocity of Wind is not stationary

Humidity is stationary

Carbon Monoxide is stationary

UV Rays is not stationary

Intensity of Light is not stationary

Rainfall is not stationary

Direction of Wind_NorthWest is stationary

Direction of Wind_SouthEast is stationary

Direction of Wind_SouthWest is stationary

Clouds_Altostratus is stationary

Clouds_Cirrocumulus is stationary

Clouds_Cirrostratus is stationary

Clouds_Cirrus is stationary

Clouds_Contrails is stationary

Clouds_Cumulonimbus is stationary

Clouds_Cumulus: Fluffy is stationary

Clouds_Lenticular Clouds is stationary

Clouds_Mammatus Clouds is stationary

Clouds_Nimbostratus is stationary

Clouds_Stratocumulus is stationary

Clouds_Stratus is stationary
```

The output of this function provides the list of features with its corresponding stationarity indicators.

Let us now make the data stationary by differencing it and rechecking the values of the dataset.

Code:

```
df = df.diff().dropna()
```

```
for column in df.columns:
    check_stationarity(df[column])
```

Output:

```
Temperature (Min) is stationary
Temperature (Max) is stationary
Pressure is stationary
Velocity of Wind is stationary
Humidity is stationary
Carbon Monoxide is stationary
UV Rays is stationary
Intensity of Light is stationary
Rainfall is not stationary
Direction of Wind_NorthWest is stationary
Direction of Wind_SouthEast is stationary
Direction of Wind_SouthWest is stationary
Clouds_Altostratus is stationary
Clouds_Cirrocumulus is stationary
Clouds_Cirrostratus is stationary
Clouds_Cirrus is stationary
Clouds_Contrails is stationary
Clouds_Cumulonimbus is stationary
Clouds_Cumulus: Fluffy is stationary
Clouds_Lenticular Clouds is stationary
Clouds_Mammatus Clouds is stationary
Clouds_Nimbostratus is stationary
Clouds_Stratocumulus is stationary
Clouds_Stratus is stationary
```

In this step, let us initialize a **VAR** model with the first 990 records of the dataset.

Code:

```
model = VAR(df.iloc[0:989])
```

Let us further determine the optimal number of lags, up to a maximum of, for the VAR model based on various criteria like AIC, BIC, FPE, and HQIC.

Code:

```
lag_order = model.select_order(maxlags=5)

print(lag_order.summary())
```

Output:

```
VAR Order Selection (* highlights the minimums)
=====================================================
         AIC        BIC        FPE        HQIC
-----------------------------------------------------
0       67.18      67.30*     1.504e+29   67.23
1       65.01      67.99      1.713e+28   66.14*
2       64.45      70.30      9.812e+27   66.68
3       64.42*     73.13      9.538e+27*  67.73
4       64.55      76.12      1.098e+28   68.95
5       64.78      79.22      1.401e+28   70.27
-----------------------------------------------------
```

The VAR Order Selection table in the preceding output shows the results of selecting the optimal lag order for a VAR model. The following statistical criteria were used to evaluate the goodness of fit for different lag orders:

- **Akaike Information Criterion (AIC)**: This value balances the goodness of the model fit with its complexity.
- **Bayesian Information Criterion (BIC)**: This value is similar to AIC, but with a stronger penalty for models with more parameters.

- **Final Prediction Error (FPE)**: This value is used to estimate the model's prediction error.
- **Hannan-Quinn Information Criterion (HQIC)**: This value is another criteria for model selection.

Let us now fit the VAR model to the data using the selected lag order based on the lowest AIC.

Code:

```
model_fitted = model.fit(maxlags=5, ic='aic')
```

In the next step, let us forecast the next 'n' steps (10 steps in this case) using the fitted model and convert the forecast array into a data frame with appropriate dates and column names.

Code:

```
n_forecast_steps = 10


forecast = model_fitted.forecast(df.iloc[0:989].values[-model_fitted.k_ar:], steps = n_forecast_steps)


forecast_df = pd.DataFrame(forecast, index = pd.date_range(start=df.iloc[0:989].index[-1], periods=n_forecast_steps + 1, closed='right'), columns=df.columns)
```

Let us finally print the forecasted results.

Code:

```
print(forecast_df['Rainfall'])
```

Output:

1972-09-17	0.999183
1972-09-18	-0.576733
1972-09-19	0.469374
1972-09-20	0.006213
1972-09-21	-0.235691

```
1972-09-22    0.082648
1972-09-23    0.033987
1972-09-24    0.015170
1972-09-25   -0.076186
1972-09-26    0.049970
Freq: D, Name: Rainfall, dtype: float64
```

Let us now look at the actual data for Rainfall.

Code:

```
df['Rainfall'].tail(10)
```

Output:

```
Date
1972-09-17   -1.0
1972-09-18    1.0
1972-09-19    1.0
1972-09-20    2.0
1972-09-21   -3.0
1972-09-22    0.0
1972-09-23   -1.0
1972-09-24    2.0
1972-09-25   -2.0
1972-09-26    0.0
Name: Rainfall, dtype: float64
```

In the next step, let us calculate the RMSE for the data.

Code:

```
rmse_results = rmse(df['Rainfall'].tail(10), forecast_df['Rainfall'])
print(rmse_results)
```

Output:

1.6462090753959264

The RMSE for the Rainfall data, considering the actual values, appears to be high. This model needs to be refined further for better accuracy.

In the final step, let us plot the data and check actual vs. predicted values for Rainfall.

Code:

```
plt.figure(figsize=(12,6))
plt.plot(df.tail(10)['Rainfall'], label='Actual')
plt.plot(forecast_df['Rainfall'], label='Predicted')
plt.xlabel('Time')
plt.ylabel('Value')
plt.legend()
plt.show()
```

The output is displayed as follows:

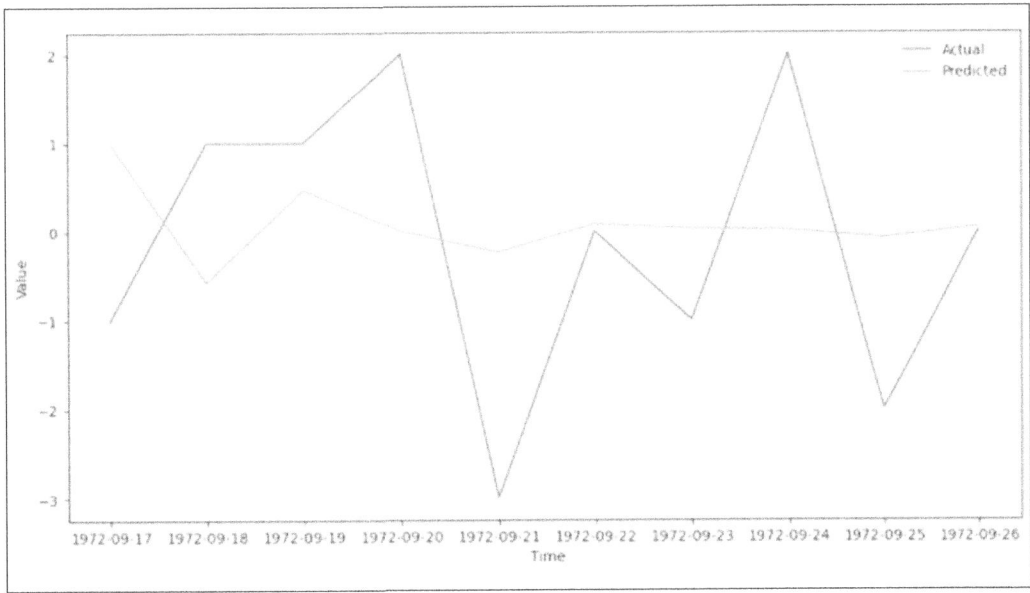

Figure 9.1: Actual vs. Predicted - VAR

The plot in *Figure 9.1* also signifies that the model parameters need to be fine-tuned further to get better predictions.

This is an example of applying the VAR model on a dataset, and these steps can be followed on different multivariate datasets for forecasting. With this understanding, let us proceed to the next model of this chapter, which will be VECM.

Applying Vector Error Correction Model

The Vector Error Correction Model (VECM) is an extension of Vector AutoRegression (VAR) model. This model is more effective for the non-stationary data that are co-integrated. If a variable of a time series dataset is non-stationary but still moves along with another non-stationary variable over a period of time, then the data is considered to be non-stationary and co-integrated. VECM is a model designed to capture both short-term changes and long-term equilibrium among co-integrated time series data. It is used when we have multiple non-stationary time series data that are co-integrated. The most important aspect of VECM is the Error Correction component, which handles the short-term correlations of the data to bring them to their long-term co-integration.

The concept of VECM is attributed to two main research papers as follows:
- The paper titled - `Some Properties of Time Series Data and their Use in Econometric Model Specification`, by Clive W.J. Granger in 1981.
- The paper titled - `Statistical Analysis of Cointegration Vectors`, by Søren Johansen published in the *Journal of Economic Dynamics and Control* 12.2-3 (1988): 231-254.

Library Documentation

The model documentation and parameters for VECM are available in the statsmodels documentation at:

https://www.statsmodels.org/dev/generated/statsmodels.tsa.vector_ar.vecm.VECM.html#statsmodels.tsa.vector_ar.vecm.VECM

VECM in the statsmodels library has the following class structure and parameters:

`class statsmodels.tsa.vector_ar.vecm.VECM`

`(endog,`

 `exog=None,`

```
exog_coint=None,

dates=None,

freq=None,

missing='none',

k_ar_diff=1,

coint_rank=1,

deterministic='n',

seasons=0,

first_season=0
)
```

The parameters of the model as described in the library are as follows:
- **endog**: This parameter is used to input the 2-d endogenous response variable.
- **exognd**: This parameter is used to input the deterministic terms outside the cointegration relation.
- **exog_coint**: This parameter is used to input the deterministic terms inside the cointegration relation.
- **dates**: This is an optional parameter used to input the datetime.
- **freq**: This is an optional parameter used to input frequency.
- **missing**: This is an optional parameter used to input missing values.
- **k_ar_diff**: This parameter is used to input the number of lagged differences in the model.
- **coint_rank**: This parameter is used to input Cointegration rank, which equals the rank of the matrix and the number of columns of alpha and beta.
- **deterministic**: This parameter is used to input deterministic terms.
- **seasons**: This parameter is used to input the number of periods in a seasonal cycle.
- **first_season**: This parameter is used to input the season of the first observation.

For more details and understanding of the parameters, refer to the **statsmodels** documentation.

Let us now proceed with the implementation of VECM on multivariate time series data.

Application of VECM on Time Series Data

In this example, we will be demonstrating how to use a Vector AutoRegression (VAR) model for time series forecasting of **WeatherData.csv**.

Let us start by importing the following libraries needed for this example.

Code:

```
import pandas as pd

import numpy as np

from statsmodels.tsa.api import VECM

from statsmodels.tsa.vector_ar.vecm import coint_johansen

from statsmodels.tools.eval_measures import rmse

import matplotlib.pyplot as plt
```

In the next step, let us load the dataset and set the Date column as the index, parsing it as date objects. Take the first 1000 records from the data.

Code:

```
df = pd.read_csv('WeatherData.csv', index_col='Date', parse_dates=['Date'])

df = df.head(1000)
```

Let us further process the data by dropping the unnecessary column **Unnamed: 0** and converting the categorical variables, **Direction of Wind**, **Clouds**, into dummy or indicator variables. This step is necessary because VECM models require numerical input.

Code:

```
df.drop(columns = 'Unnamed: 0', inplace = True)

df = pd.get_dummies(df, columns=['Direction of Wind', 'Clouds'], drop_first=True)
```

In the next step, let us define a function, **check_stationarity**, to test each time series in the dataset for stationarity using the Augmented Dickey-Fuller test. If the p-value is greater than 0.05, the series is considered non-stationary.

Code:

```
def check_stationarity(series):
    result = adfuller(series)
    if result[1] > 0.05:
        print(f"{series.name} is not stationary")
    else:
        print(f"{series.name} is stationary")


for column in df.columns:
    check_stationarity(df[column])
```

Output:

Temperature (Min) is stationary

Temperature (Max) is stationary

Pressure is stationary

Velocity of Wind is stationary

Humidity is not stationary

Carbon Monoxide is not stationary

UV Rays is not stationary

Intensity of Light is stationary

Rainfall is stationary

Direction of Wind_NorthWest is stationary

Direction of Wind_SouthEast is stationary

Direction of Wind_SouthWest is stationary

Clouds_Altostratus is stationary

Clouds_Cirrocumulus is stationary

Clouds_Cirrostratus is stationary

Clouds_Cirrus is stationary

Clouds_Contrails is stationary

Clouds_Cumulonimbus is stationary

Clouds_Cumulus: Fluffy is stationary

Clouds_Lenticular Clouds is stationary

Clouds_Mammatus Clouds is stationary

Clouds_Nimbostratus is stationary

Clouds_Stratocumulus is stationary

Clouds_Stratus is stationary

The output of this function provides the list of features with their corresponding stationarity indicators.

We will not be making the variables of this data stationary, unlike the VAR model, since we need to check for cointegration of this data using the Johansen cointegration test.

Let us define a function, **perform_johansen_test**, and perform this test on the data and interpret the results.

Code:

```
def perform_johansen_test(data, det_order=0, k_ar_diff=1):
    result = coint_johansen(data, det_order, k_ar_diff)
    trace_stat = result.trace_stat
    crit_values = result.trace_stat_crit_vals
    eigenvalues = result.eig

    print("Johansen Cointegration Test Results:")
    print("-----------------------------------")
    for r in range(len(trace_stat)):
```

```
            conclusion = "not rejected" if trace_stat[r] < crit_values[r, 1]
            else "rejected"
            print(f"Null hypothesis of rank = {r} is {conclusion}")
            print(f"Trace Statistic: {trace_stat[r]:.2f}, 95% Critical
            Value: {crit_values[r, 1]:.2f}")
            print(f"Eigenvalue: {eigenvalues[r]:.4f}\n")
```

perform_johansen_test(df)

This test returns the following four values that can be used to interpret the test:
- **trace_stat**: The trace statistic tests the null hypothesis of **r** cointegrating relationships against the alternative of **n** cointegrating relationships.
- **trace_stat_crit_vals**: The trace statistic critical values are the critical values for the trace statistic at common significance levels of **90%**, **95%**, and **99%**.
- **eig**: The **eig** is the eigenvalues for the test.
- **cvt**: The **cvt** is the Critical Value Table for the test.

The output of this test is as follows:

```
Johansen Cointegration Test Results:
------------------------------------
Null hypothesis of rank = 0 is rejected
Trace Statistic: 9661.67, 95% Critical Value: nan
Eigenvalue: 0.4493


Null hypothesis of rank = 1 is rejected
Trace Statistic: 9066.23, 95% Critical Value: nan
Eigenvalue: 0.4361


Null hypothesis of rank = 2 is rejected
Trace Statistic: 8494.45, 95% Critical Value: nan
```

Eigenvalue: 0.4230

Null hypothesis of rank = 3 is rejected
Trace Statistic: 7945.60, 95% Critical Value: nan
Eigenvalue: 0.4056

Null hypothesis of rank = 4 is rejected
Trace Statistic: 7426.48, 95% Critical Value: nan
Eigenvalue: 0.3995

Null hypothesis of rank = 5 is rejected
Trace Statistic: 6917.52, 95% Critical Value: nan
Eigenvalue: 0.3861

Null hypothesis of rank = 6 is rejected
Trace Statistic: 6430.52, 95% Critical Value: nan
Eigenvalue: 0.3828

Null hypothesis of rank = 7 is rejected
Trace Statistic: 5948.92, 95% Critical Value: nan
Eigenvalue: 0.3718

Null hypothesis of rank = 8 is rejected
Trace Statistic: 5484.98, 95% Critical Value: nan
Eigenvalue: 0.3614

Null hypothesis of rank = 9 is rejected

Trace Statistic: 5037.46, 95% Critical Value: nan

Eigenvalue: 0.3492

Null hypothesis of rank = 10 is rejected

Trace Statistic: 4608.84, 95% Critical Value: nan

Eigenvalue: 0.3468

Null hypothesis of rank = 11 is rejected

Trace Statistic: 4183.75, 95% Critical Value: nan

Eigenvalue: 0.3428

Null hypothesis of rank = 12 is rejected

Trace Statistic: 3764.89, 95% Critical Value: 334.98

Eigenvalue: 0.3312

Null hypothesis of rank = 13 is rejected

Trace Statistic: 3363.44, 95% Critical Value: 285.14

Eigenvalue: 0.3225

Null hypothesis of rank = 14 is rejected

Trace Statistic: 2974.90, 95% Critical Value: 239.25

Eigenvalue: 0.3143

Null hypothesis of rank = 15 is rejected

Trace Statistic: 2598.41, 95% Critical Value: 197.38

Eigenvalue: 0.3076

Null hypothesis of rank = 16 is rejected

Trace Statistic: 2231.53, 95% Critical Value: 159.53

Eigenvalue: 0.3001

Null hypothesis of rank = 17 is rejected

Trace Statistic: 1875.41, 95% Critical Value: 125.62

Eigenvalue: 0.2899

Null hypothesis of rank = 18 is rejected

Trace Statistic: 1533.81, 95% Critical Value: 95.75

Eigenvalue: 0.2767

Null hypothesis of rank = 19 is rejected

Trace Statistic: 1210.50, 95% Critical Value: 69.82

Eigenvalue: 0.2743

Null hypothesis of rank = 20 is rejected

Trace Statistic: 890.51, 95% Critical Value: 47.85

Eigenvalue: 0.2596

Null hypothesis of rank = 21 is rejected

Trace Statistic: 590.52, 95% Critical Value: 29.80

Eigenvalue: 0.2578

Null hypothesis of rank = 22 is rejected

Trace Statistic: 292.96, 95% Critical Value: 15.49

Eigenvalue: 0.2460

Multivariate Time Series, Metrics, and Validation 285

```
Null hypothesis of rank = 23 is rejected
```

```
Trace Statistic: 11.16, 95% Critical Value: 3.84
```

```
Eigenvalue: 0.0111
```

Let us further interpret these test results.

The null hypothesis is rejected for each rank tested from 0 to 23. This is indicated by the trace statistics being higher than the corresponding critical values. Critical values are present from rank 12 onwards. The test results suggest that there are multiple cointegrating relationships within the dataset, up to the highest rank tested. The eigenvalues for each rank are generally decreasing, but all are significant, even for higher ranks, indicating strong evidence of cointegration across multiple variables. The results indicate that we have so many cointegrating relationships. This could imply that the variables in the dataset are highly interconnected. This is expected in this dataset since it is Weather data, and the factors are related to each other in many ways. The results strongly suggest the presence of cointegration among the variables in this dataset, indicating that a Vector Error Correction Model (VECM) might be appropriate for modeling and forecasting these time series.

In the next step, let us initialize a VECM model with the first 990 records of the dataset.

Code:

```
vecm = VECM(df.iloc[0:990], k_ar_diff=1, coint_rank=1)
```

```
vecm
```

Output:

```
<statsmodels.tsa.vector_ar.vecm.VECM at 0x1884086ad10>
```

Let us now fit the VECM model into the data.

Code:

```
vecm_fitted = vecm.fit()
```

```
vecm_fitted
```

Output:

```
<statsmodels.tsa.vector_ar.vecm.VECMResults at 0x18840868fd0>
```

In the next step, let us forecast the next 'n' steps (10 steps in this case) using the fitted model and convert the forecast array into a data frame with appropriate dates and column names.

Code:

```
n_forecast_steps = 10

forecast, lower, upper = vecm_fitted.predict(n_forecast_steps, alpha=0.05)

forecast_df = pd.DataFrame(forecast, index=pd.date_range(start=df.iloc[0:990].index[-1],
                              periods=n_forecast_steps + 1, closed='right'),
                              columns=df.iloc[0:990].columns)
```

Let us finally print the forecasted results.

Code:

```
print(forecast_df['Rainfall'])
```

Output:

1972-09-17   22.488044
1972-09-18   22.810438
1972-09-19   22.548807
1972-09-20   22.623835
1972-09-21   22.576450
1972-09-22   22.634415
1972-09-23   22.591064
1972-09-24   22.614784
1972-09-25   22.601411
1972-09-26   22.610067
Freq: D, Name: Rainfall, dtype: float64

Let us now look at the actual data for Rainfall.

Code:

```
df['Rainfall'].tail(10)
```

Output:

```
Date
1972-09-17    21.0
1972-09-18    22.0
1972-09-19    23.0
1972-09-20    25.0
1972-09-21    22.0
1972-09-22    22.0
1972-09-23    21.0
1972-09-24    23.0
1972-09-25    21.0
1972-09-26    21.0
Name: Rainfall, dtype: float64
```

The forecast vs. actual data in VECM is looking much better and relevant compared to the VAR model.

In the next step, let us calculate the **RMSE** for the data.

Code:

```
rmse_results = rmse(df['Rainfall'].tail(10), forecast_df['Rainfall'])
print(rmse_results)
```

Output

1.3150022709566052

The RMSE for the Rainfall data, considering the actual values, appears to be meaningful and lower compared to the VAR model. This model can be refined further for better accuracy.

In the final step, let us plot the data and check actual vs. predicted values for Rainfall.

Code:

```
plt.figure(figsize=(12,6))
```

```
plt.plot(df.tail(10)['Rainfall'], label='Actual')
plt.plot(forecast_df['Rainfall'], label='Predicted')
plt.xlabel('Time')
plt.ylabel('Value')
plt.legend()
plt.show()
```

The output is displayed as follows:

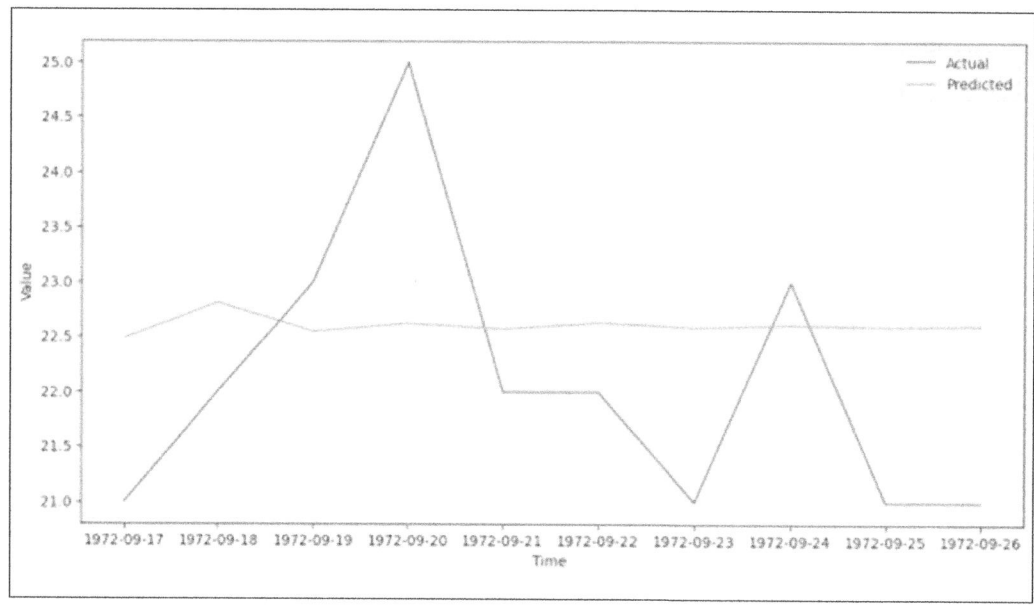

Figure 9.2: *Actual vs. Predicted – VECM*

The plot in *Figure* 9.2 signifies that the model parameters might need slight fine-tuning, but it is much better than the VAR model and closer to the actual values, even though the randomness is not well captured.

This is an example of applying the VECM model on a dataset, and these steps can be followed on different multivariate datasets for forecasting. With this understanding, let us proceed to the next model of this chapter, which will be VARMAX.

Understanding VARMAX

VARMAX (Vector AutoRegressive Moving Average with eXogenous inputs) is an extension of the VAR (Vector AutoRegression) and VMA (Vector Moving Average) models. Similar to VAR and VECM, this model also handles multivariate time series data. As the name implies, the three components of VARMAX are VAR, VMA, and exogenous inputs. Exogenous inputs are external factors that can impact the time series data without being a feature within the dataset.

The foundations of VAR models were laid by Christopher Sims in his 1980 paper "*Macroeconomics and Reality*", and the concept of incorporating moving average (MA) components in vector time series models was included from the univariate ARMA (AutoRegressive Moving Average) models, which were extensively developed by George Box and Gwilym Jenkins in their seminal work "*Time Series Analysis: Forecasting and Control*", first published in 1970. The exogenous input (X) was later added to these concepts as an additional factor.

Library Documentation

The model documentation and parameters for VAR model are available in the `statsmodels` documentation at:

https://www.statsmodels.org/dev/generated/statsmodels.tsa.statespace.varmax.VARMAX.html#statsmodels.tsa.statespace.varmax.VARMAX

VARMAX in the `statsmodels` library has the following class structure and parameters:

```
class statsmodels.tsa.statespace.varmax.VARMAX
(
    endog,
    exog=None,
    order=(1, 0),
    trend='c',
    error_cov_type='unstructured',
    measurement_error=False,
    enforce_stationarity=True,
    enforce_invertibility=True,
```

        trend_offset=1,

        **kwargs

)

The parameters of the model as described in the library are as follows:
- **endog**: The parameter is used to input the observed time-series process.
- **exog**: The parameter is used to input the array of exogenous regressors.
- **order**: The parameter is used to input the (p,q) order of the model for the number of AR and MA parameters to use.
- **error_cov_type**: The parameter is used to input the structure of the covariance matrix of the error term.
- **measurement_error**: The parameter is used to input whether or not to assume that the endogenous observations (endog) were measured with error.
- **enforce_stationarity**: The parameter is used to input whether or not to transform the AR parameters to enforce stationarity in the autoregressive component of the model.
- **enforce_invertibility**: The parameter is used to input whether or not to transform the MA parameters to enforce invertibility in the moving average component of the model.
- **trend_offset**: The parameter is used to input the offset at which to start time trend values.
- ****kwargs**: The parameter is used to input keyword arguments.

For more details and understanding of the parameters, refer to the `statsmodels` documentation.

Let us now proceed with the implementation of VARMAX on multivariate time series data.

Application of VARMAX on Time Series Data

In this example, we will be demonstrating how to use a VARMAX model for time series forecasting of **WeatherData.csv**.

Let us start by importing the following libraries needed for this example.

Code:

```
import pandas as pd
from statsmodels.tsa.statespace.varmax import VARMAX
from statsmodels.tsa.stattools import adfuller
from pmdarima import auto_arima
import matplotlib.pyplot as plt
from sklearn.metrics import mean_squared_error
from math import sqrt
```

In the next step, let us load the dataset.

Code:

```
df = pd.read_csv('WeatherData.csv', index_col='Date', parse_dates=['Date'])
```

In the next step, let us define the endogenous variables for the model, which will be the input independent variables.

Code:

```
endog = df.loc['2010-01-01':'2023-10-20', ['Pressure', 'Velocity of Wind', 'Carbon Monoxide', 'Rainfall']]
```

Now, let us define exogenous variables, which are external influencers that are not modeled as part of the endogenous time series system. For the demonstration of this example, let us consider **Rainfall** as the exogenous variable.

Code:

```
exog = endog['Rainfall']
```

Let us further initialize the VARMAX model with **Pressure**, **Velocity of Wind**, and **Carbon Monoxide** as endogenous variables. Set the **order** argument as **(2, 0)**, indicating an autoregressive order of 2 and a moving average order of 0. Set the **trend** argument to **n**, indicating no trend component in the model. Finally, let us include the exogenous variable **Rainfall** in the model.

In the next step, let us fit the model with a maximum of 1000 iterations in the optimization process.

Code:

```
res = mod.fit(maxiter=1000, disp=False)
res.summary()
```

The model summary gives us six tables with various parameters of the model as output.

Let us look at each one of them.

The results in *Table 9.1* have various dimensions of the model output, such as the variables that will be forecasted, model name, number of observations, values of log likelihood, and results of various tests performed on the data.

Dep. Variable:	['Pressure', 'Velocity of Wind', 'Carbon Monoxide']	No. Observations:	5041
Model:	VARX(2)	Log Likelihood	-19871.244
Date:	Tue, 12 Dec 2023	AIC	39796.488
Time:	04:08:13	BIC	39972.672
Sample:	01-01-2010	HQIC	39858.212
	-2053		
Covariance Type:	opg		
Ljung-Box (L1) (Q):	664.74, 4912.17, 0.61	Jarque-Bera (JB):	14.90, 787.99, 2463080046.77
Prob(Q):	0.00, 0.00, 0.44	Prob(JB):	0.00, 0.00, 0.00
Heteroskedasticity (H):	2.18, 2.46, 1.16	Skew:	-0.01, 0.95, -50.98
Prob(H) (two-sided):	0.00, 0.00, 0.00	Kurtosis:	3.27, 3.39, 3425.90

Table 9.1: Statespace Model Results

The result in *Table 9.2* represents the equation for **Pressure** as a variable and its corresponding coefficients.

	coef	std err	z	P>|z|	[0.025	0.975]
L1.Pressure	-0.0033	0.008	-0.414	0.679	-0.019	0.012
L1.Velocity of Wind	-0.1434	0.068	-2.112	0.035	-0.277	-0.01

	coef	std err	z	P>|z|	[0.025	0.975]
L1.Carbon Monoxide	13.9361	0	5.90E+04	0	13.936	13.937
L2.Pressure	-0.07	0.008	-8.562	0	-0.086	-0.054
L2.Velocity of Wind	2.221	0.068	32.82	0	2.088	2.354
L2.Carbon Monoxide	21.8708	0	7.40E+04	0	21.87	21.871
beta.Rainfall	34.6775	0.174	199.696	0	34.337	35.018

Table 9.2: Results for equation Pressure

The result in *Table 9.3* represents the equation for `Velocity of Wind` as a variable and its corresponding coefficients.

	coef	std err	z	P>|z|	[0.025	0.975]
L1.Pressure	-0.0039	0.169	-0.023	0.982	-0.335	0.327
L1.Velocity of Wind	0.1846	0.082	2.252	0.024	0.024	0.345
L1.Carbon Monoxide	-1.5427	0.001	-3023.202	0	-1.544	-1.542
L2.Pressure	-0.0206	0.169	-0.122	0.903	-0.352	0.31
L2.Velocity of Wind	0.794	0.083	9.522	0	0.631	0.957
L2.Carbon Monoxide	0.8793	0	3322.149	0	0.879	0.88
beta.Rainfall	0.8832	0.074	11.861	0	0.737	1.029

Table 9.3: Results for equation Velocity of Wind

The result in *Table 9.4* represents the equation for `Carbon Monoxide` as a variable and its corresponding coefficients.

	coef	std err	z	P>|z|	[0.025	0.975]
L1.Pressure	3.29E-06	0.005	0.001	0.999	-0.01	0.01
L1.Velocity of Wind	-0.0007	0.125	-0.005	0.996	-0.246	0.244
L1.Carbon Monoxide	0.0264	0.162	0.162	0.871	-0.292	0.345
L2.Pressure	1.14E-05	0.004	0.003	0.998	-0.008	0.008
L2.Velocity of Wind	-0.001	0.126	-0.008	0.994	-0.247	0.245
L2.Carbon Monoxide	0.0242	0.128	0.189	0.85	-0.226	0.275
beta.Rainfall	0.0218	0.164	0.133	0.894	-0.299	0.342

Table 9.4: Results for equation Carbon Monoxide

The result in *Table 9.5* represents the estimates of the standard deviation of each endogenous variable and the covariance between them.

	coef	std err	z	P>|z|	[0.025	0.975]
sqrt.var.Pressure	54.6937	0.112	489.761	0	54.475	54.913
sqrt.cov.Pressure.Velocity of Wind	1.464	0.051	28.893	0	1.365	1.563
sqrt.var.Velocity of Wind	1.8074	0.041	44.333	0	1.728	1.887
sqrt.cov.Pressure.Carbon Monoxide	0.0341	0.263	0.13	0.897	-0.481	0.549
sqrt.cov.Velocity of Wind.Carbon Monoxide	-0.0061	0.189	-0.032	0.974	-0.376	0.364
sqrt.var.Carbon Monoxide	0.0078	5.35E-06	1462.076	0	0.008	0.008

Table 9.5: *Error covariance matrix*

This model results also provide the following **Warnings** regarding the covariance matrix:

Warnings:

[1] Covariance matrix calculated using the outer product of gradients (complex-step).

[2] Covariance matrix is singular or near-singular, with condition number 1.89e+21. Standard errors may be unstable.

From the results from *Tables 9.1 to 9.5*, we can interpret the following regarding the model:

- The model shows significant relationships between some of the variables and their lags.
- The presence of autocorrelation, heteroskedasticity, and non-normality of residuals indicates that the model may not adequately capture all the dynamics in the data.
- The high kurtosis and significant Jarque-Bera test for **Carbon Monoxide** suggest that this variable might be particularly problematic.

- The significant coefficients for `Rainfall` as an exogenous variable in some equations indicate its influence on the system.

Given these results, it is essential to carefully interpret the model's coefficients and consider potential refinements, such as addressing autocorrelation and non-normality in the residuals or re-evaluating the choice of included variables and model order.

In the next step, let us predict using the VARMAX model and look at the results.

Code:

```
predictions = res.predict(start=endog.index[0], end=endog.index[-1], exog=exog)

predictions, endog[['Pressure', 'Velocity of Wind', 'Carbon Monoxide']]
```

Let us review the predictions vs. actuals side by side for the three variables that are predicted using VARMAX in the table in *Figure 9.3*.

	Actuals				Prediction		
Date	Pressure	Velocity of Wind	Carbon Monoxide	Date	Pressure	Velocity of Wind	Carbon Monoxide
01-01-2010	712	3.068757	0.499999	01-01-2010	729.611908	18.438828	0.460916
02-01-2010	712	3.070291	0.500001	02-01-2010	708.760128	6.895492	0.484363
03-01-2010	712	3.072039	0.499985	03-01-2010	735.04587	4.685985	0.5105
04-01-2010	712	3.073688	0.49999	04-01-2010	735.04884	4.687553	0.510497
05-01-2010	712	3.075328	0.499995	05-01-2010	735.052199	4.689223	0.510494
...	...	...	...	...	...	...	...
16-10-2023	1000	64.835214	0.500001	16-10-2023	1015.561805	62.449647	0.519225
17-10-2023	1000	64.876419	0.499986	17-10-2023	842.1897	58.053153	0.410082
18-10-2023	1000	64.917654	0.499997	18-10-2023	876.952361	58.976631	0.431829
19-10-2023	1000	64.958744	0.499997	19-10-2023	842.360261	58.133713	0.409942
20-10-2023	1000	65	0.499999	20-10-2023	842.446192	58.174048	0.409872

Figure 9.3: Actuals vs. Predicted - VARMAX

In the final step of this example, let us calculate the RMSE for the model predictions.

Code:

```
rmse_values = {}

for column in ['Pressure', 'Velocity of Wind', 'Carbon Monoxide']:
    rmse = sqrt(mean_squared_error(endog[column], predictions[column]))
```

```
        rmse_values[column] = rmse
```

```
print("RMSE values:")
for var, value in rmse_values.items():
    print(f"{var}: {value}")
```

Output:

RMSE values:

Pressure: 68.94309221068534

Velocity of Wind: 2.5266499786465606

Carbon Monoxide: 0.042084851085070714

The high RMSE values as compared to the model parameters and the data in *Table* 9.6 also indicate that the model needs refinement, and the model variables need to be reconsidered for better results.

With this understanding, let us look at some of the common metrics used for time series validation.

Metrics for Time Series

Metrics and validation are essential components of time series modeling since they help in performing model assessment, model comparison, parameter tuning, identifying model issues, validating the results, identifying overfitting, and decision-making purposes.

Some of the common metrics used for time series models are as follows:

- **Mean Absolute Error:** MAE is used to measure the average absolute difference between predicted and actual values.
- **Root Mean Squared Error:** RMSE is used to measure the square root of the average squared difference between predicted and actual values.
- **Mean Absolute Percentage Error**: MAPE is used to measure the percentage difference between predicted and actual values.
- **Forecast Bias**: This is used to measure the average over- or under-estimation of forecasts.
- **AIC/BIC**: These are information criteria that balance model fit and complexity.

- **R-squared**: R2 is used to measure the proportion of variance in the data explained by the model.
- **Residual Autocorrelation**: This is used to check whether model residuals exhibit autocorrelation.

These are the most frequently used metrics for validating time series data, although other metrics can also be explored depending on the problem being resolved.

Conclusion

In this chapter, we have learned about various multivariate time series algorithms that can be used to forecast future data for a time series.

We also looked at the parameters, documentation, and examples to understand Vector AutoRegression (VAR).

Subsequently, we explored the application of Vector Error Correction Model (VECM) for predicting time series data. Additionally, we delved into understanding VARMAX (Vector AutoRegressive Moving Average with eXogenous inputs) and applied it for predicting time series data.

Finally, we reviewed various metrics that can be used to validate time series models.

Throughout this book, we have learned various aspects and concepts that can be implemented to understand the time series data and perform forecasting on the data.

References

- Sims, C.A. (1980) 'Macroeconomics and reality', Econometrica, 48(1), p. 1. doi:10.2307/1912017.
- Granger, C.W. (no date) 'Some properties of time series data and their use in Econometric Model Specification', Essays in Econometrics vol II: Collected Papers of Clive W. J. Granger, pp. 119–128. doi:10.1017/ccol052179207x.007.
- Johansen, S. (1988) 'Statistical Analysis of Cointegration vectors', Journal of Economic Dynamics and Control, 12(2–3), pp. 231–254. doi:10.1016/0165-1889(88)90041-3.

- Jenkins, G.M. (2005) 'Autoregressive–moving average (ARMA) models', Encyclopedia of Statistical Sciences [Preprint]. doi:10.1002/0471667196.ess0075.pub2.

- Statsmodels.tsa.vector_ar.var_model.Var (no date) statsmodels.tsa.vector_ar.var_model.VAR - statsmodels 0.15.0 (+109). Available at: https://www.statsmodels.org/dev/generated/statsmodels.tsa.vector_ar.var_model.VAR.html#statsmodels.tsa.vector_ar.var_model.VAR (Accessed: 12 December 2023).

- Statsmodels.tsa.vector_ar.VECM.VECM (no date) statsmodels.tsa.vector_ar.vecm.VECM - statsmodels 0.15.0 (+109). Available at: https://www.statsmodels.org/dev/generated/statsmodels.tsa.vector_ar.vecm.VECM.html#statsmodels.tsa.vector_ar.vecm.VECM (Accessed: 12 December 2023).

- Statsmodels.tsa.statespace.varmax.VARMAX (no date) statsmodels.tsa.statespace.varmax.VARMAX - statsmodels 0.15.0 (+109). Available at: https://www.statsmodels.org/dev/generated/statsmodels.tsa.statespace.varmax.VARMAX.html#statsmodels.tsa.statespace.varmax.VARMAX (Accessed: 12 December 2023).

Index

A

aggregated features
  creating 152-154
Akaike Information Criterion (AIC) 272
area plot 90, 91
ARIMA application
  on time series data 161-167
Augmented Dickey-Fuller
    (ADF) Test 109-111
autocorrelation
  about 114, 115
  reviewing 114
Autoregressive Integrated
    Moving Average (ARIMA)
  about 158
  components 158, 159
  model documentation 159-161
AutoTS
  code 56-59
  documentation 56
  functionalities 56
  installation 56
  using, for time series libraries 55

B

bare metal hypervisor. See type 1
    hypervisor
Bayesian Information Criterion
    (BIC) 272
box plot 78-81

C

candlestick plot 91, 92
Convolutional Neural Networks (CNN)
  applying 256
  on time series data 258-263
  parameters 257, 258

D

dataset 158
deep learning-based approach
  developing, for time series
    forecasting 242-248
descriptive statistics
  about 99
  mean 100
  median 100, 101
  mode 101-103

double exponential smoothing 172-174
double exponential smoothing
   application
   on time series data 174-178
dtypes property 97

E

expanding window statistic
   computing 134-139
expanding window statistics
   computing 133
exponential moving averages
   calculating 139-142
exponential smoothing models
   about 167
   application, on time series
      data 168-172
   double exponential
      smoothing 172-174
   double exponential smoothing
      application, on time
      series data 174-178
   model documentation 167
   triple exponential smoothing 178
   triple exponential smoothing
      application, on time
      series data 179-183

F

Final Prediction Error (FPE) 273
finance and economics usage
   about 2
   credit risk analysis 6, 7
   economic condition analysis 7, 8
   market risk analysis 4, 5
   stock market analysis 3, 4

G

Gated Recurrent Units (GRUs)
   about 248
   applying 249
   concepts 248
   core components 248
   on time series data 251-256
   parameters 250, 251
Gaussian Process
   about 198, 199
   on time series data 199-203
Gaussian Process Regressor (GPR) 198
gradient boosting
   implementing 221, 222
   on time series data 225-228
   parameters 223, 224

H

Hannan-Quinn Information
      Criterion (HQIC) 273
healthcare usage
   about 16
   disease detection 18, 19
   disease prediction 18, 19
   patient feature analysis 16, 17
heat map 84-88
Hidden Markov Models (HMM)
   applying 192
   on time series data 194-198
   parameters 193
histogram 81-83

I

interaction terms-based features
   creating 149-152

K

K-Nearest Neighbors (KNN)
   about 212
   applying 212
   on time series data 213-216
   parameters 212, 213
Kwiatkowski Phillips Schmidt
      Shin (KPSS) Test 112-114

L

lag-based multivariate features
  creating 148, 149
lag-based univariate features
  creating 126-129
library 168
line plot 74
Long Short-Term Memory
    (LSTM) networks
  about 232, 233
  core components 232
  on time series data 235-242
  parameters 234, 235

M

machine learning-based approach
  developing, for time series
      forecasting 203-207
Matplotlib
  about 62
  exploring 62
  usage 62-64
Mean Absolute Error (MAE) 165
Mean Squared Error (MSE) 165
metrics
  using, for time series
      models 296, 297
multivariate feature engineering
  about 143-148
  aggregated features,
      creating 152-154
  interaction terms-based
      features, creating 149-152
  lag-based multivariate
      features, creating 148, 149

N

NumPy
  code 40-42
  documentation 39
  functionalities 40
  installation 39
  using, for time series libraries 39

P

pair plot 88-90
Pandas
  code 29-39
  documentation 28
  functionalities 28
  installation 28
  using, for time series libraries 28
partial autocorrelation
  about 116, 117
  reviewing 114
Plotly
  about 71
  exploring 71
  usage 71-74
Plotly time series visualization
    libraries
  about 90
  area plot 90, 91
  candlestick plot 91, 92
Prophet
  code 43-55
  documentation 43
  functionalities 43
  installation 43
  using, for time series libraries 42
Prophet algorithm
  exploring 183, 184
  on time series data 184-189
Python time series visualization
    libraries
  about 62
  Matplotlib, exploring 62
  Plotly, exploring 71
  Seaborn, exploring 64

R

Random Forest
  implementing 216
  on time series data 219-221
  parameters 217, 218
rolling statistics
  calculating 130-132
  exploring 118-122
Root Mean Squared Error (RMSE) 165

S

sales and marketing usage
  about 9
  campaign analysis marketing 13, 14
  customer segmentation 15, 16
  inventory management 11-13
  retail sales forecasting 9, 10
  seasonality analysis 10, 11
  seasonality planning 10, 11
scatter plot 75-78
Seaborn
  about 64
  exploring 64
  usage 64-70
Seaborn time series visualization libraries
  about 83
  heat map 84-88
  pair plot 88-90
security, in cloud. See cloud security
simple exponential smoothing 167
stationarity analysis
  about 108, 109
  Augmented Dickey-Fuller (ADF) Test 109-111
  Kwiatkowski Phillips Schmidt Shin (KPSS) Test 112-114
  performing 108

Support Vector Machine (SVM)
  applying 207
  on time series data 209-211
  parameters 208, 209

T

time series application
  about 2
  finance and economics usage 2
  healthcare usage 16
  sales and marketing usage 9
  transportation and traffic management usage 21, 22
  weather and climate analysis usage 19, 20
time series data
  inspecting 96-99
  loading 96-99
  overview 2
  parameter 168
  preparing 22-24
time series decomposition
  exploring 103
  level 104
  noise 104-108
  seasonality 103
  trend 103
time series libraries
  AutoTS, using 55
  NumPy, using 39
  Pandas, using 28
  Prophet, using 42
time series plots, with Matplotlib
  about 74
  box plot 78-81
  histogram 81-83
  line plot 74, 75
  scatter plot 75-78
triple exponential smoothing 178

triple exponential smoothing
    application
        on time series data 179-183

U

univariate feature engineering
    about 126
    expanding window statistics,
        computing 133-139
    exponential moving averages,
        calculating 139-142
    lag-based univariate features,
        creating 126-129

V

Vector AutoRegression (VAR)
    about 267
    concept 267
    on time series data 268-276
    parameters 268
Vector AutoRegressive Moving Average with eXogenous inputs (VARMAX)
    about 289
    on time series data 290-296
    parameters 290
Vector Error Correction Model (VECM)
    about 276
    concept 276
    on time series data 278-288
    parameters 277

Made in the USA
Las Vegas, NV
09 July 2024

92059122R00177